ƒP

# Charles Jennings and Lori Fena

**Foreword by Esther Dyson**

**The Free Press**
**New York London Toronto Sydney Singapore**

# The HUNDREDTH WINDOW

## Protecting Your Privacy and Security in the Age of the Internet

*f*P

THE FREE PRESS
A Division of Simon & Schuster, Inc.
1230 Avenue of the Americas
New York, NY 10020

Designed by Deirdre C. Amthor

Manufactured in the United States of America

10   9   8   7   6   5   4   3   2   1

Library of Congress Cataloging-in-Publication Data

Jennings, Charles
    The hundredth window : protecting your privacy and security in the age of the Internet /
Charles Jennings and Lori Fena : foreword by Esther Dyson.
        p.    cm.
    1. Computer security.  2. Internet (Computer network)—Security measures.  I. Fena,
Lori.  II. Title.

QA76.9.A25 J46 2000
005.8—dc21
                                                                          00-022527
ISBN 0-684-83944-X

# Acknowledgments

This book on the great turn-of-the-century Internet privacy and security debate has benefited greatly from many private, off-the-
record, conversations with people who shall remain anonymous,
ranging from Internet business leaders and technology architects, to
strangers on airplanes and dinner party guests. From these conversations, it is clear that few other contemporary issues can evoke
such immediate and highly personal concern, or elicit such a wide
variety of personal views.

Our public acknowledgment to those who contributed to this
book must begin with the volunteer board and hard-working staff of
TRUSTe, the Internet privacy assurance organization we founded.
Special thanks goes to Gigi Wang and Susan Scott, the original executive directors of TRUSTe, and to Bob Lewin, their successor.
They have worked tirelessly to improve privacy practices on the Net,
and to develop guidelines for meaningful industry self-regulation.
The discussions and debates inside TRUSTe about these guidelines
helped us appreciate the complexity of the privacy issue, and the dif-
ficulty of finding easy answers to the many questions raised by it.

## Acknowledgments

With respect to the actual research and writing of the book, Russell Shaw made an enormous contribution by providing many of the "Tips and Tricks" found at the end of each chapter, and by helping in other ways too numerous to mention. We could not have finished this book without him.

Much of the research at the heart of this book has been provided to us by Dave Chen and his staff at GeoTrust, an Internet technology company with a special focus on privacy issues. David Garrick, a researcher for GeoTrust, deserves special thanks for his efforts in compiling the "Privacy Incident" log that can be found in Appendix B of this book.

Various friends contributed to our understanding of the technical side of Internet privacy and security—notably, Frank Tycksen of Preview Systems, P. S. Kohli of Intel, Dave Remy of GeoTrust and Pete O'Dell and Michael Hudson of Supertracks. With respect to the development of privacy standards and privacy and security assurance programs, Caroline Buck Luce, Topher Neumann, Geoff Turner and Laura Brown of Ernst & Young's Center for Trust Online have been especially helpful, and supportive. Regarding the rights of individual citizens, or netizens, Executive Director Tara Lemmey and others on the hard-working staff of the Electronic Frontier Foundation have been important contributors—not to just to this book, but to the preservation of basic freedoms in a wired world.

A number of people read early drafts of the book and provided us with invaluable insights, comments, and criticisms. These include: Ron Lunde, Craig Berkman, Lucy Garrick, Dr. Susan Buys, Deborah Robertson, Jan Nichols, Nancy Murray, Nick Nicholas, Dick Luebke, and David and Rebecca Kennerly.

Our editor, Paul Golob, played an essential role in the development of this book. To the extent we have succeeded in communicating complex Internet technology terms and concepts in understandable, mainstream English, he deserves much of the credit. Heartfelt thanks also to our agents Lynn Chu and Glen Hartley, who helped us turn a personal passion into a marketable book. And to Melissa Hovis, whose organization skills and good sense helped keep our writing on track and on schedule (more or less), and whose personal commitment to the project went well beyond the call of duty.

Finally, we'd like to thank our wonderfully supportive spouses, Christine Jennings and Edward Zyszkowski, who in this case also served as researchers, contributors, editors, critics, and, most important, believers.

*Applied Science is a conjuror, whose bottomless hat yields impartially the softest of Angora rabbits and the most petrifying of Medusas.*
                    —*Aldous Huxley,*
                    Tomorrow and Tomorrow and Tomorrow *(1956)*

# Contents

*Foreword by Esther Dyson*                                                xi
*Introduction*                                                            xv

1  Invasion of the Data Snatchers                                          1
2  The Hundredth Window                                                   21
3  Something Digital This Way Comes                                       55
4  Privacy and Net Culture: Sex, Spies, and Video-Scrape                  83
5  The Datanet Rules                                                     107
6  From E-Commerce to Information Economies                              129
7  Who Can You Trust?                                                    149
8  The Privacy Game                                                      185
9  Private Lives, Public Networks: The Next 500 Years                    213

*Appendix A:*
*Playing It Safe on the Web: Consumer Dos and Don'ts*                    223

*Appendix B:*
*Online Privacy Violation Incidents*                                     231

*Notes*                                                                  247
*Glossary*                                                               253
*Index*                                                                  269

# Foreword

What is privacy? That is a very complicated question, and even this book is only a start at giving the answer. It lays out, eloquently and in detail, the range of issues that comprise personal privacy in the age of the Internet. But in the end, privacy is personal, and the full answer to the question depends on you, the individual involved.

Nonetheless, it is clear that the concept of privacy, the threats to it, and the means to achieve it, are all changing as a result of our new computer-based lives. Privacy used to be achieved through the sheer "friction" of everyday life: distance, time, and the lack or inaccessibility of records. Information didn't travel well, and most people who wanted to escape their pasts could simply move to a new location. Most things people did produced no records, and what records there were existed on paper: hard to find, difficult to duplicate, and subject to being lost, faded, or destroyed.

Yet at the same time, people had little privacy from others they knew: storekeepers, employers, family, and neighbors. The poor lived with one another and often slept several people to a room; the rich lived with servants.

Now, the picture has changed. You can escape your surroundings through the Net, but at the same time your actions and words can easily catch up with you—through the Net. And it's not just the Net—it's electronic toll roads (exactly when did you leave that party?), credit-card transactions (we know what hotel you went to), vendor databases (what book you bought), cell-phone records (whom you called), and much, much more. At work, your arrival and departure times may be recorded, along with your Web searches and your sick days. Your pharmacist may know more about you than any single doctor, and so forth.

What makes all this information more scary is people's new ability to combine it: the products you bought from a variety of different merchants; your sick days plus someone else's hotel bills. It is not the routine use of this information to send people marketing materials that most people find so troubling; it is the thought that someday someone might put the wrong (or right) pieces of information together to find out more than you want them to know.

At the same time, most people are happy to have others know who they are and treat them as individuals. It's convenient to have a vendor know your shoe size, your seating preference, your "regular" grocery order. It's pleasant to be greeted by name and to be offered a book, a stock, or a rental car that matches your preferences.

So the solution is not to stop progress, to eliminate the collection and use of data, or to deny ourselves the efficiencies and conveniences that the new technology affords. Rather, the solution is to put control of the data back where it belongs—in the hands of the individuals who generate it. By and large, that doesn't mean passing new laws, but setting new expectations instead—getting individuals to demand the terms and conditions they already have a right to.

This won't come about from a single set of laws or from actions by a single sector of society. It will result from a variety of interacting forces, many of them outlined in this book. The government needs to enforce statutes against fraud and misrepresentation, while private organizations such as TRUSTe and BBBOnline can encourage companies to disclose their data policies—and enforce them if they are breached. Industry associations can encourage their members to behave better, and to promote trustworthy data policies as a consumer benefit. For their part, consumers need to take the trouble to protect themselves, much as they lock their cars and secure their homes. Investors and insurers need to pay attention to the liabilities that companies incur through unsafe or unsavory data practices, and to understand the benefits of trust for vendors who behave well.

All these interacting forces will help match the benefits of a data-rich society with the human comfort that comes from knowing one's private information is secure. Of course, the world will never be a perfect place, but with the kinds of warnings and solutions that Charles Jennings and Lori Fena describe, we will be able at least to move it in the right direction.

ESTHER DYSON

# Introduction

We are writing this book in the first days of the twenty-first century—and in the beginning of the third act of The Rise of the Internet, the most important technology drama of our lifetimes. In the opening scenes, an unprepossessing system of interlinked computers rose out of the great telecommunications cloud and brought something truly unique to the world stage: a communications network where every node could connect with every other, without anyone in control. In Act II, the Internet hit the big time, blasted away at everything from stock markets to bookstores to airlines, sucked up every information system in its path. . . . and changed everything it touched. All in all, an impressive performance.

But now, at the turn of the century, the novelty and excitement are wearing thin, and the Internet's wild first wave of innovation, market-making and exuberance is coming to an end. As the curtain rises on Act III, we see a different picture emerging.

The Internet has grown up. It's become smarter, faster, cheaper, stronger, bigger, more mature. And more dangerous.

This worldwide communications medium is also getting

flashier, as faster transmission rates begin to open new channels for online entertainment. Websites of all kinds are able to offer ever more highly customized services. And the Internet's impact on the global economy grows more significant with each passing day, as the "network of networks" becomes the "market of markets."

Underneath all this change is a fundamental shift in Internet architecture. A shift toward the Internet becoming a "smart information environment," instead of a mere hub-and-spokes system of pipes and switches; a shift toward being "always on," and thus becoming a constant presence in our world. The Internet, we are realizing, is not just an interesting technology. It is a profoundly important new world. It is, above all, a new thing that moves and changes with frightening speed. Yesterday's loose, unorganized maze of interconnected networks is fast becoming a slick, smart, and almost seamless information environment. New digital devices of all kinds—ranging from stereo-top boxes for the storage of digitally downloaded music to biotransmitters for the monitoring of heart rhythms—are being designed specifically to jack into the network and are hitting the market in unprecedented numbers.

It all adds up to the emergence of a wholly new information realm—an ingenious "infosphere" where connected devices of all kinds intelligently exchange data, anytime, anywhere. With or without human intervention.

This book is not so much about the technology of this transformation—mesmerizing and wondrous as it is—but about the impact it will have on each of us, personally, as modern human beings.

Our main subject is the role of electronic networks and information technology in our lives. This is hardly an original theme. Except that it's the information in information technology that's our focus here, not the technology itself. We're interested in how information moves and behaves in the network. How it is collected, controlled, and exchanged. How it is bought and sold. When it serves the greater good, and when it does not.

And our interest is not in just any information, but a special kind of data known in the information trade as personally identifiable information, or PII. PII refers to anything in an electronic network that can be linked in some way to a flesh-and-blood human being; to someone with a name, an address, and a life; to you, for example. (If data—such as, say, your click trail through a website—can be traced back to you, it's PII. If the same click-trail data cannot in any way be connected to you personally, it's not.)

The concept of PII—the idea that data belongs in a special class when it is tied to an actual, identifiable human—is especially helpful when we try to come to grips with questions involving privacy, technology, and commerce. PII is like uranium: quite valuable, but more than a little dangerous when it falls into the wrong hands. It has become so important that Wall Street analysts are valuing some companies based on the quantity and quality of their customer PII profiles; privacy advocacy groups and governmental regulatory agencies around the world are closely monitoring PII collection and use, and considering a staggering amount of new legislation; software developers are reengineering their products to become "PII-compliant"; even new sniffers (the network analysis tools used by software engineers and hackers) are in the works for the express purpose of tracking PII inside large information systems. Yet most users of the Internet, even active ones, have very little idea what PII is, how it is collected, where it is stored—or even why it is important.

PII matters because privacy matters. And personal privacy will matter more and more as Act III of the Internet continues to unfold.

If you use the Internet at all, a great deal of PII about you is scattered around the public network already. Once collected and organized, these data can be stacked together to produce a new kind of electronic identity—in other words, an online profile about you containing the most private details of your life. These profiles can open a path to your door. Many different types of people and organizations can use this path to find you, and find out things about you, for a wide variety of purposes. Not all of which are pleasant—or legal.

As we enter a brave new millennium, the truly dynamic uses of PII are just beginning. Rich profiles about each of us—containing information about our tastes and preferences, our Web surfing habits, our computer configuration, our past behavior—are just starting to be assembled and put to use in ways that leverage both the reach and speed of the Internet. Merchants, employers, police, journalists, health care providers, financial institutions, tax collectors, advertisers, website operators, and personal information brokers, among others, collect and use these profiles routinely. Soon there will be more information about us passing through the network than is known by our very best friends.

Much of the appeal of this later-stage Internet lies in the ability of online merchants to deliver, quickly and at discounted prices, goods and services that are customized especially for us. PII is the lifeblood of this kind of service—and many customers are more than happy to donate their fair share of personalized data with the expectation of getting good deals, rare products, or a steady stream of up-to-the-minute information. When all systems are working properly, and fairly, the Internet industry's ability to know your tastes, preferences, and needs can be a wonderful thing.

And yet PII collection and manipulation via the Internet have a dark side as well. In fact, personal information about you can easily make its way into a seamy world where identity theft, online fraud, online revenge, identity spoofing, racial redlining, and various forms of harassment and stalking are real threats. This dark side of the data flow is more than just the exhaust of our hot new Internet Ferrari; it's a clear and present danger on the road ahead.

Ultimately, whether in five years or fifty, the changes taking place in information architecture today will have profound consequences for each of us. What will happen when anyone with a computer, and a phone line can obtain instant, low-cost access to highly personal information about us and our families? What will such access mean to businesses, which often collect and use such information, but which have their own privacy and confidentiality concerns as well? What will such pervasive public access to PII mean to government and social institutions? What will it mean to the pursuit of happiness and other quests of the human soul?

We believe that PII levels about each of us will soon approach a kind of critical mass (both in depth of detail and in degree of access), and that the unprecedented public accessibility of private information will generate a considerable hue and cry in response. Consequently, we believe, a tension between the growth and optimization of the Internet, and the growth and optimization of what is uniquely human, will arise and might perhaps produce a dynamic equilibrium, a new solution that can balance the societal demand for technical and economic growth with individual needs for privacy, dignity, and freedom. This book is an exploration of the new Internet privacy and security landscape, in search of this solution.

## *TRUSTe and Full Disclosure*

The Internet privacy and security zone is terrain we know fairly well. Four years ago we founded the Internet privacy assurance organization TRUSTe (www.TRUSTe.org). We have remained active, unpaid volunteers for TRUSTe ever since. Lori still serves on its board of directors, as chairman.

TRUSTe now has over one thousand licensees in its online privacy assurance program. Participating websites agree to post and adhere to privacy policies in exchange for the right to display the TRUSTe seal on their site. TRUSTe does not make judgments about how these licensees collect and use data, so long as they openly disclose their PII practices to site visitors. Disclosure by a website of how it treats private information not only leads to accountability but also builds user trust and confidence. And what's true on the Web is also true in analog media, including books such as this one. And since studies of cross-cultural assimilation have shown that self-disclosure is actually one of the fastest ways to build trust between people, here, then, is a little self-disclosure, from your authors.

Lori is currently chairman of the Electronic Frontier Foundation, a prominent Internet electronic rights advocacy group, and has served on the board of directors of such Internet firms as Critical Path Beatnik, and Urbanite. Charles is founder and CEO of Supertracks, an Internet company that provides services for the distribution of music directly over the Web, and chairman and co-founder of GeoTrust, a provider of systems and services that support trust and transparency on the Net; and co-founder of Preview Systems, a public Internet company. Individually, we have actively supported, through investment or consulting, a number of other Internet companies as well, most of which have been directly or indirectly involved in computer and Internet security issues.

Privacy-loving though we are, no one has ever accused either of us of being shy about expressing our opinions. Here, therefore, are our beginning biases and opinions:

- We are aggressively pro-privacy. We consider respect for individual privacy a bedrock human value. We believe that all users of the Internet need to understand—and have an inherent right to know and control—how information about them is being collected and used.
- We believe that privacy helps keep us free—free, among other things, to make and learn from our own mistakes.
- We recognize that the Internet business community is a uniquely interconnected industry operating in an unusually transparent environment; and feel that the pioneers of this in-

dustry have, for the most part, operated with surprisingly high ethical standards if perhaps not yet enough care and sensitivity about the confidentiality of private personal information.

- We believe that the business stakes surrounding privacy, the use of PII, and the development of customer trust are huge (fortunately), and that the development of new technologies of trust will be central to the solution of ongoing trust, privacy, and security issues and, indeed, the continued growth of electronic commerce.
- We are certain that some of the most powerful and beneficial uses of information technology in the years ahead will be the very ones that require the greatest amounts of personal information in order to be effective (medical treatments are a prime example, but there are many others).
- We believe that government has a very important role to play with respect to the use of PII for business and other purposes, and that this role begins with leading by example, getting its own PII practices in order and making sure people's names, addresses, auto license plate numbers, and government dossiers that were collected for a specific citizen-to-government purpose don't end up online or resold.
- We believe, further, that government should concentrate on enforcing existing laws well, and tackling very specific and obvious problems, before rushing to pass generic, vague, or unenforceable privacy regulations.
- We value and protect our own personal privacy as best we can, often to the extent of heading into the backwoods of Alaska or Oregon, respectively, without so much as a beeper. We believe that preserving fully private experiences is a vital part of retaining our cultural and environmental heritage.

We should also disclose now, lest there be any confusion, that this book is not intended to be a sober treatise on privacy and public policy. On the other hand, neither is it a hands-on how-to guide to Internet privacy and security for the technologically sophisticated. If you're anxious to get really technical (or really wonky) about Internet privacy and security, we'll point you to a few good sources. But our goal in this book is different, and perhaps more ambitious. We're trying to make sense of this new information environment and what it means to families, schools, businesses, political institutions, and most important, ordinary personal lives.

We are concerned, frankly, that the free flow of personal information might radically alter our world in ways many of us would find disturbing. Consequently, we hope to encourage you to participate in the growing public debate about privacy, and to help support the establishment of new ground rules of information collection and distribution—primarily through choices you make every day, on the Web and off.

Along the way, we will provide "Tips and Tricks" for making pragmatic, everyday decisions about privacy and security, especially when you are online. We will discuss the use of credit cards, home addresses, cell phones, Net cams, online financial systems, and the whole question of risk and exposure in the Internet Age. We also hope to provide a framework for answering the two questions we ourselves are most commonly asked about the Internet: "How do I protect my privacy?" and "Who can I trust?"

There are no pat answers to these questions, and it would be misleading to leave the impression at the outset that maintaining privacy and security in the Internet Age is simply a matter of reading an instruction manual and following correct procedures. It is not. The Internet privacy game is more subtle, and more difficult, than that. Playing this new game requires sophistication, and even occasional obfuscation, in addition to the requisite locking of doors and barring of windows. In fact, one of the major lessons we have learned from a decade in the software and Internet industries is that there is no absolute privacy or security anywhere on the Internet—

especially given the inherent vulnerabilities in both the public network and popular operating systems (read: Windows).

For this reason, questions of privacy and security ultimately lead to issues of trust—and to highly subjective questions about particular people, companies, and service providers. In these pages, therefore, you will also find a few of our favorite backroom Internet tales, our personal picks of winners and losers in trust and privacy battles, and our own highly subjective rules of thumb about online privacy and security.

Our entrepreneurial pursuits, combined with our roles in TRUSTe, not only have provided us with front-row seats for the Net's first two acts but have afforded us bit parts in the drama itself (especially with respect to Internet public policy issues and the development of encryption applications, communications systems, and e-commerce tools).

This hardly makes us unique, of course. The Net has had more shaping hands than any invention in human history—and continues to be shaped by nearly everyone who bothers to learn its methods and master its tools. In fact, the real story of Act III, as the curtain now rises, is that most of us in the United States are now on the Internet's public stage, and before the final curtain falls, the majority of the rest of the world will be as well.

Say what you will about Internet hype—and there has been plenty of it, certainly—but there is no denying that the rise of the Net is great revolutionary theater. It's grand, it's surprising, and it's more than a little out of control. It has shaken the pillars of the global economy. It has massively redistributed wealth. And its most powerful days are yet to come.

As in all great theater, the Act III conclusion is hard to predict. At this writing, the Internet's fate, as a Hollywood screenwriter might put it, hangs in the balance of a "jeopardy fulcrum," a crucial, suspenseful moment when the plot could move in several different directions. Consider this Act III jeopardy fulcrum, for example:

*Introduction*

How will John and Jane Dough, prosperous Internet enthusiasts, react when they learn that the Internet, the all-powerful electronic network that helped create such a vibrant, exciting time in Act II, is now spying on them, selling detailed information about them, and actually helping others assume their identity?

There are a billion stories on the great network—and more and more of them involve privacy and security. It is too early to say whether the recent groundswell of public concern about online privacy will be harnessed into stronger privacy safeguards, where trust is not only implied but actually embedded into the network infrastructure. Such trust solutions would have to be easy to use, yet also technically sophisticated and highly secure. But even larger than the technical challenge is likely to be the economic one—will it pay to build a market for trust, personal security and privacy protection?

Well, we can hope. The odds of new technologies of trust and privacy protection emerging will be more favorable if high-tech and other business leaders slow down for a moment and reflect seriously on where current trends of information collection and exchange might take us should we fail to ensure the preservation of basic human decency in the online world.

What the Internet industry needs to learn in Act III is respect—respect for the privacy concerns of site visitors, e-commerce customers, and other faceless strangers across the Net. An Internet industry that is slow to learn respect will not only slow the adoption of Internet commerce and services within the mainstream population, but will very likely cause a new wave of backlash against technology (the Seattle WTO riots of late 1999 perhaps being a precursor of things to come).* What the rest of us need to learn is how this great new system of information capture, storage, and dis-

*For more late-breaking information about trust, privacy, Internet security, and other themes of this book, visit us at hundredthwindow.net.

tribution actually works and how to exercise considerably more caution, and assertiveness, when using it.

Perhaps the next thing the Internet will change is our expectations. Trust is the expectation of fair and honest dealing, and trustworthiness is the fulfillment of such expectations. If we expect and demand trustworthiness on the Net—not just in the delivery of goods and services but in the use of our private, personal information—perhaps both our expectations and the true promise of the Internet as a creative social force will be fulfilled.

●　　●　　●

With this goal in mind, we begin our tale.

# 1

# Invasion of the Data Snatchers

*I fear the loss of my obscurity. Genuineness grows best in the dark.*

—*Aldous Huxley*

A generation or two ago, the data of daily life, to the extent that it was recorded at all, was "entered" on file cards and bond paper, stored in snap-ring binders and file cabinets, and kept under lock and key. Copying information required the use of carbon paper— and considerable human effort. A real-time commercial transaction meant pulling cash from your wallet and collecting the change. The only identifying number the typical American had was a social security number—a nine-digit code that was generally kept in strictest confidence, in accordance with the strong privacy guarantees of the initial social security program. Even as late as the 1960s, before computers were networked, the only individual transactions recorded on a daily basis were ones that involved financial credit, taxes, or governmental benefits.

The Hundredth Window

Today, social security numbers are used everywhere, from schools to stock brokerages, to track you through life. Credit cards leave a wide trail of purchase records. Copying information is as easy as point and click, cut and paste. The data of daily life—your daily life—is collected at supermarkets, at the workplace, over phone networks, at the drugstore, and at every website you visit. And these are just the hot spots.

List marketers, credit profilers, information brokers, and other legal vendors make a business out of collecting and trading electronic data profiles of you. They participate actively in what amounts to a thriving online flea market for PII. It is your data—personal facts about you—that are being bought and sold. That's the best-case scenario. The worst case is that the information in your personal data profiles is not really about you, but accidentally about someone else. If that person has a criminal past, a poor credit history or a habit of posting hate messages on the Web, you are in for trouble.

There is so much electronic information collection going on in our lives that we have become quite accustomed—even numb—to it all. But recall your grandparents' lives for a moment, lives lived without direct mail, e-mail, or credit cards; lives lived in an era when personal behavior was at most a matter of local gossip, not a widely accessible public record. And then join us as we imagine a typical day in your thoroughly modern life.

*7:00 a.m. Wake up, turn up heat, take shower, dry hair, make and drink coffee, use up remaining milk in refrigerator.*
You can still wake up at home with some expectation of privacy. You know that your shower, at least, is private. Chances are no one is monitoring the simple tasks you perform in order to get ready for the day.

*7:47 a.m. Log onto the Internet to check news and stock portfolio; check e-mail on personal account.*
Now you have plunged into the data zone, where every move

you make will be captured in a computerized system. Your identity travels the Net with you, leaving a solid, easily traceable trail. Every click of your mouse is being recorded somewhere far, far from your hard drive, and every transaction you complete will be stored and analyzed.

**8:31 a.m. Turn down heat, open/close garage door, depart house.**
The local utility may be specifically monitoring your heat consumption in order to run its systems more efficiently and to anticipate high-load periods. If you use an electronic garage door system, anyone with appropriate equipment can monitor its use—from a distance—to determine when you leave home, though this requires hard-core electronic surveillance. As you drive off from your house, your car's trip computer records the start of today's journey.

**9:10 a.m. Drive into the city, use E-ZPass automatic toll payment to make commute faster.**
In New York as well as many other major metropolitan areas, toll collection has become automated through systems such as E-ZPass. However, as this system speeds you through the toll booth, your car is being identified and information about your whereabouts is being collected and stored. New York City police detectives have successfully subpoenaed this information and used it as evidence in court. (Cars are moving billboards containing a critical piece of PII—your license plate number.)

**9:12 a.m. Answer cell phone in car regarding a hot new business deal.**
At first the cell phone cuts out, of course, as you cross the bridge. But then you reconnect, perhaps aware that cell phone transmissions and receptions are recorded for billing purposes, but probably not caring in the least. But then you realize that cell

3

phone calls can be intercepted. While that possibility is somewhat remote, you shudder at the thought that a business reporter might be lurking in the sea of traffic alongside you, ready to eavesdrop on your call. The thought passes, and you hit the speed dial to return the call.

*9:30 a.m. Have breakfast meeting with prospective customer; pick up the bill with a credit card.*

The credit card companies—the banks as well as the payment processors—are some of the biggest collectors of personal data about you. Plastic is often handier than cash, and sometimes it is essential, but it is never anonymous. Credit card data warehouse operators are expert at mining information about what you buy to better understand your behavior as a consumer. This can result in directing marketing efforts that target your likes and dislikes—but this information is not in any way regulated, and nothing precludes it from being sold to whoever wants to buy it. The biggest privacy leak in most people's lives can be found in their wallets, where they keep their credit cards.

*10:46 a.m. Go into office building, use electronic badge to enter parking area, building, restroom, and work area.*

Electronic badges, like E-ZPass and cell phones, can locate you in a particular place at a particular time. So can the video cameras in the parking lot, elevator, and building lobby, all of which are now online in a closed-circuit network, with feeds to both a security control room and the executive suites. Ostensibly, this data is owned and held in confidence by your employer for security purposes only. But this data can be used for other purposes as well, such as in job reviews and employee disputes. Incidentally, alarm systems that require you to punch in a specific personal identification number, or PIN, to gain entrance also store a record of your coming and going.

***11:10 a.m. Check/send e-mail from work account; log onto Internet to research the competition and gain access to analyst reports.***

Not only are Internet access providers collecting information about your every online click, your employer may also be doing the same—and legally it is within his or her rights to do so if you are using your system at work. So beware! (And please stay off those porno sites when you're at work—it could be embarrassing when the boys in the server room check your log sheets.) Also, e-mail records have been used extensively in legal actions—and have even bitten the grand titan of software, Bill Gates—so understand that what you dash off in an electronic note lingers on, perhaps forever.

***1:38 p.m. Go to Amazon.com to buy a book, and recommend it to a client's management team.***

Amazon.com has established itself as the premier online vendor of books, in part by offering personalized service. This is accomplished by collecting information about your likes and dislikes regarding particular titles and comparing these with the likes and dislikes of the countless others who frequent their site. (The process is known as "collaborative filtering" and involves a set of cutting-edge technologies that are being used increasingly in e-commerce.) The Amazon folks do post a privacy policy on their site and try for the most part to behave like a responsible, privacy-sensitive merchant, but nonetheless, the company's databases contain a great deal of personal information about the subject matter that most interests you and stimulates you. This information in some ways is even more sensitive than the more generic payment data that a credit card company records—and in at least one controversial program, Amazon did use this information to disclose publicly what books were most popular among employees of certain well-known companies.

**2:00 p.m. Participate in business alliance conference call using a teleconference service bridge.**

Many of the phone companies that provide this type of teleconferencing service require you to provide your identity to access the call—for security reasons. It is worth noting that this information is logged into these companies' database systems and can be accessed if required by the purchaser of the service or by law enforcement officials.

**4:10 p.m. Use your always-on Internet access at work to visit an online wedding registry, in order to make it easy for friends and family to buy gifts online for the big wedding.**

Getting married soon? No problem—there are many websites ready to come to your rescue and help you prepare all the details. Many such sites require that you enter virtually your whole life story before you can be listed in their nuptial registry. Moreover, when people purchase gifts for you via the registry, the site operators get a very accurate profile of your friends and family as well. Whenever entering detailed personal information via the Internet, regardless of how seemingly innocuous the purpose, be sure to read the site's privacy policy to understand how the information you are providing is to be used. The way to do this is to search for a link (usually on the home page) that says "privacy policy." Read this policy! If it claims that the site operators can, essentially, do whatever they please with your data, you might be well advised to look for an alternative. (Here's the kind of language in a privacy policy to avoid: "In an effort to bring you more exciting offers from our partners, we reserve the right, from time to time, to share information about you with these partners. . . .")

**6:15 p.m. Log onto favorite travel site to purchase tickets and select seat for upcoming business trip.**

The proliferation of new travel services on the Internet is a direct result of the low cost of entry into this field and the relatively low cost to operate and maintain such a site, compared to a bricks-and-mortar travel agency. In this highly competitive arena, the ability of travel retailers to gather and analyze information about your travel patterns is an important competitive asset. This information is often resold to carriers within the travel industry but can also be used to gauge your relative wealth and amount of leisure time. This kind of information is gold to the direct marketing industry—and online travel agencies can and do trade this gold in order to expand their margins. Traveler, beware.

*7:30 p.m. Review, edit, and put final touches on upcoming speech; e-mail presentation to conference organizers for reproduction.*
Companies that run conferences generally keep copies of your presentation for their files and distribute them to conference attendees as well. Some conferences actually publish presentations on their website. This may not be a problem, but it is helpful to remember that your ultimate audience could include competitors or investors.

*8:17 p.m. Exit building, using badge to exit prepaid underground parking.*
It's the end of another high-voltage day. Somewhere, someone knows what time you left the building. In fact, he or she may even have noticed how tired you looked as you passed the networked security camera.

*8:35 p.m. Stop in at grocery store to pick up milk and Häagen-Dazs ice cream; use discount card and make a quick cash purchase.*
Many people don't realize that a supermarket discount card is more than just a convenient substitute for coupons. The computer-

ized scanning systems linked to your personal discount card capture information that your grocery can use to maintain a profile of you and your family—one that includes all your eating and drinking habits. This information is valuable to others as well, such as insurers, employers, and direct marketers. Do you really want total strangers to know about that fondness of yours for pinot noir?

*9:10 p.m. Collapse in easy chair; order dinner from Waiters online.*
You should not be surprised when your friendly gourmet delivery service addresses you by name when they pick up the phone, anticipates your usual order, and offers to bill it to your Visa card (which they have on file). The incredible convenience of instant, customized service comes to you courtesy of the caller ID feature in the phone system, which in turn is hooked up directly to Waiters-on-Wheels's customer file and credit card billing system. They know your dinner routine better than you do. Tonight, when the waiter arrives, he asks, "Would you like us to call your cell phone at the usual time while you're on your way home, just to make it a little easier?" Over the seared ahi and saffron rice, prepared just the way you like it, you begin to wonder if perhaps these waiters know you a bit too well.

*10:43 p.m. Log onto an Internet health site to research father's illness; request information.*
Although you know the information you are requesting is for your father, the site owners don't. The pharmaceutical company that sponsors the site receives your information and sends the materials you requested to your postal address. What you don't realize is that you are now entered in their records as a person who possibly has a troublesome illness and, therefore, may be a potential customer. If the pharmaceutical company also resells its database to insurance companies, they and other data brokers may miss the

nuance inherent in the phrase "may have this illness." They might not even have any idea of how the information in the database was compiled. Two months later, though you are a healthy thirty-seven-year-old woman, you receive a free sample of an herbal supplement that is reputed to help treat prostate cancer.

*11:34 p.m. Call your phone message service to arrange a 7:00 a.m. wake-up call; turn in for the night.*
Your first data log of the day ahead has already been recorded.

• • •

The modern information landscape has indeed changed greatly from that of our grandparents. Try as we might, we can no longer avoid the scrutiny of the data collectors, even if we avoid using that most obvious of data-entry tools, the computer keyboard. Computers and sensors are now embedded in the most mundane environments, and data is frequently collected about us without our volunteering it. To the many skills required to successfully make your way on life's journey, add one more: personal privacy protection.

Every day, millions of everyday people—the amateurs, let's call them—willingly provide personally identifiable information about themselves to the data collection pros. This information may include a name, a phone number, an address (home, business, or e-mail), and any number of other unique identifiers (social security number, credit card number, driver's license number, even the image of a face, retina, or set of fingerprints)—but it must have at least one such identifying element to be useful. To be true PII, the information must always contain a hook—a way to snag and reel in the unique identity of an individual human being.

PII hooks can be found in all sorts of information files. Imagine a massive computer directory, with thousands of electronic file folders, each containing a specific PII profile. The information in the files could be about anything from college grades to stock trades—but every scrap of data in the files would come with a PII string attached. In this meta-directory, you might find, in a random perusal, such folders as Driving Records, Reading Habits; Gambling Histories; Records of Disciplined Soldiers, Attitudes about Abortion; Telephone Records; Airline Travel Preferences, Genetic Profiles, Conference Attendees, Asthma Sufferers, Purchasers of Palm Pilots, Mortgage Holders, Subscribers to *Playboy* Magazine, and on and on. When we speak of PII profiles, these are the kinds of categories that such profiles contain (though not all categories will be found in each profile).

While there is no single PII profile system, the advent of electronic computer networks is currently creating something quite similar: linked access among the many different computer directories that currently store PII. More and more PII-tagged information is being entered, stored, and traded via a common electronic grid. And the pros—along with another group we'll meet later, the cons—are getting better and better at using this grid for all kinds of purposes.

The real news about PII—about the collection and use of information about *you*—is that its use is compounding. Like the interest on a long-term debt, personal information that has made its way into the hands of the data collection pros feeds upon itself and grows exponentially. The more that is known about you—and the more pros who know about you—the easier it is for the next pro to learn still more. Connect the dots between the PII folders labeled "Home Phone Numbers," "Buyers of Outdoor Clothing," "Websites Visited," and "Truck Owners," and a gun merchant is able to build a new file called "Potential Buyers." Soon he is on the phone, calling people whom he suspects support the Second Amendment, drive pick-ups, and wear "camo" windbreakers. And this is a relatively benign example. Connect the dots between "Women Drivers

10

Under Twenty-One"—a database that contains home addresses—with "Lingerie Buyers" and "Online Sex Chat Visitors," and you get quite a different picture. It is this ability to connect, with electronic ease, dozens to literally thousands of isolated bits and pieces of information about an individual human being that is dramatically changing the rules and raising the stakes of privacy protection in modern society.

Exchanges of PII take place via a variety of electronic and non-electronic means, in virtually every segment of modern life. Amazingly, they often happen almost subconsciously. We want money from a cash machine; we want service from a doctor; we want product warranty protection for a new purchase; we want to visit a news site on the Web; we want a discount on groceries—so we provide information about ourselves. We barely stop to think about where this information about us is going, who will get it, where or how long it will be stored, what it will be used for, or generally what the consequences may be.

Yet make no mistake: there *are* consequences—potentially serious ones. Such as when personal, private, confidential financial information obtained from information brokers is used by phone solicitors to convince elderly citizens they need phony annuities. When the mother of a stillborn child receives birthday greetings from direct marketers for several years on the anniversary of her child's death. When the age and e-mail address of a ten-year-old is obtained online by a convicted sex offender. When detailed home phone records of a CEO are purchased over the Internet by a competitor. Or when a youthful indiscretion, a past disease, a reckless e-mail, or even a data-entry error by some unseen, unknown person enters the public digital record forever, and brands someone, accurately or inaccurately, for life.

Perhaps you are aware of the risks of modern society's ravenous hunger for facts about you. After all, you have chosen to read a book about privacy, so your awareness of privacy issues is likely well above average. But even so, do you, practically speaking, know how to manage your own personal privacy in the data exchanges of everyday life? Do you know how to take advantage of the growing online marketplace for goods, services, information, and entertainment, without being compromised by the equally robust online market for personal data?

These are the horns of the modern privacy dilemma. Privacy matters—but how much? Personal data is sensitive, but where are the lines to be drawn between privacy and accountability? Information is power, and information about specific people is very powerful, but what precisely should be the limits of its use in business and trade? No one knows, and few agree.

There is little true consensus in the business and technology world about how matters of personal privacy should be handled, and there are no simple answers to the tough privacy questions being raised by new information technology. The sooner a common consensus is reached, however, the better. Without one, privacy issues will become a major obstacle to continued growth in the electronic marketplace.

The payoffs of privacy policy consensus, and the risks of not achieving one, are compounding almost daily. Indeed, the whole personal privacy landscape has as least temporarily turned into a kind of shambles—an Alice in Wonderland game that nearly everyone plays, but according to a hodgepodge, random set of rules. Perceptive observers—a group that includes the CEOs of Microsoft, IBM, and McGraw-Hill and the chairman of the Federal Trade Commission—understand that this state cannot continue. It's far too unstable.

Consider the following data points:

- Polls are showing privacy concerns at an all-time high. (See box, pages 37–38.)
- The United States and Europe are in the midst of a serious

trade disagreement over how personal data is to be collected and managed.

- Privacy policies of individual companies vary tremendously, as does compliance with these policies (largely self-generated and self-enforced).
- Privacy preferences vary tremendously among individuals as well (the Internet spectrum is from the cleverly anonymous to people who proudly webcast their entire lives—including their most personal moments—on their sites).
- Courts around the world are awarding significant damages to consumers and Internet users over claims of privacy violation. (See the article on US Bancorp in Appendix B.)
- Over one hundred new privacy laws were introduced in the 105th (1997–98) U.S. Congress, nearly four times the number introduced in the 1993–94 session.
- New technologies of data collection, Internet monitoring, online surveillance, data mining, automatic mailing, personal searching, and identity spoofing are rolling out into the electronic marketplace every month.
- Personalized, customized products and services over the Internet—most of which require users to provide more personal information than they ever have given to companies before—are creating one of the hottest growth sectors in the entire economy.
- Networked databases, the applications that store and manage personal information, are becoming more powerful, more intelligent, and more interoperable. But much more significant is the fact that PII is moving from proprietary databases out into the clear on the Internet—a trend that may have profound privacy implications.
- The rising use and increased durability of private company e-mail is creating both serious human resource concerns and significant legal liabilities for corporations.

- "Legitimate" information brokering—the buying and selling of personal information—is now a billion-dollar industry in the United States.
- Illegitimate identity theft aided by online technologies has been cited by the FBI as one of the fastest-growing white-collar crimes in America.
- Parents, students, law enforcement officials, AIDS and cancer patients, gynecologists, politicians, film stars, multimillionaires, and anyone ever divorced—to name just a few special categories of note—are becoming increasingly sensitive about specific privacy risks they now face because of electronic data sharing.
- And not surprisingly, public polling also shows that average citizens are becoming extremely confused and anxious because of all of the above.

If you are dealing with privacy issues today in business, you and your company should understand that privacy can no longer be ignored. Governments are getting restless, consumers are strongly pro-privacy in opinion polls (if not yet consistently in the voting booth or the marketplace), and many of your competitors will likely be using privacy positioning soon as a competitive advantage. Internal privacy policies governing company-to-employee relations will also become increasingly important for employee recruiting and retention and for legal risk management. Over 80 percent of Net users in a recent survey said they would like to see companies require privacy training for all employees. Bottom line: privacy management is a new core competency you must have. If your company does not yet have a privacy policy "owner" who is knowledgeable about privacy issues and empowered to manage them, get one soon.

For government officials, our advice is: keep one foot on the gas and the other on the brake. Continue to respond to rising public concern about privacy by focusing on the most obvious problem areas—such as children's privacy and identity theft. Rattle the saber of regulation, but use it sparingly. Avoid slowing down Internet commerce, which is much more dependent than you might realize on free-flowing, chaotic marketplace experimentation. Before thinking too seriously about managing privacy in the marketplace, manage it first in all government operations (government databases often being the easiest, cheapest source of personal information). But understand that personal privacy will continue to be a major social and political issue in the decades ahead. And stay up to date— privacy is a dynamic, evolving field.

If you are collecting PII as an Internet outlaw, hacker, con man, or online peeping tom, look out. As the privacy heat rises, you'll be the first to pay the price. Fun-and-games time is over. Expect a massive new commitment to fighting info-terrorism and cyber-crime in the very near future. Even minor data thieves may get swept up in the net.

For everyone else—consumers, citizens, Net surfers, parents, etc.—the first thing to realize is that, for all practical purposes, personal privacy is no longer a right, but a skill. Your government— even if you live in privacy-sensitive Europe—will fall far short of offering full protection. Technology is moving too fast. When you interact with an electronic network, you are venturing into strange new territory where facts about you stick like flies to flypaper. Read the signposts—especially company privacy policies as posted on the Internet. If you find your personal privacy being attacked by some online menace, look for help.

Learn as much as you can about how data is collected and used in this new online environment: from now on it's going to be an increasing part of your life. Never give out personal information frivolously—unless you like having companies and people know as much as possible about you. And especially, "vote" for privacy whenever possible by supporting trustworthy merchants with strong, clear privacy policies and practices.

There. That's the easy part.

## Tips and Tricks for Chapter 1

**Lie.** When in doubt about the trustworthiness or integrity of a website operator, if user registration is required, lie. A survey by Boston Consulting Group for TRUSTe revealed that fibbing tended to be a very popular response from users when they were asked to give PII to a website. Although we don't endorse wholesale lying as a practice, we do believe it is a good strategy when you are uncertain of a site's policies. And don't feel too bad if you do fudge your identity a bit—you will not be alone: 30–40 percent of online registration info given over the Web is bogus!

**Tell the truth.** When you do find a company or website you trust, be as open and honest as you can, especially when such information can help provide you with better, more personalized service. MyExcite or MyYahoo, for example, have a great deal of information about the authors' highly personalized needs for information about privacy and technology—and even know our zip codes (in order to personalize our weather reports). Failing to give correct information to Excite or Yahoo!—known to us to be trustworthy information partners—would be foolish.

**Create an alias.** The same Boston Consulting Group survey cited above also revealed that many Internet users had set up a system of false identities for e-mail purposes. The idea was to give out one particular e-mail-address alias whenever registering at a website (especially when registering at a site likely to do considerable direct marketing), while keeping another main identity for friends, family, and business associates. As this e-mail box fills up with promotional inquiries, you can track how companies use and resell the addresses they collect.

**Seed the market.** "Seeding" is a monitoring practice used by privacy assurance organizations such as TRUSTe. The idea is to seed the marketplace with a specific set of unique identities that can be uniquely traced to a single information transaction. If Bill Gates wanted to see if America Online really protected his personal privacy, what he might do is register only at AOL as Willie X. Gates, while putting in correct data everywhere else. In this way, whenever he encountered this particular name—in spam e-mail, in junk mail, or in a telemarketer's call—he would know precisely where it came from. This can be a good way to discover the sources of your own PII leaks, online or otherwise.

**Firewalls: they aren't just for geeks anymore.** In the corporate computing world, firewalls are security systems intended to protect an internal company network against unauthorized entry from the outside. Now firewalls are available for your home computer, too.

Some security suites, including WRQ's AtGuard 3.1 and Aladdin Knowledge Systems' eSafe Protect Desktop 2.1, come equipped with firewall capabilities that let you control access to your PC from other computers. To activate these firewalls, these programs will ask you to create rules describing who can have access to your computer, when they can use it, and what types of activities are permitted.

**Erase your steps.** Most modern Web browsers store a list of the Web pages you've recently visited. This information is stored in the History files and cache. Maybe you want to keep this info away from snoops.

Here's how to erase these entries:

**Netscape Communicator.** Go to the Edit menu and click

Preferences. Then click again on Preferences, and an expanded menu will appear. Choose Cache. Select Clear Disk Cache, and all URLs in the cache will be erased. To clear the History window, choose Preferences from the Edit menu, click the Navigator category, and then click Clear History.

**Microsoft Internet Explorer.** To empty the History folder, go to the Tools menu. Choose Internet Options, and then click on Clear History. To clear the cache, open Windows Explorer and access the directory C:\windows\temporaryinternet files\, and mark all files for deletion.

Some software programs go even further. Weberaser (http://www.weberaser.com/) allows you to specify any file or the contents of any folder on your computer for deletion, erase the most recently used document list from the Start menu, and remove all entries from the Windows Start menu's Run and Find command pull-down lists.

**List your phone number, but not your address.** When your street address is listed in the phone book along with your phone number, you're leaving the door wide open for junk mailers, pesky phone solicitors, and even more mischievous types. That's because most Internet-based people finders and their CD-ROM–based cousins simply copy telephone directory listings into their databases. Once your name, phone number, *and* address are stored in such fashion, it's a simple matter for a computer program to gather all names and addresses by zip code and then move it to a mailing list. Combined with Internet dynamic map systems and a GPS-locator in a car, anyone could beat a path to your door in no time.

If you want people to be able to contact you without making your home vulnerable, ask the phone company to list only your phone number in the next edition of their book. Be aware that this may take a while: most phone books come out only once a year, and the cut-off date for listings changes is usually three or four months before new volumes are distributed.

**Use a "human" anti-spam cop.** Bright Mail is a free spam filtering service that uses a combination of software and real people to evaluate and detect spam being sent to your e-mail box. It shunts offending mail into a Gray Mail folder on your e-mail utility, which you can then read if you wish. More information is available at http://www.brightmail.com/requirements.html.

# 2
# The Hundredth Window

*When speaking of computer systems, never use the word*
*"secure."*
   —*Donald H. Rumsfeld, former U.S. Secretary of Defense*

*Alice could never quite make out, in thinking it over after-*
*wards, how it was that they began: all she remembers is, that*
*they were running hand in hand, and the Queen went so fast*
*that it was all she could do to keep up with her: and still the*
*Queen kept crying "Faster! Faster!"*
   —*Lewis Carroll,* Through the Looking Glass

Privacy. Independence. The right to be left alone.

To Americans, these words have a sacred ring, echoing from the depths of our national character. From the "Don't Tread on Me" era in revolutionary America to the Wild West days of the lonesome cowboy, respect for individual privacy has long been as American as apple pie, with ice cream on top.

Though it has been recognized in various Supreme Court decisions, a fundamental right to privacy is not among the hallowed privileges of citizenship enumerated in our Constitution and Bill of Rights. Perhaps this is because in the sparsely populated frontier territory of our founding fathers, where information moved at horsespeed and homestead lots were measured in acres, a lack of privacy was the least of one's worries.

But make no mistake: in the warp-speed USA that is accelerating into the twenty-first century, individual privacy is no longer a "natural" resource in abundant supply. And consciously or subconsciously, every American citizen knows it.

Personal privacy is being abraded, primarily as a by-product of incredibly powerful new data collection and data processing technologies, networked together with unprecedented ease. Indeed, the reach and penetration of the Internet is all but rewriting the rules of personal privacy, as third parties—information brokers, direct marketers, private detectives, and stalkers included—can learn the attitudes, life histories, contact information, and even physical location of individual people with the click of a mouse.

Privacy is a lot like clean air. There was plenty of both once, but technology has made each considerably less plentiful. Modern transportation, refrigeration, and industrial production clearly have reduced the amount of clean air in our atmosphere—but we've been making progress of late. We have cars that run cleaner, refrigerators that don't pump out fluorocarbons, and industrial plants that voluntarily conform to tough international standards. But making these changes required considerable public effort, and the job remains unfinished. Just ask anyone who has recently visited Mexico City.

To keep privacy from going the way of the Mexico City airshed, we'll need the privacy-enhancing equivalents of catalytic converters and nonventing refrigeration on the Internet. We'll need global business standards for the collection and use of PII. We'll need, in short, a concerted technical effort, combined with the political will to reshape the information rules of our world.

The privacy-as-clean-air metaphor, however, ultimately breaks down. The quality of privacy cannot be measured in a parts-per-million analysis, since quality standards change according to context (children? health? criminal records?), according to culture, even according to individual needs and preferences. Personal privacy is complex, individualistic, sensitive stuff. Also, unlike fresh, clean air, it is not an absolute good. Does anyone want to accord pedophiles, bomb throwers, computer virus programmers, or government officials absolute anonymity?

The truth is, privacy in a post-Internet world is something we are only beginning to understand. We all know that in real life it's okay to step close and peer into a café window, while it's not okay to do so outside a bedroom window. It's good business in the real world to get to know one's customers—to ask how Jason is doing in Little League, for example, or whether Kathy likes her new job. But what are the rules in cyberspace?

## *The Price of Privacy*

It's not just the social mores surrounding privacy that are changing, but also the economics. Personal information about us—as consumers, as citizens, as parents, as employees or business partners—is becoming more and more valuable. In fact, increasing numbers of people are choosing to cash in on it. Witness the phenomenon of Free PC, a fledgling start-up company that burst onto the Internet scene by offering to give away ten thousand computers with free Internet access in exchange for agreeing to receive a continuous stream of online advertising (presumably for the life of the computer.) Applicants also had to fill out a detailed personal questionnaire, so that ads could be customized to their specific tastes and needs. (Public opinion polls about privacy notwithstanding, there was no shortage of takers for this promotion.) Even short of this extreme, nearly all Net users make regular trade-offs with respect to personal privacy—whether to get customized news at the MyExcite Internet portal, or a king-sized bed in a top-floor hotel room via the online travel and reservations site Expedia.

But the bustling commercial trade in PII does not stop there. A conscious decision to trade a good or service for someone's e-mail address is one thing; it's quite another to provide an Internet service that allows customers to discover a neighbor's bank balance or read an ex-lover's phone bill. In fact, there is an entire underbelly of PII trading that goes on each day, largely unnoticed and essentially unregulated, that would shock most people. It's an even bigger issue when one of the biggest purveyors of PII is our government at all levels, local, state, and federal. Government agencies require citizens to give PII in order to drive a car, own property, pay taxes, etc.; however, this information is not only often made accessible to others, it is sometimes even aggressively marketed by government agencies to individuals and companies, including some who have operations on the Net.

Given the dynamics of Internet growth and the thrust of information technology, it's safe to say that this market for highly personal information—information about each and every one of us—will continue to expand, riding a new wave of seamless information sharing between interlinked systems. As a result, with respect to how much others know, or can know, about us, we'll soon be waking up in an entirely new world.

## The Internet Bazaar

Imagine the Internet as a world of its own—a lively, colorful labyrinth, an electronic bazaar filled with sights, sounds, facts, rumors, delights, dangers, stores, sideshows . . . and people. Very real, often very smart people.

All the great human archetypes are represented: Merchant, Mother, Scholar, Thief, and so on. All are either manipulating or inadvertently triggering technology that connects each to each other. To this new carnival they come by the millions, to explore, to mingle, to learn; to communicate, to play games, to make money.

A surprising number in the crowd are on a mission to collect personal information about other people. Some go about their work covertly, picking the information pockets, as it were, of those wandering through the bazaar. Others, the more sophisticated, more ethical ones, collect huge amounts of personal information, but with permission of the subjects. Both types, and others, are part of the hot new PII trade that is all the rage. And for good reason. Here in the Internet marketplace, information about people is literally more valuable than rubies or gold.

Now, picture the Internet that you use—that is, your own computing platform, and all the links to the online world that make up what we might call your personal "computing environment." Picture this personal computing environment as a grand villa located at the edge of the thriving Internet bazaar. (We know, it may be hard to think of that old Pentium II running Windows 98 as a grand villa, but work with us here.)

You are the lord or lady of this villa. You want to take advantage of this wonderful and exciting Internet marketplace bazaar just outside your door, but you also want to keep out the spies and pickpockets, as well as the con men, vandals, and thieves.

A thick stone wall surrounds your living quarters. In the wall are precisely one hundred doors and windows. These gaps in your stone wall perimeter allow you to see out into the grand bazaar, and to come and go. They are also the spots where you are most exposed, where you may be vulnerable to outside surveillance or even attack.

## The Hundredth Window

Let's assume you are a security-minded owner. You have put stout iron bars in the window openings, shuttered the windows tightly, and put locks and bars on each door. You've even hired an expert to come to your palace and inspect each of your doors and windows, making improvements where necessary, and generally tightening up your defenses. Are you now secure?

Out on the old Silk Road in the steppes of Asia, perhaps you would have been. On the new Electronic Highway, you are not. Because even with the best intentions, and even with an abundance of resources, one of your windows will eventually pop open. Or will be left open accidentally. Or will be pried open by someone on the outside wanting to come in. On the Internet, many of your one hundred doors and windows may not even be under your control; leaving one of them open can be someone else's mistake, without your ever knowing about it. Furthermore, many of the windows — especially those of the operating system variety — often do not close at all, in a security sense. And no matter how many bars and locks you have on the other ninety-nine openings in your villa's stone wall, if you leave just one window open and unguarded, you will be vulnerable. In computer security parlance, that one opening is called the "hundredth window."

It's hard to accept, but the fact is, each and every one of us today who regularly uses the Internet has a hundredth-window problem. We're living in our virtual villa on the edge of the wild, wonderful, and dangerous Internet bazaar, and we have a window open. Our online privacy and security can be compromised, no matter how vigilant we might think we are.

How could this have happened? How could a system so vital to world commerce, communication, and security be so essentially flawed?

There are several answers. First, architects intentionally designed modern computing systems to maximize information sharing and to enable the remote control of a particular PC by network system administrators and other technically adept users. Consequently, certain windows and doors have been put in the system to make it easy for administrators to manage the network—and these openings are generally unknown to the average Internet user. The rise of the Internet did bring some local control back to the desktop, but most browsers and websites were not designed for user control or privacy. In fact, most of them were add-ons that demanded that Internet technology do just the opposite: amass as much data about site visitors and customers as possible. Very few sites or Internet technology companies were funded using business models in which their hot new technology would carefully abstain from collecting any personal data. One of the reasons that network computing systems are as vulnerable as they are is that they were designed that way, on purpose.

But even when the technology is airtight, other problems pop up. For example, suppose during a household remodeling job, a contractor forgets to close and lock one of the house doors after installing a new appliance. It happens, and that kind of thing can happen in the online world as well.

For example, a phone company employee—we'll call him Harold—experienced this firsthand when a super-high-speed direct subscriber line was installed in his home as part of a trial program. Within a month of getting high-speed DSL access to the Internet, Harold discovered a "Read Me" file on the hard drive of his home PC system. He opened the file and started reading. It was a warning note from a fellow DSL subscriber, alerting him that his hard drive was now exposed and accessible to others in his local loop. Needless to say, Harold made sure that the phone company's engineers corrected the problem.

Essentially, the problem in Harold's case was a failure to take the proper precautions when using DSL. Unless a user specifically resets the network defaults in the PC, or installs snoop-resistant "firewall" software that will protect against unwarranted access to his computer files from the outside, a DSL connection from a telephone company acts as if it is a part of the local PC's "Network Neighborhood" feature. Someone on the same DSL network using the Network Neighborhood pull-down menu from another computer could access Harold's hard drive directory directly . . . and read or delete any file in his computer. Oops.

This gaping hole in Harold's computing environment arrived courtesy of the phone company's new service. The Network Neighborhood open window was a holdover from the days when DSL was a business-only product. Then, the system administrator at each business would be savvy enough to recognize the issue and install appropriate firewall software. As the product migrated to the consumer market, however, there were no local experts in place to configure the system properly. The situation called for Pacific Bell to redesign their product before releasing it to the home market, or at least alert subscribers to this security/privacy leak, but they themselves were just starting to realize the importance of computing security in the home. Frankly, this type of security breach occurs even more frequently on cable modem systems where users find themselves sharing a common connection (cable companies generally being less sensitive about privacy issues than phone companies).

But even when you think you've sealed all the cracks around your doors and windows and added a firewall for additional protection, a team of focused experts with better tools can outsmart you. Consider the case of David Lee Smith, the reclusive computer programmer who pleaded guilty to writing and launching the data-corrupting Melissa virus that struck computers across the country in February 1999, and is generally regard as the most widespread and costly computer virus in history. The reclusive Smith had enough technical savvy to bring down the e-mail servers of companies around the world, but not enough, apparently, to keep his online identity private. (FBI officials, with a big assist from America Online, discovered a "digital fingerprint" on the virus and traced it back to Smith's New Jersey apartment.)

If a sophisticated computer programmer with an obsession about privacy had a hundredth window open in his personal computing environment, chances are we all do. In fact, given the legitimate security concerns raised precisely because of cybercreeps like Smith, the fact is that hundredth-window vulnerabilities in the network, exploited occasionally to identify wrongdoers, might actually add to overall security rather than decrease it. (We don't really want guys like Smith dropping virus bombs on the Net with impunity, do we?)

We're not saying that following the digital cookie crumbs back to Smith's door was a trivial task. He thought he had been logging onto fully anonymous Internet sessions. For the most part, they were. But he left a window open. It may have been a difficult-to-access secret entrance, but it still left him vulnerable. And that's the point: this vulnerability exists for all of us, in varying degrees, whenever we are online.

The "hundredth window" is a kind of computer security fable, told to remind technicians of essential computing vulnerabilities and to teach them the important lesson that an interlocking chain of security is only as secure as its weakest link (which is where computer security systems are usually broken). Part of the art of computer system security, therefore, is the continual strengthening of the weakest links in the computing chain. This type of activity takes place all the time. Even though obvious vulnerabilities remain in the system after the work, in relative terms, the security of a system is always stronger when the weakest link has been strengthened.

In private local systems, constantly upgrading and strengthening these weak links is a fairly manageable task. But in an open, global, public network such as the Internet, it's all but impossible. We have been speaking of the hundredth window essentially as a PC security problem, but it also applies to Internet privacy, in spades. Because with respect to the flow of information on the Net, it's not only the cracks and openings in your personal computing environment that contribute to a loss of privacy, but the entire architecture of the Web—a system that was not at all designed to protect private information.

This essential design character of the Internet—decentralized, open, and unstructured—has enormous implications for security, for privacy, for commerce, and for society. Not for nothing is the Internet called a public network: except when being used by true experts, there is virtually nothing private about it.

This simple fact is about to profoundly change our lives.

## Gossip at the Speed of Light

A billion computers. All connected, all exchanging information with each other, all the time.

That's the vision of Intel, the world's leading manufacturer of the microprocessors that power the machines that, increasingly, empower the world. When you consider that another Intel goal is to go from the 6 million transistors on a single microprocessor today to a billion transistors per chip by the year 2012, well, let's just say we're headed toward a public network with a ton of processing horsepower. A network thousands of times more powerful than the Internet today. Now, hold that thought for a moment as we consider the ways that information courses through this massive system.

The Internet utilizes an innovative communications architecture. In terms of personal privacy, the significance of this architecture has been that suddenly, for the first time in human history, the tools and systems used to collect and manage information have become interconnected. A personal fact about John J. Hoosier of Indiana can be "scraped" off the Internet by Ravi K. Brahmin in India and shared instantly with Gretchen Fjord, a Web merchant in Norway, who can, in the next instant, get back in touch with Mr. Hoosier directly, by phone or e-mail.

Imagine buying lunch several years from now. You walk in, touch one square on a computer screen to order the daily special, and place your hand on the pad nearby to pay for it. The pad is a biometric device that identifies you and plugs you into the global money grid without your having to sign a check, carry a card, or remember a PIN or password. Instantly, your handprint is scanned, your identity is authenticated, your electronic banking account (run by a company, let's say, in the Netherlands) is debited, and the burrito joint gets the same amount credited into its merchant account. The bank not only verifies that you've got enough money in the account, it also signals to its marketing partner, an online ad-serving company in Toronto, that you are a high-value customer. The Toronto company quickly flashes you a personal message on the desktop PC where you ordered your burrito. Would you like free nachos with that, courtesy of First Cyberbank of the Netherlands?

As you enjoy your kelp-and-avocado burrito, with nachos, the transaction doesn't stop. The transaction details are sent to a company in Ireland, to be data-mined. The resulting personal profile about you is in turn shared with a direct marketing company in New York, which will connect this profile with other profiles about you. After a bit of cross-referencing, the New York company decides (automatically) to pique your interest in a trip to Cabo San Lucas via a phone call later that evening.

But that's still not all. The result of this profiling and data mining may reveal patterns about you as an individual purchaser that, well after the purchase, become available to all kinds of companies, and even government agencies, years after the transaction. Given the seamless new network infrastructure that is in place now, trading and distributing even complex personal profiles and histories is suddenly as easy as picking up a phone, or clicking a mouse.

The Hundredth Window

In the old days—say, twenty to thirty years ago—when most information about people was still being stored in cramped file drawers or dusty boxes, the very real barriers of locks, security guards, geographical distance, communication costs, and political boundaries provided consumers with considerable privacy protection (from all but the local gossip). The private details of life were generally private, and certainly safe from bank employees in the Netherlands, data-mining analysts in Ireland, and direct marketers in New York; but, as technology marketers love to proclaim (quite correctly), the Internet changes everything. Even the privacy of burrito eaters.

## *They Know Who You Are*

The Internet has created an unprecedented arena of human interconnectivity, but it is not just this increased connectivity that is changing the privacy landscape. The second major driver of change is the fact that the Internet and information technologies generally are greatly reducing the number of anonymous transactions in society and replacing them with ones that involve an exchange of PII. Everyday activities like reading the newspaper, shopping, traveling, and communicating often used to take place without a trace of personal information being left behind; in this age of Web-based newspapers, credit cards, e-mail, and e-commerce, such fleeting anonymous transactions are rarities. Records of what we read and buy, where we go, and whom we communicate with are everywhere.

And not only is more information about us being captured, but the various information devices that collect and manage the data are themselves becoming networked, and thereby rapidly becoming more and more powerful.

Joining the great Internet parade are new or beefed-up software applications, databases, fiber-optic lines, wireless communications systems, search engines, neural nets, Net-cams and Net-mikes, electronic commerce-management tools, mailing list management software with million-recipient capability, smart cards with circuit chips that can store information about you as well as your personal identification number, electronic wallets that allow you to pay for Internet purchases with a credit card or deduction from your checking account, and thousands of other tools and devices.

As if engaged in a game of hyperactive leapfrog, each new technology leaps off the last one's back, leveraging the power of other technologies already in the grid. As a result, it's not only the network's raw processing power that is growing exponentially, but also its reach—into ever more devices, which collect and transmit ever more data. Each successful new component in the system makes the other parts stronger, helps the information input/output become ever more precise, increases the demand for even newer devices that can further leverage the power of the network—thus driving the technology marketplace to run, like Alice in Wonderland, faster! faster!

By now, however, the dynamic pace of Internet Age technologies is old news. We know that an awesome global electronic marketplace is springing up around us. We know that Internet-linked microprocessors will inhabit the smallest nooks and crannies of our lives, bringing real-time communication capability to everything with even a scrap of computational intelligence—from dishwashers to dashboards, from postage meters to potted-plant soil readers. What we may not yet understand is that the impact of all these networked data-swapping devices will be profound, and that tsunami-sized waves of new PII will soon be flowing into corporate databases, government files, news media, direct marketing lists, commercial websites, and individual PCs.

Among the gazillion bits of information that will flow each day through this network of connected devices will be a sizeable number that spell out your:

- exact location and patterns of movement, at any given moment
- address and phone number
- financial status, buying habits, and credit record
- health history and profile
- academic grades, driving record, marital history, criminal record, military record, political, social, and religious affiliations . . .

. . . to name just a few of the more than two hundred categories of personal information that certain online companies track right now. Much of this information about you is probably in the public network today. If you are an active Internet user, some of your PII is being used somewhere in the digital world, by somebody, almost every day. As the network encompasses devices beyond the desktop, you won't have to touch a keyboard or mouse to trigger the network or sensors that capture data about you. The swipe of a frequent user card, a password entered at an ATM, a cellular call, passage through the E-ZPass toll booth, an online search or purchase, renewal of a driver's license, the reading of news online—each of these activities can expand a growing PII profile that will follow you like a new partner in the dance of life.

As computing power grows, and as the number of connected computers climbs toward a billion and beyond, the ability of each computer in the global electronic grid to know and reveal things about you will grow as well. Information about you will increasingly be profiled, shared, and cross-referenced. A new profile created about you by one company will compound with existing ones created by others to produce an ever deeper, ever more useful picture. As these better, more complete pictures of you and your behavior emerge, their worth will grow also. Increasingly, they will become valuable not just as marketing fodder but as products in and of themselves. Companies where you shop or work will be joined by your neighbors, friends, enemies, lovers, in-laws, bankers, lawyers, and others too numerous to mention as anxious purchasers of this new kind of information product. Indeed, complex individual human profiles, complete with various direct links to that individual, will be among the most precious resources in the entire global marketplace.

What do the dynamics of the growing sophistication of PII collection and management mean to the rest of us? Simply this: more and more people are going to know more and more about you and your family. Unless you are very careful—and fairly skillful—the coming "digital metabolism" of a billion interconnected computers will soon be on your trail, tracking you like a hungry bloodhound.

Is this an overly paranoid picture? Well, as Andy Grove, long-time Intel CEO and author of the best-selling book *Only the Paranoid Survive,* has suggested, there's nothing like a little healthy fear to focus the mind and improve performance. And if it's improved performance with respect to privacy protection that we want, we'd better get very focused very quickly, because when it comes to collecting and distributing juicy digital data streams, the Net is just getting warmed up.

## The Coming Sentient Internet

Ponder this for a moment: in the United Kingdom today over 300,000 cameras are mounted on street corners, in subways, and in other public places, transmitting live video streams to police stations via online networking. One station in London now uses facial-recognition software in combination with a closed-circuit network of 140 street cameras to spot criminals in crowds. Japan, Singapore, and parts of the United States, including New York City, are also experimenting with similar online video surveillance systems. And as is always the case with technology innovation, where use in one sector quickly spreads to others, networked video surveillance capability is quickly expanding outside law enforcement, notably onto the Internet. At this writing, over two thousand Internet sites now feature "spy-cams" which transmit real-time sound and pictures of unknowing subjects.

This may be only the beginning. Technology futurists such as Paul Saffo are predicting that the first decade of the twenty-first century will produce a "sentient" Internet—a highly sophisticated information-gathering network linking hundreds of thousands of biometric input devices, millions of tiny video cams, tens of millions of optical scanners, and hundreds of millions of computer keyboards from around the planet. Daily life will be recorded as never before, and the resulting data and personal identity profiles constructed with this data will become widely available throughout the entire realm of connected computers. This live, sentient network, say the futurists, will not only know who you are and what you've done, but *what you're doing right now*. Privacy invasions, then, will become real-time events, and often quite unexpected ones.

Predicting the future of "sentient-network" technology is a hazardous task, but projecting Internet trends at least some distance into the future is a necessity if we are to devise strategies for personal privacy protection, industry self-regulation, and e-commerce growth—all worthy goals. Technology trends clearly suggest a growing capability to conduct electronic surveillance, track personal data, build personal profiles, and deliver them to anyone, anywhere. However, this is not the same thing as saying that technology *should* always do these things. (Any more than atomic bombs should be exploded because they can be, or life support devices should be kept on indefinitely simply because they work.) Countervailing factors such as public opinion, government regulation and industry self-regulation, changing consumer behavior, and other "soft forces" can shape technology development in ways that are quite surprising . . . and productive.

## *Privacy As a Public Issue*

We now find ourselves living in a world where, as leading computer visionary David Gelernter wrote a decade ago in his prophetic book *Mirror Worlds,* technology is essentially able to convert "the *theoretically* public into the *actually* public. What was always available in principle. . . . becomes available in fact."

For many people, the technology-enabled trend of making heretofore private parts of our lives "actually public" is happening much too fast. The data-hungry Internet, where more than seven of eight "dot-com" sites collect some form of personally identifiable information, is increasing public concern about privacy and causing a wholesale reexamination of privacy issues in all forms of commerce. According to one recent poll, nearly 80 percent of adults say the increasing use of computers and the Internet is reducing personal privacy.

In our daily lives, perhaps unwanted e-mail, or "spam," is the most obvious invasion of our online privacy. You will begin to realize that online privacy is about much more than spam and other forms of nuisance marketing, however, if:

- Your fiercest business competitor gets detailed records of your phone calls and travel itineraries, online.
- You learn that a live satellite image of your house—at a level that shows real-time car movement—can be accessed online.
- Your online identity is stolen.
- Your daughter suddenly shows up on somebody else's spy-cam.

These kinds of things are happening on the Internet today. More privacy intrusions are coming. Some would even say that we have lost so much of our personal privacy to the computing age that

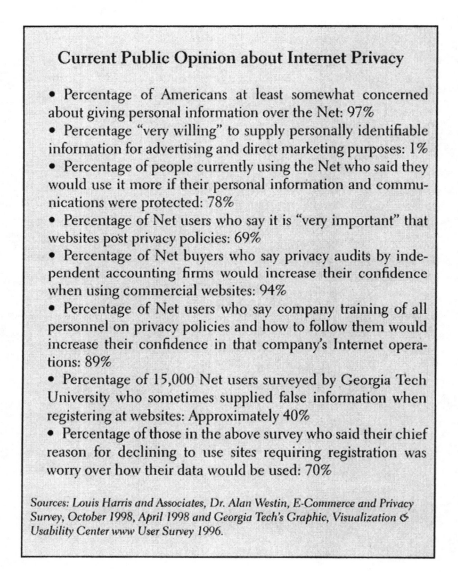

## Current Public Opinion about Internet Privacy

• Percentage of Americans at least somewhat concerned about giving personal information over the Net: 97%

• Percentage "very willing" to supply personally identifiable information for advertising and direct marketing purposes: 1%

• Percentage of people currently using the Net who said they would use it more if their personal information and communications were protected: 78%

• Percentage of Net users who say it is "very important" that websites post privacy policies: 69%

• Percentage of Net buyers who say privacy audits by independent accounting firms would increase their confidence when using commercial websites: 94%

• Percentage of Net users who say company training of all personnel on privacy policies and how to follow them would increase their confidence in that company's Internet operations: 89%

• Percentage of 15,000 Net users surveyed by Georgia Tech University who sometimes supplied false information when registering at websites: Approximately 40%

• Percentage of those in the above survey who said their chief reason for declining to use sites requiring registration was worry over how their data would be used: 70%

*Sources: Louis Harris and Associates, Dr. Alan Westin, E-Commerce and Privacy Survey, October 1998, April 1998 and Georgia Tech's Graphic, Visualization & Usability Center www User Survey 1996.*

we should just get used to it. "Privacy is gone," claimed Sun Microsystems CEO Scott McNealy. "Get over it."

And yet our experience has shown that true privacy—that age-old friend of lovers, artists, conspirators, and saints—*can* survive alongside powerful network technology. *If* we act. If we realize that the rules are changing and that old assumptions about personal privacy and security no longer apply. If we understand that in a fully and powerfully interconnected world, whether we like it or not, privacy requires vigilance.

The government is not going to protect your online privacy—at least, not much. You must learn who you can trust, and who you can't. And you can start by being very careful about trusting anyone—especially a CEO with a stock price to defend—who says that privacy is dead.

## Twenty Reasons Why You Should Care About Internet Privacy

Regardless of how the Internet and related information systems shape up over the next decade or two, we can confidently expect certain near-term changes in our daily lives resulting from increased use of technology that is currently either in R&D labs or already in the marketplace. That the world's massive interconnected computing environment will steadily increase in size, strength, and sophistication, and extend further into your life, is beyond question. Predictions about its specific impact are more difficult, but we have nevertheless compiled a list of twenty privacy- and security-related phenomena that will come creeping into modern society with increasing force. These are the things you should indeed be paranoid about; and remember, it's not paranoia if you are really being watched.

**Spam.** A torrent of electronic marketing promotions are headed your way. One large Internet news site currently sends *50 million* promotional e-mails per month, albeit with user consent. More than 50 percent of commercial websites now use promotional e-mailing as a marketing tool. (See the Spam Filter tip, page 46.)

**Identity theft.** The FBI calls this the fastest-growing white-collar crime in America. Using PII acquired from a variety of sources—ranging from government databanks and online directories to stolen credit card receipts and rummaged garbage—computer-savvy thieves construct a phony new "you" which they use to purchase goods on the Internet, fraudulently receive government benefits, withdraw savings, and more. Though online credit card companies now limit consumer financial liability in the case of credit card fraud to $50, the consequences of identity theft can be quite serious. Most annoying is the fact that, after experiencing identity theft, you may have trouble proving that *you* are *you*—thereby hampering your own ability to use electronic services. You may also have your identity blended with someone else's as a result of identity theft. Erroneous and damaging credit reports can be particularly troublesome in a massively connected online world. (Protection against identity theft is one of the strongest arguments in favor of personal vigilance with respect to personal privacy online, because the more PII about you circulating in the network, the easier it is for someone to reconstruct your identity.)

**Identity spoofing.** This form of online impersonation usually does not involve intent to defraud but can nonetheless be quite malicious and dangerous. The most common kind of identity spoofing is pretending to be someone you're not, in a newsgroup, chat room, or e-mail message. Adept computer users can "spoof" not only your name but your actual e-mail address, so the message appears to be fully authentic. Though some identity spoofing is good-natured and humorous, other forms can be quite vicious—as in the case of the spurned lover who took on his ex's identity and left postings in sex chat groups. He not only described her supposed fantasies of being raped but gave out her name, address, and apartment security code. She learned about the ruse when a man showed up at her apartment door, offering to play out the fantasy. Fortunately, her apartment door was locked at the time.

**Packaged PII products.** A flourishing new market will develop for products and services, publicly available over the Internet, that sell complex information profiles about individual people. Today, on AltaVista.com, you can plug in a name and get not only an address and phone number but also a detailed map of the neighborhood where your "subject" lives. At TML.com, for $10 a month, you can key in automobile license plate numbers and get names—which can be used at AltaVista.com to get maps, and at onestopinfo.com to get just about anything else you'd want to know about your subject. Shortly, we should expect powerful, flexible Internet applications that bundle these and other kinds of personal information search functions into a single offering. Some will be free, some quite expensive (and extensive).

**Electronic monitoring of the workplace** via networked video cams that will provide managers with real-time remote surveillance capability and through routine screening of employee e-mail. (Surveys show that between 25 and 40 percent of all employers monitor their employees' e-mail.) Some of the results of video surveillance will even make their way outside the office and onto the Internet, as recently happened in the case of a secretary whose boss's hidden video cam caught her urinating in the corner of his office. (Perhaps she was unhappy with her stock options.)

**E-redlining.** The proliferation of accurate, electronic ZAG profiles (Zip code, Age, Gender) makes it possible for companies to screen out certain less profitable, more risky demographic groups. This practice has been used in the offline database world for some time. When it is used to discriminate on the basis of race or ethnicity, it is illegal—offline or on.

**Electronically enabled stalking** by sexual predators, political extremists, "dirt" peddlers, and other unsavory types. A recent case in Florida where the owners of cars parked at an abortion clinic were identified via the services of PII purveyors on the Internet, and then harassed at their homes in person and by telephone, is an example of the political variety of such stalking.

**Unauthorized, illicit spy-cams** feeding video onto the Net. One such Internet camera was installed in the men's dressing room of a popular fitness center in Vancouver, Washington (to name just one incident of many). The spy-cam fed images of men undressing and taking showers onto the Internet for several months before it was discovered.

**Mouse-prints.** Tools that track your behavior online—to record what sites you visit and even how long you stay there—are proliferating. The resulting information, which can be parsed down to the time spent viewing specific marketing messages, and in which order, can be very valuable. When such data is linked to PII and compounded with information from other sources, a very deep individual profile emerges. The notorious "cookies"—blocks of data that websites can deposit in your computer for future identification purposes—are but one of many technologies being used for this purpose.

**Industrial espionage** can be expected to increase across the board, but with a number of new twists—such as the acquisition, by a company's competitors, of detailed travel patterns and phone call records of its top executives. A number of companies on the Internet now promote such services on a fee basis. Traditional espionage will also include electronic methods. One British company found that its intranet had been hacked. . . . and then several months later was surprised to discover a product identical to one they'd designed suddenly on the market. The competitor, based in a foreign country, had enlisted local British hackers to crack the company network and steal the design in exchange for sophisticated hacking tools. The foreign company beat the Brits to market by two weeks.

**Hacker vandalism.** At a Rand Foundation conference attended by one of the authors, a high-ranking U.S. official revealed that a single branch of the military reported over five thousand full-root-access hacks into their computers in a single year. (Full-root access essentially means that the hacker has complete control over the computer in question.) Though most such incidents today go unreported—it's both embarrassing and a further security risk to go public with the facts—hacks in the past three years have shut down a phone system operating in five states, taken over temporary control of the computer monitoring a space shuttle flight, and wrought havoc at a major weather prediction center, to name just a few of the more notable incidents. Much of this activity falls in the category of youthful high jinks, but a growing trend toward politically motivated hacking, or "hactivism," is rising as well.

**Cellular spying.** Laptop computers equipped with the appropriate software can now be used as cell phone interception devices, simply by maneuvering them to within the required range (about a mile, in most cases) and scrolling through and selecting a specific frequency from many presented on the screen. Even more insidious, however, is the use of cellular locating technology to pinpoint and follow the movements of a particular cell phone user as he or she travels around the neighborhood, or around the world.

**E-revenge.** This category includes the posting of slanderous or even salacious content about others in newsgroups, online community chat groups, and other realms of Internet publishing. Certain Internet sites are currently soliciting and even paying for revealing photos of ex-lovers and spouses from the angry and disgruntled, in order to put them on public display on the Web.

**Electronic lifestyle monitoring,** such as the kind that links supermarket purchasing patterns to insurance actuarial tables and to individual policy rates for health and life insurance. (Too much liquor and butter in that shopping cart? That'll be an extra $50 a month on your life insurance, please.) A database developer in

Boston told us that he had been recruited, unsuccessfully, to work on just such a project.

**Party line–style online snooping,** especially in the case of high-speed cable networks providing Internet access to an entire neighborhood of up to 500 homes from a single node. Standard and relatively simple computer security practices can prevent that teenage genius next door from gaining access to your private files, but a great many people will learn the hard way why such practices are necessary.

**"Linda Tripping."** This is the term information brokers now use for the recording and distribution of supposedly private phone conversations. The Internet twist on the old wiretap game is to record a conversation, encode it as an audio file, and then send it as an e-mail attachment to interested, or titillated, third parties. The rise of Internet telephony will make this unseemly practice much easier, since all the tools needed to capture phone conversations can be conveniently located on the desktop, just a click away.

**Identity reverse-engineering.** Health care providers, among others, have long understood that even an anonymous information profile can sometimes be traced back to an individual person. If the health histories of all the employees at a certain company become publicly available, for example, an individual familiar with the workforce might be able to put two and two together to find out that Jack has a heart condition or that Amy has herpes. A similar process, supported by sophisticated information technology, can be deployed to reconstruct personal identifiers, thus making it possible in certain cases to convert anonymous information to PII.

**Fan/flame sites.** We can expect a proliferation of websites that track and monitor in great detail the lives, loves, triumphs, and tragedies of every sort of celebrity and public figure. One unfortunate consequence of this trend is that misdeeds, stupid remarks, compromising photo sessions, and other potentially embarrassing remnants of a celebrity's past will gain a new permanence and tend to linger forever. While this phenomenon will not affect most people directly, it could have considerable impact on the political process.

**Universal identifiers.** Much like fingerprints, Intel's Processor Serial Number feature, built into its Pentium III microprocessor, allowed individual computer users to be traced when they accessed the Internet. This technology led to a modest consumer boycott of Intel products on privacy grounds. The proposed national health ID advocated by the National Centers for Disease Control is another of many examples. A number of European countries, including Denmark and Germany, already have such unique identifiers. They have long been resisted in the United States but could emerge in this country under certain conditions.

**Broken promises,** such as happened when GeoCities sold customer information to third parties despite published policies to the contrary. This case led to Federal Trade Commission penalties, but many more instances of companies violating their own privacy policies can be expected. Many of these violations are inadvertent, but still significant.

• • •

As the above list makes all too clear, the consequences of having private information fall into untrustworthy hands can be serious, even disastrous.

But this list of risks, scams, and threats is only one side of the picture. Yes, we all now have a hundredth window open—an essential vulnerability that we must manage. And yes, private information about us is flowing around the planet as never before. But there is also a positive side to this new information landscape, a side that it would be extremely foolish to throttle, distort, or destroy. It's a dimension that can reshape our world in dramatic ways and actually enhance our quality of life. It is to this positive side of the information infosphere that we now turn.

## Tips and Tricks for Chapter 2

**Build a personal firewall.** ConSeal Private Desktop for Windows 95/98 is a personal firewall that safeguards your PC's connection to the Internet. Designed for the nontechnical user, this privacy management tool stops all of the most common attacks, including "denial of service" (an attempt to disable your Internet access account) and direct log-ons from cyber-stalkers. Unless you first identify an "object" (software application or Java applet) that comes to you over the Internet as "trusted," ConSeal Private Desktop will block it from appearing on your computer. (http://www.signal9.com/sales/cpd/index.html)

SyShield lets you configure the type of firewall access you want on your home computer. It decides to allow or deny every incoming Internet packet based on your security level choice. If it senses any potential hacking or attacking attempts, SyShield will close your Internet connection and send a warning message to your computer screen. (http://www.sybergen.com/why/comp-txt.htm)

**Install a spam filter.** Spam Buster comes armed with an arsenal of more than 150 text-based filters. These are based on several criteria, including message subject (such as the word "rich") message header, and sender (a blacklist of almost 17,000 known spammer e-mail addresses and domain names). Spam Buster also has the ability to filter messages on the basis of size. In the Spam Buster dialog box, you can view, edit, and delete these filters, as well as create your own red lights, according to your preferences. (http://www.contactplus.com/spam/spam.htm)

SpamKiller squashes annoying spam in several disqualifying categories such as sender, subject, message text, e-mail header (including X-Mailer and other X headers), and country code. Because some country codes are known to be used by spammers, this can be a useful feature. SpamKiller will also check for invalid e-mail addresses and determine whether or not the sender and reply-to addresses are identical. (http://www.spamkiller.com)

**Find an infomediary.** As predicted by McKinsey consulting gurus John Hagel and Arthur Armstrong in their book *Net.Gain*, 1999 saw the rise of a new breed of privacy player on the Internet. Dubbed "infomediaries" by Hagel, these new companies act as information intermediaries, meaning that they collect and store your PII and help you make intelligent choices regarding the exchange of this data with others (especially companies). Infomediaries offer a measure of convenience (you don't have to refill the same online forms all the time) and protection (when they are set up correctly). The market for infomediary services is still at an early stage, but if you are interested in this type of service, two initial leaders worth looking at are Lumeria (at lumeria.com) and Privaseek (privaseek.com).

**Guard the home.** Meaning, in this case, all the data that can be used to link you uniquely to your home. This includes your street address, obviously, but also your phone number, your social security number, credit card numbers and even automobile license plates. As information about you proliferates on the Web (as opposed to just being stored in various private, offline databases), and as data-searching agents become more plentiful and more powerful, you'll want to be especially careful about giving out any of this data indiscriminately, since it can be used to establish the location of your residence. Protecting your home address calls for special care, because even though quite a number of bad things can happen when your privacy is compromised, few are worse than actually having your personal living space invaded. And since information put on the Web today will live for a very long time, available to search agents, now is the time to begin taking precautions.

You'll have to give out your address, of course, when ordering physical goods online—today, this can't be helped. (As we go to print, United Parcel Service has announced its intentions to provide a universal indexing service that would allow you to insert your private UPS ID number instead of your actual home address. It is a terrific idea, but one that will mean that UPS's own internal privacy will have to be airtight.) But even now you can greatly reduce your risk of PII leakage by trading with reputable online companies, preferably ones with both privacy policies and certification by a privacy seal program such as TRUSTe or the Better Business Bureau online. For the time being, our best advice is to insist on trading online only with companies that agree specifically in their privacy policy not to sell or distribute physical addresses. Also, be sure to keep your home address out of newspapers, online bulletin boards, chat groups, and telephone books and all other local directories.

It should go without saying, but since we're all new to this online world, we'll say it anyway: Be sure to tell your children not to give out your phone number, home address, or school name to online chat groups, websites, or online merchants. For younger children, even giving out their real names is not a good idea.

**Remove your name.** The Direct Marketing Association has an active program that enables you to remove your name from many (but not all) direct marketing databases. Removing your name is quite simple—simply send a card to the Direct Marketing Association, P.O. Box 9014, Farmingdale, NY 11735. (This removal is binary; you are either removed from all DMA lists or none. But you can start over and send your name to a few select companies if you want to receive e-mail promotions or catalogs.)

**Know and then upgrade your browser's encryption strength.** The newest versions of Netscape Communicator and Microsoft Internet Explorer offer 128-bit encryption strength. If you're running Communicator and are not sure what the encryption capabilities are, you can check it by going to the Fortify.net website and typing "https://www.fortify.net/sslcheck.html." For Internet Explorer, click on the Help menu, then select the About IE button and read the Cipher Strength info.

To download a 128-bit encryption version of Netscape Communicator (Windows or Mac), visit http://www.netscape.com/computing/download/.

To download a 128-bit encryption version of Microsoft Internet Explorer (Windows or Mac), visit http://www.microsoft.com/windows/ie/ie5/.

For the average Internet user, the first security enhancement to consider is the upgrading of the browser so as to take advantage of stronger encryption and other security enhancements.

**Use filters.** Virtually all modern e-mail applications have strong filtering features—many more than are deployed by average users. Use the Help menu in your e-mail client application to read about how the filters work in your system. Filters not only can screen unwanted mail, such as promotional spam or boring entreaties from that pesky ex-boyfriend, but using them can also help you manage your e-mail more effectively, by sorting the mail as it comes into your in-box.

**Crumble those cookies.** "Cookies" are small bits of code that are deposited onto your local computer by websites that you visit. Cookies are not necessarily invasive, especially when they come from site vendors with responsible privacy practices. But they are frequently deposited in your computer without your knowledge and consent, and they do provide both an externally accessible record of your online travels and a convenient hook for various data collection schemes.

Check to see whether cookie files have been deposited on your computer. (You may be shocked to see how many there are.) If you have a PC, look for a file on your hard drive labeled "cookies.txt" for Netscape browsers and the directory \windows\cookies for IE browsers. If you use a Macintosh PC, look for a file called "magic cookies." It will enable you to remove cookies from your hard drive or block the delivery of new batches of cookies. In the pull-down menu on your browser's feature bar, look under the headings Preferences or Options.

To banish cookies in Netscape Communicator: Go to Program Files\Netscape\Users\(Your) User Name, and delete the cookies.txt files. All cookies will then be deleted.

To delete them in Microsoft Internet Explorer: Go to the Windows\Profiles\UserName\Cookies directory and delete the files you don't want.

Certain browser add-on programs can handle this as well as let you specify which cookies you'd like retained or erased. *PC Magazine*'s PC Labs website has a list of such programs, with download links, at http://www.zdnet.com/pcmag/stories/reviews/0,6755,2311289,00.html.

WRQ's @Guard utility allows Web users to choose whether cookies report information about them back to a site. The software also allows you to accept cookies from sources you trust, such as subscription sites.

Consider a subscription-based encryption service. Until now, people who wanted to prevent websites from collecting private information had to use proxy sites such as Anonymizer.com. When you use them as a jumping-off point, proxy servers operating at hub sites block other websites from gaining access to user information.

But proxy sites come with drawbacks. For example, proxy sites are typically unable to accept cookies. Although some Internet users hate them, others find that cookies can be useful for eliminating the hassle and saving the time of repeatedly entering passwords and other information.

New programs, currently being developed and expected to be released soon, use software that you download and install on your PC to encrypt personally identifying information, including your Internet address.

**Websites are easy to duplicate but URLs are not.** Since digital graphics are easy to copy, whole websites can be "spoofed" and made to appear legitimate when they are anything but. Such a site may also have a URL address very similar to the one it is trying to pass itself off as, but it cannot exactly duplicate the URL. Here's a hypothetical example: http://www.barnesandnobel.edu (instead of http://www.barnesandnoble.com). A famous knock-off was the porn site Jennycam, which is not to be confused with the G-rated web-cam site Jennicam.

One helpful resource that allows you to specifically check a website's URL is Network Solutions Internic WhoIs Server (http://www.internic.net/whois/). Type in the site's address where it says "Get a Web Address or Search Our Database for Availability." If the address is in use, it will show who has registered it and the address. Additional information such as contact name, phone number, and a company address may also be posted.

Use "Mail Controls" to guard your privacy on AOL. Type "Mail Controls" in AOL's Keyword bar. You'll come to a page with Parental Controls and Junk Mail settings. To use Mail Controls:

Make sure that you are signed onto AOL using a master screen name. (Master screen names include the first screen name you created when you joined AOL as well as any other screen names that have been designated as master screen names using Parental Controls.)

Click the Set Up Mail Controls button below. A screen will appear that displays all of the screen names on your account.

Select the screen name for which you'd like to set Mail Controls.

Click EDIT. A screen will appear, allowing you to set Mail Controls for the screen name that you have selected. Among other functions, you can use Mail Controls to block incoming e-mail from addresses you specify.

*To use Parental Controls.* AOL has four Parental Controls category levels. You can choose from the Kids Only (ages 12 and under), Young Teen (ages 13–15), Mature Teen (ages 16–17), and General Access (ages 18 and older) categories. Each category has a different level of access to information on AOL and the rest of the Internet, as well as to features that allow a member to communicate with others online (including Instant Message conversations, chat rooms, newsgroups, and e-mail). Using the Custom Controls accessible from the Set Parental Controls window, you can adjust the controls to best suit your child's maturity level—or your own.

Smart cards may be getting too smart. The day may not be too far off when one card you carry around with you will store credit card information, your driver's license, your frequent flyer numbers, and even a biometric sensing device that will be able to identify you based on your fingerprints or other physical traits. While smart card vendors will doubtlessly position this as a convenient time-saver—fewer cards to carry around—privacy advocates are nervous because of the potential for disparate pieces of information about you to be tied together. Others worry about the potential for abuse if enough data about you fell into the wrong hands.

As this technology edges closer to reality, watch the public debate that is sure to hit the headlines.

# 3
# Something Digital This Way Comes

*It's great to be great, but it's greater to be human.*
—*Will Rogers*

The twentieth century was an era of spectacular, unprecedented technological progress. But this progress clearly came with a sociological price, and throughout the century ordinary citizens worried greatly about technology's impact on society and its tendency to butt into our private lives.

Personal privacy issues, in the modern sense, first surfaced in Stalinist Russia and Nazi Germany, where personal information was collected on a mass scale and used by tyrants for horrific ends. In the English-speaking world, however, the first real crescendo of popular concern about privacy and modern technical progress came just as computing was getting started, in 1949. The catalytic event was the publication of George Orwell's *1984*—a response to Stalinist-style totalitarianism.

This classic satire depicts a cold, cynical world subject to an omnipresent Big Brother who spouts "doublethink" slogans ("War is Peace," "Freedom is Slavery") and whose eyes on giant billboards follow everyone everywhere. The loss of personal privacy is a central theme. Big Brother serves as the figurehead of a ubiquitous entity known simply as "the Party." Using powerfully invasive surveillance technologies to track its citizens' every move, the Party manages—quite successfully—to control the mass of humanity by stamping out independent thought and political dissent.

Orwell's novel took its place beside an earlier classic with a similar vision of a dark, managed future, Aldous Huxley's *Brave New World*. Together these two bitterly satirical books reshaped the modern debate about privacy, each using a similar clever ploy: they pitted privacy against technology.

These two learned British authors, both remarkable men with wide-ranging interests and careers, captured the public imagination and influenced political rhetoric for a generation, tapping into growing public anxiety about scientific progress. By 1949, only seventeen years after *Brave New World* was published, science had given birth to atomic bombs, television, computers, and even advanced psychological brainwashing techniques. New forces were being unleashed upon society—and with remarkable prescience, both men looked deeply into the nature of these forces and imagined dark new worlds.

Orwell's *1984* had the greatest immediate impact, almost overnight adding a new vocabulary of privacy violation to the English language. When a government became too intrusive, it was behaving like Big Brother. "Orwellian" became a sinister adjective, ready to be pinned onto anything deemed a threat to individual privacy and freedom, from mainframe computers to Nixon's bungling burglars. "1984" itself became a shorthand term for a future run amuck. From 1949 until the end of the Cold War four decades later, few works of fiction shaped political debate like those of

George Orwell, and none had a bigger impact on the issue of privacy than *1984*.

Today, it is Huxley's *Brave New World* that has proven the more prophetic of the two books. It certainly is more pertinent to mankind's current dilemmas with information technology. In Huxley's world, it is not a Soviet-style, truth-destroying dictatorship that mankind confronts, but insidious social progress and soul-numbing technology, all created with good intentions. High-tech wonders such as the Prozac-like drug Soma, the virtual-reality-like "feelies," and genetically engineered test-tube babies are used to create a society without anxiety, pain, disease, suffering—or any real privacy. And as Huxley deftly shows, with the loss of privacy comes a loss of identity and will.

The technologies in *Brave New World* are amazing. If Huxley were reincarnated today as a high-tech entrepreneur, he could probably bag millions from Silicon Valley venture capitalists with his "feelies" concept alone. But in Huxley's false utopia, the progress that these technologies bring is a fool's bargain. Ultimately, it is only in the wilds of the desert, living the life of a "savage" in the private spaces far away from the wonders of technology, that our humanity can be fully experienced and preserved.

For nearly half a century, these two novels have served as distinct poles of an ongoing debate about privacy, government, and technology. On the one hand, we have those (on the right and the left) who, like Orwell, fear a centralized Big Brother state, strongly believe in holding government in check, and value individual freedom over state control. On the other side are those, like Huxley, who are deeply suspicious of new technologies and the businesses that build them, and who value the human dignity of all people. This is an oversimplification, but these two extremes still resonate in the polarized political debate about privacy—an issue that today is being actively debated in nearly every major political capital in the world.

One thing both Orwell and Huxley got right was the power of technology to abrade personal privacy. We share both Orwell's concerns about centralized governmental control of information and information policy and Huxley's worry that technology can, if not carefully watched and moderated, insidiously erode core human values. And yet, though hardly Pollyannas about the role of technology in our lives, we approach the whole issue of information technology and man's relationship to it with considerably more optimism than either Orwell or Huxley. The reason? Fifty additional years of history.

## Digital Metabolism Rising

Some experts—including, notably, Arno Penzias, a 1978 Nobel laureate and discoverer of cosmic microwave background radiation—maintain that the Internet has come into existence more out of a need for computers to communicate with one another than from any real human need. However strange this notion might sound, there is no denying that today's computing environment is indeed one odd beast. Computers are now fundamentally in charge of the most important human communications systems, routing message units this way and that according to dynamic changes in the state of the system itself. This decentralized routing of tiny packets of information by machines themselves—rather than by humans pushing buttons and executing arcane computer code—is a powerful innovation. It is, in fact, the brilliant insight at the core of the Internet. From this insight has come the foundation of a whole new information architecture, a new machine-driven model of information flow that will dominate the social debate about individual privacy and freedom in the next fifty years, much as fears of Big Brother and intrusive centralized government bureaucracies have for the last fifty.

It is a slippery slope, this massive new digital terrain. The heart of its value, and the source of its power, lies in the free flow of information it enables. And yet it is precisely this same free flow of information that must be dammed up, at least in part, if the deep human need for privacy is to be satisfied.

To understand the nature of this dilemma, it is first important to understand a few basics about the technology itself. And a half century after Orwell's and Huxley's visions, this is the information platform that matters: the public, packet-switched Internet; overlaid with the World Wide Web and its ingenious Universal Resource Locator (URL) protocol, which gives every digital machine in the universe a unique address; powered by inexpensive microprocessors that double in processing speed every eighteen months, according to the oft-cited Moore's Law; connected to powerful data-filtering and pattern recognition technology, which can store, sort, retrieve, and generally work magic with information; all linked together via fiber optics, satellite communications, and other sophisticated high-bandwidth transmission systems that can virtually eliminate barriers of time and distance.

Roll this all together, and what you've got is some really potent technology, with potential to increase prosperity, longevity, and self-actualization—or strip us of our most essential and enduring values.

This particular technology set, however, is just a foundation. Soon a wide variety of new applications and services will build upon this foundation and extend the reach of information technology much, much further into daily life, while exponentially expanding the free flow of information in our world.

We often tend to think of this digital infrastructure as merely a set of information conduits and girders, but it's really something more than that, something altogether new and different. It routinely confounds expectations, upsets markets, changes rules, and breaks down barriers. It's evolving faster than a flu virus, and growing like a teenager. With a nice sci-fi touch, George Dyson, the author of *Darwin among the Machines*, calls this quick new thing "the digital metabolism."

It's important to understand that in Dyson's metaphor, the digital metabolism is not a computer; rather, *computers are its cells*. The metabolism itself is the great global network of interconnected information devices—our planet's new pulsating nervous system. It can, indeed, seem eerily biological. The new global network has a "body" that consists of about a hundred million *microprocessors* all jacked-in to a big grid, all speaking the same language. It has a fairly stable nervous system consisting of billions of *strings of code* that waft through the millions of connected semiconductors in this network body. These code strings instruct the processors in much the same way DNA instructs organic cells. Like an unstoppable two-cycle engine, the interplay between these two elemental parts (the *instruction* and the *machine*) keeps driving the whole Internet revolution right on down the tracks, code-to-chip, code-to-chip—*information to cell*.

While information technology probably has not yet crossed the threshold of emergence as a true life form, the Internet's explosive growth and unpredictable twists and turns demonstrate that when we speak of network-era computing, we're no longer talking about data processing as the key function of computers. Mere data-processing power, no matter how fast and efficient, could not have spawned the socioeconomic phenomenon of Internet companies such as Yahoo!, eBay, and Amazon.com. The social tumult ushered into our world by Internet-era computing is far greater than anything operational efficiencies alone could have caused. It is no longer the processing of information in back rooms by massive computing systems that is changing the world, so much as the distribution and general availability of massive amounts of information, from anywhere, to anywhere, over this new widely decentralized computing grid. It is not the ability to crunch data that is changing our world today; it is our ability to mold it into forms that seem, almost, to take on a life of their own. And that know all about us.

## *Info-Power*

If the telephone was about talking, and the television about entertaining, then the Internet, this network of all networks, is about *knowing*—knowing about everything and everyone. Therein lies its power, and its risk.

To suggest that the Internet has a lifelike side is not to say that modern computing really is some sort of mystical dance of the sugar plum fairies, driven by unseen forces. Dyson's biological model notwithstanding, networked code/chip interplay is hard science, growing out of exacting human engineering, executed with extraordinary precision. The sites of some of the most difficult engineering feats of the modern world are giant semiconductor production facilities called fabs. In Arizona, Israel, Ireland, Singapore, Oregon, and other planetary supply points, these fabs stamp out code-bearing chips and send them marching forth into the world, eager to network and serve. When these chips later connect online, they form the elemental structure of the information cloud we call the Internet. And they fuel the tornado of information processing power that resides within it.

With the great force of the Internet, of course, comes great economic potential; and when harnessed properly, the Internet is perhaps the mightiest economic force in history.

Take the case of Exxon, for example—hardly the kind of company one would think of as a high-tech firm. According to the *Wall Street Journal*, Exxon reported that during the first eight years of the 1990s, information technology improved the odds that its wells would strike oil from once in eleven tries to once in every five—resulting in savings of hundreds of millions of dollars per year. Similarly, pharmaceutical companies report that the average time to bring a major new drug to market has been cut nearly in half, solely on the strength of new information technology.

As we mentioned in Chapter 2, information technology drives forward by leaping ahead on its own back, and it's important to keep in mind that new info-tech applications are always applied first to the growth and development of their own kind. The first use of every new Intel microprocessor, for example, is to help in the design of its successor. The first and most advanced use of the Web as a product delivery system (as opposed to a product ordering system) is in the industry sector called electronic software distribution, or ESD. Using ESD technology, publishers of software applications, Web tools, and Internet plug-ins are able to deliver their products directly over the Web, selling "virtual products" that never take a physical form (no CDs, no shrink-wrapped boxes). The first customers in the ESD market were webmasters and other Internet technicians, who loved the fact that they were able to get new software and Web tools instantly over the Internet, rather than having to wait during manufacturing and distribution cycles that might take months. They could get new tools faster, and thus go to work sooner building a better network, which in turn could deliver more tools. And so on.

ESD runs on an economic model that uses this spiraling, rich-get-richer cycle that is the hallmark of networked technology. This cycle is known in contemporary economics as the Law of Increasing Returns, and it accounts for much of the economic growth in all markets over the last decade. If you doubt its economic force, consider the impact it has had on the software marketplace over the past five years: just try to find a retail storefront in the shrink-wrapped software business these days. Five years ago they were on busy urban streets everywhere; now even the former sector leader, Egghead Software, has closed all its stores and sells only over the Internet. Within five years, network economic forces collapsed one whole sector of the software industry marketplace (retail software stores) and built another in its place (ESD online).

The key to this kind of raw economic power unleashed by the Internet is the free flow of information. It is an awesome power, but one that increasingly will need to be tempered to fit human needs as well as those of technical and economic systems.

As the last decade has clearly shown, the Internet is both a creator and a destroyer. And it hits technology markets first. People in information technology fields, therefore, are probably the ones most aware of its full power — its power to improve life, its power to disrupt it. And technologists are the ones most aware of its big secret, as well: This amazing, fast-growing "metabolism" is still in its embryonic stage.

Fifty years ago, the only electronic software in the world consisted of a few strings of code in the storage buffers of primitive, vacuum tube–powered ENIAC computers. These first-generation systems had nowhere near the power of a single laptop of today. Now, in a single Internet moment, trillions of bits of information can be transmitted from any one cell in the network body to any other around the earth — part of a global information system that is constantly adapting, evolving, and self-organizing. That's quite a growth curve. The question is: Where is all this growth heading? Where will info-tech systems be fifty years from now?

Some people see the relentless push of information technology and envision a truly scary future where all personal privacy will have been sacrificed on the altar of technology. Their fears are based on the rapid growth of data-collection and data-manipulation capability over the last fifty years and on projections of where such growth might take us if it continues. These fears are certainly not unwarranted; but they probably underestimate the power of information systems to self-organize and continuously self-correct. It is in this context, in fact, in examining this question about the likely interplay between information technology and human privacy needs in the future, that reflection on the works of Huxley and Orwell can prove quite helpful.

The respective visions and fears of these two writers can be debated forever, and perhaps will be, but one thing we can say for certain is that neither of these brilliant, prophetic men saw even a glimmer of the Internet on the horizon fifty or sixty years ago. In fact, they would have been shocked to learn that a technology so chaotic, so decentralized, and so fundamentally open and pliable in its structure would become the dominant technology on earth. Neither could they have imagined a new media form so varied in its content—or so diverse in motive and purpose. And least of all could they or anyone of their generation have predicted the tremendous economic windfall created by the birth of the Internet and its emergence as a global, free-market engine of commerce. Indeed, few predicted the rise of e-commerce even a decade ago. Frankly, there has never, ever been a prosperity machine like the Internet in the late 1990s. Just ask anyone selling real estate in Silicon Valley.

What both Orwell and Huxley couldn't yet know was that a central equation drives information network systems: information in, power out. *Power* in the economic, social, political, and even physical sense. The new digital metabolism not only absorbs information, it harnesses it, with muscular potency. Like a laser that fuses scattered light waves into a single and very powerful coherent beam, today's digital technologies transform scattered fragments of data into meaningful beams of information. Beams that are often turned inward first, in order to drive improvements and growth in their own systems, but which ultimately are focused outward, toward society at large.

It is this tendency of information systems to readjust constantly, to take dynamic new shapes in order to fit into new environments and new conditions, that should give us some degree of optimism with respect to privacy and technology. Because if we can shape our social, political, and market environments properly, technology will adjust to our needs.

But still, one can almost hear Orwell and Huxley asking, as these systems grow, will the importance—and, indeed, the freedom—of individual human beings be reduced as a result? What kind of world will we inherit once the information tides have reached their crest? Will it be a dark neo-Orwellian realm, except with the twist, perhaps, of corporate multinational big brothers ruling a global digital cabal? Will it be a Brave New WorldNet, a heartless technology environment that saps our dignity and reshapes our lives into something that, today, we might consider less than completely human? Or will it be some fabulous and relatively benign new world, one that is as unimaginable to us today as the Internet was to Orwell and Huxley?

Fortunately, unlike the subservient flesh-and-blood creatures who manned the digital controls in the ominous visions of Orwell and Huxley, we still have the power—at least for now—to decide our digital fate. Frankly, our challenge is to do at least as well at the technology controls as the generations that followed Orwell and Huxley. For, no matter how jaded your view of humanity's travails over the last fifty years, at least this much must be said of the people of the latter half of the twentieth century: they preserved much more freedom, democracy, prosperity, and, yes, even more privacy in the face of a bewildering array of new technology than the two British sages would ever have thought possible.

Of course, the latter twentieth century's biggest achievement may well have been merely to preserve life, by avoiding the ultimate in technology overload: thermonuclear war. Both Huxley and Orwell came to be quite pessimistic on this score and would have been shocked to discover that these weapons of mass destruction have not been used in war since the bombing of Hiroshima. But though the threat of nuclear war has greatly diminished, the threat of global terrorism has not. This latter threat is often mentioned by those who support limiting privacy—and to some extent, their argument is compelling. As author David Brin argues in his recent work *The Transparent Society*, some new balance between privacy and transparency will be necessary in the coming age in order to protect against a new, technically enabled, wave of crime, terror, and fraud. Yet however much the growing digital metabolism breeds new horrors and risks, we should not let these risks seduce us into giving up our fundamental human values.

As John Philpot Curran said two centuries ago, "Eternal vigilance is the price of liberty," and the battle to preserve individual freedom and privacy in this era of a global information environment will be fatiguing indeed. To this end, it is vital that we stay informed about the ever-proliferating technologies that make up the growing digital metabolism. At the end of the day, the real power of the Internet and other information systems, as George Dyson's sister, Internet futurist Esther Dyson, has suggested, lies in the hands of the people who learn the technology and use it.

Information technology does have its cold, dark side—but its shadows can in no way alter the fact that in this great digital metabolism something wondrous is being born. Something that does indeed carry within it a tremendous capability to do good. The very fact that information technology has managed to emanate and thrive in our world for half a century, without falling into the traps of Orwellian tyrannical control, Huxley-style mass cultural homogenization, or the cataclysmic loss of personal privacy both these authors feared, should in itself be cause for optimism. If not genuine celebration.

## *Don't Solve Problems!*

Perhaps a focus on the dark side of the privacy issue—seeing privaly as a zero-sum game, where data given out is a "privacy loss"—is the wrong approach.

For years George Gilder, one of the technology prophets of the Internet Age, has been traveling in business circles as a kind of John-the-Bandwidth, preaching the good news of the coming digital millennium. One of his key teachings has been the importance of full-fledged optimism, which he serves up in the form of a mantra, delivered with arms flailing, to open his frequent keynote addresses at Internet conferences.

"Don't solve problems," Gilder insists. "Pursue opportunities! Don't solve problems!"

This forward-looking management principle is a business dictum that was first pronounced by Peter Drucker, the preeminent management guru of our time. The idea is that in a time of rapid growth and large opportunity, obsessive problem-solving drains resources and constrains organizational thinking just when creativity and innovation are most needed. Companies mired in the details of a messy and persistent problem may miss the terrific new opportunity just around the corner. Often, when companies pursue new opportunities, old problems seem to solve themselves. This is particularly true in an environment with the kind of rich information-feedback loops enabled by Internet technologies.

When examining how personal information flows through the world, it would be a great mistake to concentrate on only the problems created by personal information exchange. As commentators have pointed out throughout the twentieth century, technology is plainly a two-sided coin. One side is Risk, the other is Opportunity. The more times technology comes up Opportunity, the more times we win. And often, even with the most overt technology Risk, all you have to do is turn it over to find Opportunity.

Take online video surveillance, for example. Yes, it's spooky, scary stuff. But it has a useful social purpose, too. The most popular application of Internet video system technology in the U.S. market right now is, perhaps not surprisingly, nanny cams. Kindercam.com, a provider of remote childcare monitoring via the Internet, claims it will have more than three thousand real-time, online video cameras installed at daycare centers in the year 2000. Use of hidden nanny cams in the home is also growing. With these systems, concerned parents wishing to keep an eye on their children's caregivers can log onto a private URL and in real time, to see what's happening at home or at daycare. What could be more innocuous—or, given news headlines over the last decade, more justified?

And yet, there have been strong objections to online nanny cams—from nannies and from the staffs of childcare centers. Lawsuits have even been filed by staff members, citing an invasion of privacy. Cameras have been pulled from some centers—with the result that technology and privacy concerns have reached a kind of sensible equilibrium: concerned parents increasingly have the option to send their kids to certain centers that continue to deliver video feeds to the Internet; and privacy-sensitive staff workers have the option to work only at centers that do not.

As is so often the case, the same technologies of surveillance, intelligence gathering, PII management, and others that often reduce personal privacy can also make many positive contributions to our world. Networked video surveillance systems help secure buildings and workplaces. Huge government databases filled with PII are used to issue social security checks, counted on every month by millions of the most needy U.S. citizens. Lifestyle tracking systems that, with your consent, can monitor your compliance with medical advice are increasingly important tools in health and wellness programs, and the tracking of individual health histories plays an incredibly important role generally in both medical research and patient care. Even fake identities can occasionally play a positive role in society (for example, the federal witness protection program). Beyond these familiar instances are many lesser-known uses of PII collection and management that are at least benign, if not actually quite positive. A few examples:

- *Compacks.* Yes, Internet professionals are going to have faster, better, cheaper access to ever more detailed e-profiles about you, but many companies will use these profiles to provide you with new kinds of highly personalized products and services, many of which are proving very popular. (These services are called *compacks,* short for *complex packages* of goods and services.) Compacks put you in *your* favorite seat on airplanes, notify you of market activity and industry information about *your* stocks, and not only can provide you with information about *your* favorite music albums, but in some cases can even enable you to have new music that suits your tastes sent to you on a trial basis (these systems use predictive, neural net logic). None of these services, or hundreds of others like them, can be delivered without the provider of the service keeping detailed information about *you* in its systems.

- *Customized health care.* Online PII linked to your health history can save your life by alerting you or your doctor about the potential for an adverse drug reaction, or enabling emergency care workers quickly to become aware of allergies, existing conditions and other personal health parameters in the case of an accident or other health crisis. Online storage and management of personal health data can in fact greatly facilitate the sharing of information across many medical specialties and, as patients change health plans, between various health care organizations.

- *Online relationships.* Clear lines of public safety and decency must be drawn to protect against sexually related stalking and spying, but online systems are also helping bring a new kind of companionship to many people. Such relationships often require revealing much about yourself, including your actual identity. One result is the spawning of many legitimate romances, some even leading to marriage. Cyber-dating is one of many online tightropes where both disclosure and protection of personal data must exist, however precariously, side by side.

- *Dollars for data!* More companies are collecting information about you—but an increasing number will soon be either paying you for it directly or bartering with you by providing "free" goods and services. This trend of offering value-for-value in an information exchange is likely to become one of the most important trends in the online privacy arena.

- *Accountability.* The availability of a PII profile about you on the Internet can be quite unsettling—but the same online technology used to assemble and distribute it can also be used to check the credentials of doctors and stock brokers, to find deadbeat dads, to identify felons and illegal aliens, to discover lies on resumes, and generally to improve professional accountability.

- *ID numbers.* The Intel Processor Serial Number feature mentioned in Chapter 2—which gives every computer a unique identifying number that cannot be changed—can potentially be used to identify individual network users and track their online behavior in positive ways. Making individual machine IDs readily available to all PII collectors makes selling and trading consumer information between merchants and others much easier as well. But chip IDs are also a powerful security tool for e-commerce in the areas of digital content distribution, software asset management, fraud control, and even antivirus systems. Clearly, having the PSN turned on automatically and without user consent is potentially a privacy-violating technology; but having it available to be turned on in order to take commercial advantage of certain "trust markets" is not only worthwhile but desirable.

This list could go on, but the point is that the technology used to collect, manipulate, and distribute PII is far from a single-sided coin. In fact, rather than being the result of some nefarious industry or government conspiracy, development and use of information technology is increasing for a single compelling reason: *as a society, we want it to.* We are continuing to behave in ways—through our purchasing, our investing, our work, and even our votes—that not only support the development of stronger information technologies but also continue to expand the free flow of information in our world.

This does not mean that society as a whole approves of each and every new technology application and feature. Indeed, public opinion polls clearly show that many aspects of Internet technology make large numbers of people downright squeamish. But the continued growth and public acceptance of the Internet and other information systems does suggest that simplistic attempts to put the technology genie back in the bottle in the name of privacy protection are not only misguided but probably irrelevant. Our planet's digital metabolism—the technology of sophisticated, networked information management—is on a major roll, ready or not.

The question is: What's the smartest way to live with this new beast?

•　　•　　•

In succeeding chapters we address the core question of how to live with the growing phenomenon of the Internet and related technologies, especially with respect to issues of trust, privacy, security, and accountability, in ways that both uphold traditional human values and pursue new technology-enabled opportunities. As we explore these matters further, however, we freely admit we will be using as a working hypothesis the belief that society (as it becomes ever better informed, of course) will harvest increasing benefits from new information technology, while for the most part avoiding its worst consequences. The method for achieving this kind of continuing advancement will be to allow technology developers a relatively free rein, so that innovation and expansion can proceed apace — but then to use the Net to learn quickly from the inevitable mistakes, and respond with the forces of public opinion, marketplace behavior and, when clearly necessary and only as a last resort, government regulation.

Take the specific issue of private health information, for example, which we have noted above. The possibilities for abuse of this kind of PII in networked information systems are immense — and indeed, a good number of abuses have been documented. In a notable example in 1996, a Department of Health worker in Florida, after accessing computerized records, sent the names of four thousand HIV-positive citizens to the *Tampa Tribune* and the *St. Petersburg Times*. Abuse of private health data can be unauthorized and illegal, such as in this Florida case; or, it can be fully legal and authorized, such as when supermarket and drugstore chains sell private prescription drug records to database marketing companies — a practice that the *Washington Post* in 1998 reported was widespread in Washington, D.C. (Companies named in the story stopped the practice after the story came out, but such practices undoubtedly continue elsewhere.)

Even these are mild abuses compared to what could happen if private medical records begin to leak out onto the Internet (and indeed, networked health organizations do have their own hundredth-window problems). Imagine a publicly posted crack — not unlike one that opened the doors to the databanks of Hotmail in 1999, exposing approximately 50 million users' e-mail — which could make the privately networked medical records of thousands of patients suddenly viewable over the Net. How would you feel to have all of your medical history publicly exposed?

In fact, the shift of our global information retrieval systems from a stand-alone propriety database to a shared, networked model that leverages Internet systems means that, absent any direct action to avert it, health information may well begin to become part of the personal profiles that even now are so widely traded over the network.

But information technology can adapt with amazing speed. Even now, opportunity seekers in the Internet and computer security fields are tackling the health information privacy/security issue—and new technological solutions will soon emerge. With tamper-resistant encryption applications, private health records will become both *generally accessible,* available to a small number of patient-authorized health care workers (such as a dentist, a physician, a pharmacist, and a naturopath); and *highly secure,* so that access by these workers is similar to that of bank employees accessing a vault (during open hours). The security, in this case, will come from both the obfuscation of the information using public-key cryptography— only those with the proper set of keys can open private health files and read them—and from the secure audit trails that such systems can provide. The fact that everyone accessing private health records in such a system will be recorded, and leave a digital footprint of the visit, will in itself be a powerful aid to privacy protection, as everyone viewing the information becomes more accountable for its continued confidentiality.

Thus the problem of protecting the privacy of online health records is solved faster by letting technology adapt to the specific needs of both the medical industry and patients than by debating health privacy policy as a kind of contentious, zero-sum game, with privacy advocates on one side and the medical and insurance establishments on the other. It is solved by new Internet-based applications that leverage the dynamism of open network technology in order to provide much better solutions on several levels, privacy included, and that ultimately make personal health data a more effective and focused tool for improving health and fighting disease.

On the other hand, the value inherent in this opportunity can only be captured if the technology that enables the collection, storage, and retrieval of personal health information is designed to be privacy-friendly and deployed in ways that take privacy concerns seriously. Yet since public opinion polling clearly shows that high levels of privacy protection are an absolute requirement of online health information systems, if they are to be used by consumers, it is reasonable to expect that such protective steps will be taken when it comes to health information especially. (Visit wellmed.com or webmd.com to view the first of these new online health and medical sites.)

Ultimately, the fair and proper use of technology—in the ways that contribute most to the common good—depends on a sometimes delicate balance between technical efficiencies and human expectations. The quality that, above all, keeps this scale in balance is trust.

## Trust Environments

The kind of layered, encrypted, authorized-access-only system described above is known, in computer security terms, as a "trusted system" or "trust environment." In computing circles, trust is actually a technical term having to do with specific levels of verification and authentication. In fact, the trusted systems segment of computing is one of the most complex in the industry, one that uses some of the industry's most arcane tools.

Trusted systems make online credit card transactions possible. They are the basis of private e-mail exchange and of the content protection of online digital "goods" such as software, music, and video. At their core, the purpose of trusted computing systems is very simple: to enable authorized access to information—and authorized access only, thereby bringing elements of real-world human trust to the data streams of the Internet.

Some of the most advanced work in trust systems today is being conducted at the Santa Fe Institute in New Mexico, where new trust and security models are being patterned after the workings of biological immune systems. The foundation of this work is the insight that in simple biological organisms, immune systems work by keeping certain things out of a cell, while letting everything else in; in advanced creatures (humans, for example), immune systems function by letting only certain things in, and keeping everything else out.

In the digital metabolism of the Internet, info-tech systems have reached a level of complexity sufficient to move to an advanced immunology model in safeguarding privacy and promoting trust. With all of us living in our open-window houses, it will no longer do to plan to keep certain specific rogues out of our personal system; we will have to begin moving toward environments where we let only specific trusted people in.

For these types of systems to work, and work well, those operating them will have to understand considerably more than is generally known today about human trust and its relation to information technology systems. But given a closer integration of human trust and technical schemes for security and authentication, perhaps these new tools can provide us with opportunities to have our technology cake and eat it too—with a privacy frosting. It is our demand for these systems—indeed, our *insistence* on them—that will create opportunities that will spur the market to build the tools that will enable networks to self-correct and solve the pervasive problem of privacy loss. (The very same privacy loss problem, of course, that the Internet and other advanced information systems would otherwise exacerbate.)

Many social dimensions of the online world influence the trust, or lack thereof, in information technology. These dimensions include sex, identity, new legal and political jurisdictions, Internet rating systems, online espionage, and online journalism, to list a few of the more prominent.

We will now pause in our examination of network technologies, therefore, and spend a chapter exploring some of the very odd social changes that new info-tech tools are stirring up in modern society. It's a strange brew, certainly, consisting of cultural and commercial oddities that could only have been spawned on the Net—and that may in the end determine if our online privacy, and indeed our liberty, are safeguarded and secure or fall into a scenario straight out of Huxley or Orwell. These two great writers might not have envisioned the precise form of the Internet, but they did foresee the great Information Revolution it has spawned. And they gave us warning about the very real threat to human civilization that technologies represent when, under the guise of efficiency and order, they rob the individual of the ability to control his destiny. Or his data.

## Tips and Tricks for Chapter 3

**Encrypt your e-mail.** When you send e-mail, you probably assume that the person you send it to is the only person reading it. Hopefully that's true, but it doesn't work that way all the time.

By using encryption and digital signatures, secure e-mail programs can minimize these risks. Encryption programs encode text into incomprehensible cipher text for transmission over public networks, and then, once received, decode it. Most e-mail programs use public-key encryption, a process that requires a pair of keys—one on each end—to encode and decode messages. The key length dictates the security of the messages. As in monster movies and basketball, "size matters"—the longer the key, the tougher it is to break. The current industrial-strength standard is 512-bit encryption, yet even keys of this size have been compromised under "brute force" attack. (A brute force attack is one that uses massive parallel computing power to break the code, as if by sheer strength, rather than through cunning.)

Digital signatures prove that you are who you say you are and that your message hasn't been tampered with during transmission. A secure mail solution can generate a digital signature, or you can download one from a service such as VeriSign (http://www.verisign.com).

**Give Finger a farewell.** Finger is an Internet gateway that may have information about you, such as your e-mail address and the city where you live. This information is generated by some Internet service providers. The service is promoted as one that can help people find each other on the Internet, but some spammers and other privacy invaders have learned to harness it.

To find out if you're in the Finger database, type http://www.cs.indiana.edu:800/finger/gateway. When you arrive at that page, enter your e-mail address in the search keyword box. If information about you appears and you'd like it removed, contact your Internet service provider and ask them to do so. If they refuse, close your account and shift your business to another provider.

**Is your current Web session secure?** You certainly want to know this before you send any financial information to an electronic commerce website. Netscape Communicator and Microsoft Internet Explorer both have the capability of letting you know the website you're visiting uses encryption to maintain the privacy and integrity of your communications with them. Here's how to check:

Netscape Communicator: Choose Tools from the Communicator menu. Then select Security Info. A screen will appear that will tell you whether or not the website you're on is using encryption.

Microsoft Internet Explorer: When you visit a website that uses encryption, it automatically sends you its certificate. Internet Explorer then displays a "lock" icon on the status bar.

**Has the site you're about to visit been hacked?** The Archive of Hacked Web Sites (http://www.onething.com/archive/) has a list of sites—some of them major—that have been illegally entered within the last three years. Included is a description of the nature of the attack. Although you shouldn't necessarily take this information as a "red flag" alert, it can help you gauge the security vigilance, or lack thereof, of some potential data exchange partners.

**Keep your browser up to date.** To plug newly discovered security leaks or other bugs, Netscape and Microsoft frequently release updated versions of their Communicator and Internet Explorer Web browsers. Often these updates will look exactly like the previous version—but with "under the hood" enhancements that fix problems. The newer your browser, the safer it will probably be. For this reason, it's a good idea to periodically visit the website associated with the browser you are using. If there's a new edition, you can be assured it will be touted and available for download. The best place to check for new browser availability is on the Netscape and Microsoft websites. For Microsoft, go to http://www.microsoft.com/ie. For Netscape: http://www.netscape.com/computing/download/.

**Obliterate your newsgroup messages.** Newsgroup postings are fertile ground for spammers. To remove messages you posted from Deja.com's archive, just fill out the Article Nuke Form at www.deja.com/forms/nuke.shtml. Note that this removes your posting only from Deja.com, not from Usenet. To prevent new postings from being archived, use the X-no-archive option supported by the Deja.com X-header field and some Web browsers. (In the X-header field, type "X-no-archive: yes"). If you are not posting through Deja.com, or if your browser does not support X-headers, then you can still employ the X-no-archive option by typing it in as the first text line of your message.

**Watch your temper online.** A number of Internet newsgroups, websites, or chat forums engage in often-provocative online debate about such volatile subjects as politics, religion, or (believe it or not) privacy practices. That's the upside of living in a free society. Many of these sites post the e-mail address of each respondent.

By their controversial nature, some of these online debates attract people with enflamed minds as well as radical views. Too often, such online forums deteriorate into numerous postings where someone who has posted objectionable content is "flamed" (criticized hotly). The danger is that a few people may feel the need to harass those who have challenged them online. If your e-mail address is easily traceable to a geographic location or to a phone number, you may be targeted for abuse or worse. Even if you use a "handle," certain e-mail directory sites may have your name, address, and phone number in their database where someone can easily check it against your screen name. We are not suggesting that you shouldn't state your ideas vigorously. To protect your safety, however, watch the invective and name-calling.

**Leave your member profile blank to reduce spam on AOL.** More than five times as many people access the Internet on

America Online as through any other service. While AOL's growing universe of more than 15 million users is a great shot in the arm to the viability and vitality of online life, it represents a huge data-mining opportunity for spammers hawking everything from get-rich-quick schemes to graphic photos.

There are two ways to severely limit your vulnerability to this kind of intrusion on AOL. First, reveal as little as possible about yourself in your Member Profile. Spammers often visit these lists and look for interest-related keywords that can spur them to put you on their mailing list. Don't give them the chance to obtain this info. If you've already entered this info, type "Member Directory." You'll see a blue box that says My Profile. Click again; the next screen you see will be Edit My Online Profile. You may wish to remove information in the Marital Status box. If you've previously entered "single," you may have opened yourself up to Internet porn, or worse.

**"Munge" your e-mail.** Spammers, rip-off artists, and stalkers hang out on Usenet discussion boards, trolling for names. Also, many of these groups make free Internet-based e-mail mailing lists available from time to time. You can use an anonymous remailer (a service that receives your incoming e-mail messages, removes your personal identification from the e-mail header, and then sends it along to your recipient) or an auxiliary e-mail address when posting to these lists, but another creative approach is to use a technique called "munging." This involves opening up your e-mail program controls and temporarily entering a fake e-mail address in the reply-to field. After you've posted to your mailing list or newsgroup, don't forget to change it back; if you don't, people you *want* to hear back from won't be able to reach you through the "Reply" function in the e-mail program they use.

**Guard passwords on your mobile computing device.** A growing number of us use PalmPilots or other mobile computing tools. When on the go, we do not have ready access to system administrators or locked drawers at work, and it's easy to forget your password. Perhaps you've written it down in your personal address book. What if that book gets stolen along with your Palm?

A program from Zetetic Enterprises, released in 1999, lets you file system passwords securely on a PalmPilot using 128-bit encryption. Called STRIP (Secure Tool for Recalling Important Passwords), the program prevents clever hackers from using trick software to get access to those secret files. Your passwords will be far safer than if you've written them down. Plus, if you're on a harried business trip and forget your password, you won't have to tax your brain to remember it.

# 4

# Privacy and Net Culture: Sex, Spies, and Video-Scrape

*The picture-papers are more than half-filled with pho-*
*tographs of bathing nymphs—photographs that make one*
*understand the ease with which St. Anthony rebuffed his*
*temptations.*

—*Aldous Huxley,*
**On the Margin,** *"Beauty in the 1920s"*

It was a quiet street with grapefruit trees in a sunny city in the South. A group of college-age young ladies were living together in a large, homey, turn-of-the-century house with a friendly front porch and a fresh coat of paint. There was no unusual traffic to and from the house, no complaints about wild parties or visits by strange men. In fact, the neighbors had no idea anything at all unusual was going on inside. Thus it came as quite a shock when the local zoning commission declared the house to be the site of an active adult entertainment business and sent all the young ladies packing.

# The Hundredth Window

The business in question was Voyeur Dorm, an X-rated Internet take-off on MTV's *The Real World* series. Forty video cameras were mounted in the house, covering every room, streaming video of the young women's lives onto the Web "twenty-four hours a day, seven days a week," according to the site's home page. "A real-life Truman Show!" the site's headline proclaimed, in reference to the popular Jim Carrey film in which one man's life becomes a soap opera for millions of rapt television viewers.

Voyeur Dorm is not the only instance of real-time monitoring of private lives on the Net—and not all such *Truman Show* wannabes are X-rated. The personal privacy spectrum on the Internet is a full gray-scale, reflecting many individual differences and preferences. Privacy standards vary not just among different people but also according to context. Someone who is absolutely adamant about an unlisted telephone number might have no problem putting his e-mail address all over the Web. A person who would never put a credit card number on the Web might not think twice about giving it out to a stranger over the phone—a considerably more risky proposition. A model who might have no problem exposing her body on the Web may be adamant about keeping her home address off it.

To some extent privacy has always been a highly subjective matter, but now, with the Internet suddenly changing all the information rules, it can seem as if all cultural moorings have been cut loose, and we find ourselves in alien territory, where we confront:

- strange personal boundary issues, such as those created by the new wearable computers, which are capable of recording one person's daily life and transmitting it back to the Web, and raise questions about the rights of others he or she meets along the way.
- debates about the ownership of customer PII between com-

84

panies and customers, between companies and their partners, and sometimes between lawyers in court.

- jurisdictional quagmires growing out of information exchanges that pass through three or four countries in a single transaction.
- data accuracy issues — if others are assembling online profiles about you, you may want to see that they get it right, and avoid entering false information, which can sometimes be very damaging.
- new questions about the privacy of children's online journeys — and especially those of teens who, quite naturally, don't want to be spied on by parents most of all.
- and an almost infinite number of questions about what happens when what throughout history has been the most private of human affairs — sex — hits the online world.

The expanding privacy spectrum can even create new economic opportunities in society. The conceit at Voyeur Dorm, for example, was that the women were all young coeds in a college dorm, but in fact they were working women getting free room and board and what one of the women claimed was "a small stipend," in exchange for revealing their personally identifiable private parts online, while taking showers and prancing around naked in front of live cameras. (Our source here is the blonde "coed" who was interviewed on the Fox News Channel, where the show host claimed with a straight face to be interested in the impact Voyeur Dorm's closing would have on zoning laws across America. Before, of course, getting to the really important issue of what it felt like to sleep nude in front of thousands, live on the Internet.)

It's not news that some people's need for privacy doesn't include a need to close the curtains, so to speak. Nor is it news that sex is big business on the Internet and all other forms of modern media. Estimates of the total revenue in the cyber-porn business range from several hundred million dollars a year to over a billion. In fact, it's very hard to know just how much money is being generated by porn sites around the world, as their proprietors are not much given to public disclosure of what goes on behind the X-cams. We do know that one well-known X-rated site in Italy, Diva Futura, took in approximately US$22,000 between December 1997 and June 1998—but we know this only because the site, owned by Italian porn king Riccardo Schicci, who had been jailed previously on charges of running a prostitution ring, was configured in such a way that virtually all the information stored on its databases was plainly accessible online to anyone who bothered to look. Included in the publicly available data were the names, addresses, and credit card numbers of nearly a thousand members of the subscription-based website who had signed up from around the world. When this rather amazing lapse in site security became known and widely reported in the media, the exposed subscribers to Diva Futura learned a new definition of the term "naked," and were not amused.

Though the Diva Futura incident is unusual in the site's complete disregard for data security, the collection and storage of detailed member PII by porn sites is commonplace. In fact, there is probably no business sector on the Web that is more adept at collecting PII than sex site operators—but then, they got a huge assist in 1998 from the U.S. Congress.

It was dubbed the Child Online Protection Act, or COPA, a law that whizzed through Congress in a matter of days with almost no hearings, and no expert testimony from Internet insiders. It was a motherhood-and-apple-pie bill, a chance for members of Congress to show their constituents that they were protecting the nation's youth from the scourge of pornography on the Internet. Their intentions were laudable, but their execution was seriously flawed. For one of the chief means of protecting children from porn in this piece of legislation was to require age verification (eighteen years or older) of everyone visiting an X-rated site.

Cyberporn businesses and the ACLU teamed up to challenge the law, and the part relating to a ban on porno banner ads was ruled unconstitutional. At first there were also some protests about the age verification requirement—but that was before the sex site operators discovered just what a bonanza they had been handed. Because, as it turned out, there is only one good way to determine whether or not someone is eighteen or older when they show up at a site: you have to get a credit card number from them. The authentication/verification routines of credit card processing systems are the only online, real-time systems which can determine someone's age—because no one under eighteen can obtain a credit card. Thus requiring visitors to produce credit card information to enter a site would limit access to adults, and thus satisfy the demands of the law. At least that was the logic that suddenly started showing up on porn sites.

So in December 1998, when the law took effect, porn sites across the world (those in the U.S. at first, then ones in other countries as well, for whom compliance with the law was not an issue) began to require that visitors provide a credit card number in order to get "free" access to the site for a short period of time—generally, several days to a week. This did several things for the website operators—all of them good, in their minds. First, it linked visitors with a specific credit card number, so that free trials could be promoted, but limited to the number of credit cards a visitor had (one free trial per card). Better yet, it generated a ton of very accurate PII, because the credit card verification system required a proper name and even correct zip code before a card would be approved as valid. There were no charges to the cardholder's account in these free trials, so presumably the number of users willing to provide PII was much greater than would have been the case if PII collection was limited to true purchases only. And though no e-mail address is needed for a credit card authorization/verification routine, nearly all sites required that as well. (Some sites even sent passwords via e-mail to ensure that e-mail addresses were correct.) More interesting yet is the fact that many of the "cardholders" were undoubtedly fourteen- to seventeen-year-old boys who had copied down their fathers' credit card numbers—thus putting Dad's PII in places he himself might never want it to go. In at least one Web forum frequented by hard-core sex site visitors, this piece of legislation was dubbed "the Dad's Data Collection Act."

The most benign use of this data by site operators would be for sending numerous annoying e-mail promotions to their visitors regarding new offers, and to trade lists with other site operators for the same purpose. To consider other, less benign possibilities, think of filling out a porn site age verification form as the online equivalent of leaving a credit card behind in a dingy brothel. Not a pleasant thought.

The moral of this story is not just that government has a huge propensity to screw up when it is regulating systems it does not understand—though that is one inference, certainly. (It's one thing to pass a law saying that you have to be eighteen years old to enter an adult Web domain; quite another to figure out a way to do it effectively, and without unintended consequences.) The scarier conclusion, however, is that a massive amount of PII, and PII linked to credit card numbers, has been collected by porn operators around the world since December 1998. And, while we have nothing against porn site operators, personally, neither would we pick them (as a class) to be the prime holders of our national credit card number archive.

Note: If your family has an adolescent in the household, and if you or your mate has suddenly started receiving a rash of e-mails promoting porn sites, it would probably be a good time to sit down and have a talk with Junior. And to change all your credit cards.

## *Spy vs. Spy—The Sequel*

Diva Futura and Voyeur Dorm lie at one end of the privacy spectrum on the Net—the extremely transparent end. At the other end of the spectrum, we find the closeted hacker with a triple alias, sending only encrypted e-mail and sharing illegally downloaded software products and MP3 music files with anonymous online pals from around the world; or the online information broker, living on a lonely mountaintop while running a worldwide industrial espionage business, operated entirely online; or destructive cyber vandels, of the David Lee Smith variety (the Melissa virus hacker). Though one side of this spectrum is bathed in klieg lights and the other in shadows, both sides share a kind of symmetry in their extremism, and in their roles as shapers of privacy issues on the Net and drivers of Internet technical infrastructure (albeit in much the same way that wolves tend to improve the "infrastructure" of elk herds).

Interview any technically savvy pornography entrepreneur, and you will get an earful about how the porn industry has been a pioneer and major influence in every new media technology from VHS videotape to dial-in bulletin boards to live streaming media on the Net. You'll be told how it created huge chunks of Net infrastructure by having some of the first websites to require T3 phone lines and a parallel server architecture. The porn industry isn't shy about boasting of its role as an early Internet driver and pioneering force.

The role of the private-sector spy trade, however, is less well known. For one thing, a true online surveillance expert or private investigator will say next to nothing about his business or how it works. Yet this covert industry has, if anything, played an even more critical role than pornography in the technology development of the Net and in the development of tools and systems for the collection and distribution of PII.

The Hundredth Window

The story of the role of the dark arts of espionage in the use of network technologies begins with the legacy of the Cold War and a remnant of electronic surveillance that dates back two decades or more. In the last chapter we dismissed the Orwellian vision of centralized technology control as seriously outdated, and yet . . . what else could you call a global surveillance system that can monitor every phone call, fax, and e-mail crossing the Atlantic or Pacific oceans?

In his 1998 book *Exposing the Global Surveillance System*, investigative reporter Nicky Hager, citing extensive interviews with New Zealand whistle-blowers, revealed that the U.S. National Security Agency had been running a massive network monitoring program in league with at least five other Western nations, including France and Great Britain. Known as ECHELON (among other names), this top-secret electronic snooping project has now become a matter of international controversy. Hager's research — called into question in the mainstream media when his book was published — has now been widely accepted. According to an "interim study" issued in 1999 by a research branch of the European Parliament, "Hager interviewed more than 50 people concerned with intelligence to document a global surveillance system that stretches around the world. . . . [This system targets] all of the key Intelsat satellites used to convey most of the world's satellite phone calls, internet, e-mail, faxes and telexes. These sites are based at Sugar Grove and Yakima, in the USA, at Waihopai in New Zealand, at Geraldton in Australia, Hong Kong, and Morwenstow in the UK."

Using an extensive pattern-recognition system linked to the monitoring of huge flows of e-mail, fax, telex and Internet communications, combined with strong database storage/retrieval software, ECHELON is able to target highly specific subjects in the sea of global communications with the precision of a heat-seeking missile. According to Hager:

> The ECHELON system . . . works by indiscriminately intercepting very large quantities of communications and using computers to identify and extract messages of interest from the mass of unwanted ones. . . .
>
> The computers at each station in the ECHELON network automatically search through the millions of messages intercepted for ones containing pre-programmed keywords. Keywords include all the names, localities, subjects, and so on that might be mentioned [by someone ECHELON wants to monitor].

Clearly, the ECHELON program is deploying very powerful and comprehensive technology. The program's stated purpose is counterterrorism, but several members of the U.S. Congress have begun worrying about whether ECHELON has sufficient safeguards protecting against domestic political uses of the system. Regardless of how it is being used, Project ECHELON is clearly a big customer for technology from the new sector known, rather inelegantly, as "data-veillance" (technology for the real-time collection and monitoring of digital data). "The term data-veillance covers an impressive range of methods and devices," says the European Parliament's Science and Technological Options Assessment group (STOA), "including vision technology; bugging and interception techniques; satellite tracking; through-clothing human scanning; automatic fingerprinting; human recognition systems that can recognize genes, odour and retina patterns, and biometric systems." The report also mentions night-vision goggles; parabolic microphones that can detect conversations over a mile away; laser mikes that can pick up a conversation through a closed window that is in a line of sight; and cellular phone locator systems (routinely used by one Swiss company) that track the location of cell phone users to a specificity of one meter.

Especially since it came from an official government body, the

STOA report—titled "Technologies of Political Control"—raised a number of concerns, including:

- *Automated surveillance.* STOA worried that while the East German police in the heyday of their police state managed 10,000 secret informers who were needed just to listen and transcribe citizens' phone calls, ECHELON technology, using what STOA describes as algorithmic surveillance, does the job infinitely better, with a much broader sweep. And does it almost automatically. "Such automation," says the report's author, Steve Wright, "not only widens the surveillance net, it narrows the mesh."
- *Legal and illegal interception of communications* and the planting of phone "bugs" has been an issue in many European nations. However, the report claims, "planting illegal bugs is yesterday's technology. Modern snoopers can buy specially adapted laptop computers, and simply tune in to all the mobile phones active in the area by [navigating] down to their number. The machine will even search for numbers 'of interest' to see if they are active."
- *Vehicle recognition systems* have been developed which can identify the license plate on a car, then track the car around a city using a computerized geographic positioning system. Such systems are now commercially available. For example, the Talon system introduced in 1994 by the British company Racal initially was used for traffic monitoring, but it has been adapted in recent years for security surveillance as well. The system works both day and night, and can record all the vehicles that enter or leave a proscribed area in a particular period.

But the report raised an even more fundamental concern: namely, that "new technologies which were originally conceived for the Defense and Intelligence sectors have after the cold war rapidly spread into the law enforcement and private sectors." In fact, the core pattern-recognition and database searching technology that lies at the heart of ECHELON is already embedded in many, many commercial applications (optical scanning systems at supermarkets, for one). And indeed, the history of technology suggests that systems deployed in one sector of the technology world will soon pop up in others — even if the first sector is covert.

The question is, how do you feel knowing that the wide array of data-veillance technologies can now be aimed at you? And not just aimed by Uncle Sam, but by cousin Tom, competitor Dick, and ex-husband Harry? Because as surely as the database traveled from the CIA to the back offices of corporations (Oracle, the world's leading database company, grew out of a CIA technology project code named "Oracle" led by company founder Larry Ellison), ECHE-LON-like technologies are coming soon to a company, or a snoop, near you.

This is not to suggest that migration of technology from government to the private sector is a major threat. It happens sometimes, but the reverse is even more common these days, for technology development in the private sector has greatly outstripped that inside government. A teenage hacker today can have more computing power on his desktop, for example, than NASA used in putting a man on the moon.

It is not the transfer of actual surveillance and monitoring technology from government to the private sector that matters so much as the transfer of technology control more generally. The highly secretive National Security Agency (NSA) is rumored to have once employed three thousand in-agency cryptographers, who produced up to 90 percent of the agency's software, using proprietary tools. Today, the agency obtains most of its technology in the commercial marketplace, for the simple reason that it cannot keep up with the dynamic forces of technology in the free market. The agency once funded academic research in encryption, built most of its own encryption applications, and controlled the best such technology in the world almost completely. Today it's not only cheaper for the NSA to buy technology from the private sector rather than to build it, but also a better security strategy, due to the dynamic game of crack-and-patch played by builders of security technology and the attackers of their systems. Government technology development simply cannot keep up with what is coming out of the marketplace.

Consequently, over the last twenty years, the leading edge of sophisticated encryption technology development has migrated from the NSA to major U.S. corporations. From these major corporations, the core technology is quickly licensed to various software development labs, and from these labs come new applications and tools that make their way to literally tens of thousands of computers, operated by people in many different countries, for many different purposes.

Today, some of the best encryption technology—and best encryption-cracking technology—is being developed in Israel and Russia. Because of past usage-and-export regulations imposed by various governments, encryption has been the most closely controlled of all security technologies, yet even this former NSA specialty is now well outside the control of anyone in the United States government. Frankly, the era of tight government control of information technologies is over. The technology genie is out of the bottle and may never return.

This recent global dispersion of the electronic tools of the spy trade—encryption/decryption, electronic surveillance, pattern recognition, data storage/data retrieval, online tracking, communications interception, etc.—raises some of the most serious privacy and security questions in the world today. For, make no mistake, a massive proliferation in the development of information "weapons" is under way, and the Internet is proving to be one hell of a pipeline for their marketing and distribution.

Here are a few samples of what you can buy on the Internet today:

### Hidden Video Surveillance Cameras

- *Cell Phone Camera.* This "private investigators' favorite" is a black-and-white pinhole camera built into a nonfunctioning cell phone.
- *Pen Camera Set.* This new camera is discreetly hidden in a gold and silver pen set.
- *Wireless Clock B/W Video Camera.* Says the manufacturer: "We put the 900 MHz wireless video sender into this wall mounted clock allowing wireless video surveillance."
- *Wireless Clock Color Video Camera.* Operating quartz clock contains an undetectable color CCD camera.
- *Smoke Detector B/W Video Camera.* This smoke detector look-alike has the same specifications as the clock camera above, except it's discreetly built into a nonworking smoke detector. "Works great in low light!" the manufacturer exclaims breathlessly.
- *Clock Radio Camera.* "Our newest covert black and white camera is built inside a clock radio for totally hidden surveillance!"
- *Indoor or Outdoor Bullet Camera.* This tiny black-and-white camera is weather resistant and less than an inch long.
- *Sony 960 Time Lapse VCR.* The Sony SVT-5050 is a VCR that allows 960 hours of continuous surveillance and monitoring.

### Telephone Recording and Surveillance

- *12-Hour Telephone Recording System.* This telephone recording system provides long-term recording and play-back, "with amazing clarity."

- *Handset Interface.* This tool connects your telephone to any tape recorder in seconds, "for crystal clear recording of both sides of your telephone conversations."
- *Phone Manager.* Take control of your telephone recording needs with this new device that can record all of your outgoing calls automatically. It now stores up to 2000 calls for your review on its LCD.
- *Cell Phone Microphone.* This tiny microphone/earphone allows you to record conversations from up to 50 feet away while appearing to be talking on a cell phone. (The ads suggest use at a business conference filled with competitors.)
- *Shotgun Microphone.* Allows you to pick up sounds from a distance of up to 50 yards.
- *Super-Sensitive Wired Pen Microphone.* This microphone with high-gain pre-amp will pick up and record from distances up to 50 feet from sound source, and is cleverly disguised in an ordinary pen.

This is just the standard, run-of-the mill inventory. For specialty items, you have to look a bit further, but if you do you'll find such things as the laptop camera (for surreptitiously videotaping business meetings with your laptop computer) and the sticky-cam, a one-inch device that you can paste up almost anywhere, and which sends a wireless signal about one hundred feet to a recorder. The author of the STOA report mentioned above even told the *New York Times* that microprocessors with audio and video recording sensors and wireless transmitters are experimentally being implanted in live cockroaches—biological "devices" renowned for their ability to infiltrate kitchens, bathrooms, bedrooms, and other bastions of privacy. The signals all these devices emit can now be jacked into the Net, with wires or without, thus dramatically increasing their potency and reach.

Recording the sights and sounds of daily life and putting them on the Net is one thing. It's quite another, however, to have such images be retrievable in any coherent way, given the great mass of information that is available on the Internet. But that is where the shadowy worlds of cybersex and digital surveillance come full circle: in the phenomenon of video-scrape.

## Digital Faceprints

Searchable video has been one of the holy grails of the modern audio/video industry for some time. The basic notion is simple: being able to search through full-motion, digital-stored video for specific images, just the way large databases are searched for a specific word or phrase. But matching visual similarities in long streams of video has, for any system besides the human brain, proven extremely difficult.

The power and popularity of Internet search engines has also led to various attempts to bring visual-based searches directly to the Net. Virage, a builder of visual search technology, supplies leading sites such as Snap.com and iVillage.com today with a kind of video search capability, based on indexing schemes and word searches of the audio tracks in a video recording. Large relational databases storing video clips can be queried online, using Virage's technology. In the case of Snap and iVillage, a video database of the 2000 presidential campaign has been updated during the course of the race, and their online visitors can use the Virage system to retrieve all available video where George W. Bush is speaking about, say, privacy.

Audio track searches for keywords, or indexing schemes requiring human data entry in logging screen images, are the current state of the art in audio/video content retrieval, at least with respect to mainstream commercial applications. But real action in the image retrieval field—and at major research centers at the University of Michigan and Stanford—is in the use of complex mathematical algorithms to achieve what is known as facial recognition capability, in real time. The idea is to be able to use digital images to recognize a particular face among many—either to authenticate a face as a method of identification (known as one-to-one match), or to search for a face through photo archives, live video streams, or any other searchable digital media (a one-from-many search).

A company called Mr. Payroll today deploys facial recognition software to authenticate the identity of people withdrawing money at various ATMs in the United States. Imagefish.com builds systems that use "visual similarity" recognition tools to provide large enterprises with the ability to search through individual frames of video or digital archives of stock photos. (An example of large-scale visual similarity searching can be found on its website, www.imagefish.com.) But by far the most intriguing use of visual searching and facial recognition technology today is being done by Visionics, a U.K. company with roots in the surveillance industry.

Visionics's product, FaceIT (www.faceit.com), literally picks faces out of a crowd. One of its first applications has been in Newham, East London, where Visionics provided the local police with a system consisting of 144 live, networked video surveillance cameras, linked to a FaceIT recognition system. FaceIT automatically scans all the incoming video streams, searching for matches with a database containing the faces of convicted criminals. If a bank robber walks into a shopping mall, or a pedophile is seen strolling by a schoolyard, the police are notified immediately, in real time. According to the local police supervisor, the system works remarkably well. FaceIT is also being used in a "border crossing application" by the Israeli government.

FaceIT works by breaking facial images into small blocks whose color, texture, and relationship to each other are used to build what Visionics describes as a "faceprint." According to the company's website, "The faceprint contains the information that distinguishes a face from millions of others. And our latest advances allow the FaceIT engine to scan through these millions of records in the blink of an eye."

Today, FaceIT and the few other applications like it are used primarily in closed, proprietary systems. The 144 cameras in the CCTV (closed circuit television) system in Newham are part of a secure, private system, not linked to any public network. But similar technology could also be used to "scrape" (i.e., scan and search the Internet) for a face—and no doubt soon will be. Eventually, the tools needed to perform a video-scrape search on the Net could be available to anybody.

Facial recognition technology introduces a new slate of social issues. One application of visual similarity tools on the Net today involves searches for similar female models—most of whom are in a similar state of undress. As with most other new technologies in the world of audiovisual imagery, the porn industry will no doubt be first in line to use the new systems. Law enforcement and other government agencies will also be highly tempted, no doubt, by systems that can search through hundreds, if not thousands, of unique video streams, in real time, looking for one person, or for everyone ever on a Ten Most Wanted list. Or on any other list that seemed, to them, to be worth the effort.

But even these relatively isolated uses stop well short of the true privacy concern raised by this kind of technology. Things really start to get serious when faceprints, voiceprints, names, and other digitalized PII can be scraped from all the data streams collected from all the digital devices mentioned above, all flowing through the great global grid. Welcome to the information age, indeed.

## Tips and Tricks for Chapter 4

**Got a family website? Don't tell too much.** Thanks to such online communities as GeoCities and Tripod, there are hundreds of thousands of family sites. If you have a family website showing your children's pictures, don't include information like where they go to school, where you live, your phone number, or any other personally identifiable information—that's giving personal information out every bit as much as sending an e-mail or filling out a registration page.

**Sign an online behavior contract with your child.** Many families have found that working together to come up with a set of online "rules of the road" goes a long way toward helping kids have positive online experiences. One approach is to have a family Internet use agreement, or contract. Some families print and post the contract by the computer, others elect to have both parents and kids sign the document. There's an excellent sample Internet use agreement on the Internet Education Foundation's website at http://www.getnetwise.org/tools/toolscontracts.shtml.

**Watch your computer's file-sharing settings.** If you work in a small office with a few networked PCs, you may not want your co-workers to be able to see that resume you've just e-mailed to a competitor or that alternative lifestyle chat you frequent. To reduce this risk, you may want to examine your computer's file-sharing settings. If you don't want the files on your local computer accessible to others on the network, you can disable file sharing completely. To do so, double-click on the Network icon in Control Panel, then click on the Network dialog box's

File and Printer Sharing button. When you see the File and Printer Sharing dialog, clear the check beside "I want to be able to give others access to my files."

**Create different passwords for each directory.** Software security programs are now available that help prevent unauthorized access to files on your home computer. Some can encrypt every directory with a different password so that you must log in every time you access a different directory. Even if your online service provider tries to read any private files, it will be denied access. These programs may include an "audit trail" that records all activity on the computer's drives.

**Create an anonymous e-mail address at work.** Taking this step can help your online privacy, as well as your peace of mind. This is especially true if, by virtue of your position, you sometimes need to be the bearer of bad news to the public— for example, if you work at a small company and you're one of only a few customer service reps assigned to handle e-mail complaints. If a complaint is not settled to their satisfaction, some customers can take the matter personally and become angry and abusive. If enough of your real name appears in your e-mail address—such as, Jane.Koslowski@custserv.county bank.com—you could be setting yourself up for abusive phone calls at work or maybe even at home if your number is listed in the phone book.

Better to use an anonymous e-mail address, such as feedback@countybank.com. A good alternative is an actual feedback form. Your e-mail administrator or ISP can write one for you, or you can do it yourself by obtaining such inexpensive or free programs as CGIMail (http://www.nsiweb.com/cgisoftware/cgimail/), Extropia (http://www.extropia.com/), or Freedback.com (http://www.freedback.com/).

**Post a list of online safety rules near your computer.** The Eugene, Oregon, School District has six excellent "Rules for Online Safety," which it suggests that parents or children print out and tape near their computer.

The rules are posted on their website at http://www .4j.lane.edu/safety/rules.html and include:

- I will not give out personal information such as my address, telephone number, parent's work address/telephone number, or the name and location of my school without my parent's permission.
- I will tell my parents right away if I come across any information that makes me feel uncomfortable.
- I will never agree to get together with someone I "meet" online without first checking with my parents. If my parents agree to the meeting, I will be sure that it is in a public place and bring my mother or father along.
- I will never send a person my picture or anything else without first checking with my parents.
- I will not respond to any messages that are mean or in any way make me feel uncomfortable. It is not my fault if I get a message like that. If I do I will tell my parents right away so that they can contact the online service.
- I will talk with my parents so that we can set up rules for going online. We will decide upon the time of day that I can be online, the length of time I can be online, and appropriate areas for me to visit. I will not access other areas or break these rules without their permission.

**Consider using a family-friendly ISP.** Unlike filtering software, which once installed on your computer (usually) blocks access to websites with content you deem objectionable, family-friendly Internet service providers do the blocking for you, right on their server. Most charge in the same $19.95–$29.95 range as other ISPs do. The website KidShield.com maintains a list of these family-friendly ISPs at http://www.kidshield.com/isps/filteredisps.htm#top. Focus on the Family, an advocacy organization with Evangelical Christian roots, also has a directory on its website at http://www.family.org/cforum/research/papers/a0002551.html.

**Easy tech steps to help you monitor e-mail before your kids can read it.** Maybe your child shares your Internet e-mail account. You don't want him or her to read any of the porn-flavored junk that crams your electronic mailbox, or perhaps e-mails from his or her teacher. Well, certain e-mail programs can manage this problem. Microsoft's Outlook Express is one.

First go to Tools, then Options, and then Settings. In the Settings menu, uncheck the top box, "check for e-mail every xx seconds." When you do this, your incoming e-mail—both wanted and unwanted—will sit on your ISP's server until you or someone else clicks on "send and receive." Here's where you can gain a step on the commercial and smutty spammers. In succession, go to View, then Layout, then check Customize Toolbar. Next, remove the send and receive icon from the bar. You won't receive any new e-mail until you manually request it by temporarily reconfiguring the send and receive option on the Toolbar. For a sharp fourteen-year-old, this "fix" will last for about forty-eight seconds—but it's very effective with younger children.

**Don't give out your full name on your voice mail greeting.**

If you use voice mail or an answering machine, giving your full name provides unnecessary info to spammers and stalkers alike. It's a better idea to leave just your first name, or your phone number only. Here's an example: "You've reached 555-2222. Please leave a message after the tone. If this is an unsolicited sales call, we don't want any."

**Use the "second person" on your voice mail greeting.** Phone stalkers and potential thieves may interpret the revelation that a person lives alone as a sign of vulnerability. Especially for women who live alone, it's always a good idea to promote the notion that you aren't there by yourself. You could say something like "You've reached 555-2222. Please leave a message after the tone. Either Guido or I will get back to you right away."

**Lurk before you post to a chat room.** Some Internet chat rooms will post e-mail addresses of participants so that anyone else in the chat session can easily grab a valid e-mail address. Here's a hypothetical example: "Laura Gale of Atlanta (lgale@yourfriendly-isp.com) writes: I vehemently disagree with your politics." Another chat participant could then go to an e-mail address directory site and perhaps find Laura Gale's phone number and even her physical address, thus opening the door to harassing phone calls, letters or worse. Before you post in any chat room, first log on and see if they follow this practice. If they do, stay away.

**Control your e-mail forwarding.** You may send a confidential e-mail message to a colleague or friend, only to have him or her unintentionally violate your privacy by forwarding it along to someone else. That recipient might forward it to another person, and so on. Now it's possible to mark your e-mail so that it can't be forwarded to anyone else by its recipient, or even block the text of your message from being copied and pasted into a new message. The magic bullet here is InteRosa, an e-mail control technology from QVTech Inc. More info is available at http://www.qvtech.com/.

# 5
# The Datanet Rules

*Computing is not about computers anymore. It is about living.*
*—Nicholas Negroponte, Being Digital*

To a certain extent, collecting data about ordinary people is nothing new. Personal information has been collected, amassed, and stored since the days of the Roman Empire.

For the last several hundred years, this information has been recorded on paper and squirreled away in boxes or filing cabinets. "Access to PII" was slow and laborious, and meant writing a letter or standing in line in hopes of getting a clerk to open a file drawer and dig through folders. The sheer inertia of this kind of information retrieval kept most private matters private, or at least contained within a small circle of people or organizations. Instant public access to private data, on any kind of large scale, was impossible.

A single computer software application changed all that: the database. By breaking data into many small building blocks called "fields" and organizing these fields in a consistent pattern, or "schema," data could suddenly be "queried"—i.e., requested and retrieved with great specificity—at electronic speed. Query routines could pull out consistent sets of data—about left-handed baseball players, corn farmers in Nebraska, or single mothers. Huge mailing lists could be created efficiently and economically. Over time, databases increased in sophistication, and corporate users of databases began to slice, dice, and "data-mine" their massive store of customer records, so as to target offers down to the level of a single person, instead of firing randomly at a herd of nameless prospects. This task required considerable computing firepower, and for the last decade, database development has proceeded at an aggressive pace. Consequently, a turn-of-the-century advanced relational database can easily be queried to see if there is a unique left-handed, softball-playing, corn-farming single mother in Omaha.

Powerful as they are, these same databases often can't prevent people from getting multiple copies of the same mail-order catalog, or continuing to get them long after they are dead. Databases have been important tools in the Information Revolution, but they are slow and clunky compared to network data retrieval systems. While not likely to disappear anytime soon, databases do tend more and more to resemble an early life form whose body is much larger than its brain.

However antiquated computer databases may become in the twenty-first century, they clearly helped the world take a giant leap forward in information storage and retrieval in the twentieth. The database from Oracle, an early Silicon Valley company, was especially powerful, and terrifically scalable (that is to say, it can handle high-volume data storage and other demands of large corporate customers very well). In its first incarnations, the Oracle database ran on an open UNIX platform, which meant that it could run on virtually any type of computer that was running a UNIX operating system, giving it a competitive advantage against early market leader IBM, which sold its proprietary database only with its own computers. Oracle was also one of the first software companies to train an army of consultants to help support its software product—thus helping many companies not only to install its database but to use it for maximum effect in a variety of applications, including, notably, direct marketing.

When the Internet first began to explode commercially in the second half of the 1990s, Oracle databases became a key transaction management platform and served as the technical foundation of such fast-growing sites as Amazon.com, E*Trade, and CNN.com.

But databases were really not designed for the Web. Their core purpose has been to archive information rather than to transmit it at warp-speed, interacting in real time with geographically remote resources. Databases, in other words, were meant to stand as giant storage bins beside the highway, not to be part of the road itself. The design of the database, in fact, still resembles that of its architectural predecessor, the filing cabinet. Each database cabinet has its own rules, and its own way of organizing the data filed inside it, which often makes its data incomprehensible to other databases. Despite recent database industry initiatives that have tried to standardize certain internal data structures and the communications protocols between database applications, transferring information from one database to another remains problematic. Not impossible—it's far more efficient than swapping paper files—but well short of the holy grail of seamless data flow between applications.

Despite the wide use of databases in e-commerce websites, the arrival of the World Wide Web hit the information storage business like a tornado, and databases, the reservoir of almost all digitally stored PII as late as the mid-1990s, had to struggle to adapt to a strange and rapidly changing environment. Suddenly, much of the most important information in the world wasn't being stored at all; it was being *posted* on the Internet, where it could be accessed by anyone with a browser and access to a search engine. At last count, that was nearly 200,000,000 people—a very big number.

Threaded through the massive reams of data stored on Internet systems is much personally identifiable information. And not just names linked to postings in chat groups and newsgroups, but personal profiles containing contact information, behavior patterns, credit history, investment records, and even medical information. Some of this data is stored in highly secure computing environments, but a great deal of it is "in the clear," meaning that it can be accessed by anyone. Some data is partially secured, but accessible with a password or a digital certificate (a verifiable ID in digital form that can be used as a kind of ticket). In systems of this type, PII can be stored in databases behind firewalls with online access gates, and then be queried online. The query results are then posted in HTML format on the Net. (Sections of Peoplefinder at AltaVista.com provide one example.)

But as we mentioned at the beginning of this book, the Net is currently undergoing a major shift in architecture, from HTML (which is about graphic display) to XML (about data exchange). When personal information is run through an XML editor, it can easily be "coupled" online with other data, much as any Lego piece can be connected to any other. In this environment, personal profiles about us become "objects" which can be "loosely coupled" over and over again, for many different purposes. Much of this coupling can be done intelligently and automatically, with the result being nothing less than a fundamentally new information environment. Partly to contrast the coming XML-driven era with the fading heyday of the database, we call this new information environment the *datanet*.

The era ushered in by the datanet will feature much seamless exchange of private information about you, between people you do not know, for purposes you have not approved. That much is a given—there are too many PII ponies already out of the barn. For better or worse, some of your PII is about to come out of the cabinet forever, and spill out of proprietary databases as well.

# *What's in a Name?*

It's not just the technology foundations of information storage/retrieval that are changing. The economics are changing as well.

The economic trends influencing the information environment are, of course, often themselves driven by changing technology. The basic cycle seems to be: a technical innovation is introduced into the marketplace; early adopters use this innovation as a competitive advantage and gain ground on their rivals; the rivals recognize their resulting disadvantage and quickly deploy the new technology themselves — thus driving up revenue for the supplier of the technology, who gains resources that make it possible to come up with even more innovations.

But strategic demand for a particular innovation must exist before it will be deployed successfully. As the Australian technology scholar Graeme Donald Snooks argues, "Da Vinci's ideas about motive power were blocked not by problems of execution, but by the absence of demand for that technical solution. Strategic demand, not conditions of supply, is the major determinant of both technological change and economic growth." In other words, you can build it and they still may not come, unless economic conditions are right.

What, then, are the current conditions with respect to strategic demand for PII? Is there enough demand for private personal information to spur the computing industry to move the technology innovation cycle forward in a great quantum leap?

To answer these questions, it is necessary only to look at new metrics the financial markets are using to measure company value. As is quite apparent from the market valuations of Internet companies, many of the old yardsticks for measuring the worth of a company have been tossed aside. But new yardsticks have emerged to take their place, using new units of value. One of the most important of these new measurement units is the customer name. Understanding how this new measurement system works, and how it helps to explain certain seemingly bizarre new business models, helps us understand a great deal about the strategic demand for PII and how a world powered by a dynamic datanet might evolve.

Consider the potential of this hot new Internet business model: A big bank, suddenly tiring of the bricks-and-mortar banking biz, decides to go entirely digital and put all its resources onto the Web. Literally. Their cutting-edge idea is to become the prime mover in online banking by offering their core product, *cash*, at very low prices. So they launch their new e-site with an offer to sell crisp, new $100 bills at a dollar apiece (limit of one per customer).

It's a great promotion—essentially, $10 in free cash for every customer who signs up! The offer, of course, starts a feeding frenzy—and for a while, chaos reigns in the bank's back office systems. But the operations team weathers the storm, and the bank promotes its brand and transforms itself into a savvy e-bank worth billions.

Sound far-fetched? Well, on the Net, the far-fetched can quickly become routine. PeoplePC, which itself delivers a personal computer to your home and provides Internet access for $24.95 per month, recently offered a special promotion with E*Trade. The deal was that every PeoplePC subscriber who signed up with the online broker would have $100 placed in their new account, courtesy of E*Trade. And, although the promotion was designed to help PeoplePC customers start buying stocks, there was no restriction against simply closing the account and having E*Trade send them a check for a hundred bucks. The actual E*Trade payout, in other words, was no less than that of our hypothetical e-bank.

Why is the Internet economy giving rise to such promotions? We can find one answer in the case of an Internet start-up's Christmas promotion of 1998.

800.com was the brainchild of television producer John Ripper, who came from the world of direct-response TV advertising, or infomercials. He envisioned a new business model for the Internet, one that would utilize informative video clips to help sell and support high-end electronics products. The company's website was launched in September 1998, and by November, 800.com CEO Greg Drew was looking for a blockbuster Christmas promotion. Taking a page from book and music clubs that predated the Internet, 800.com announced on its website that each visitor could order three current, mainstream music CDs or DVD movies for just a dollar. It may have been a gimmick, but it was also a great deal.

It wasn't that the company was feeling the holiday spirit; its plan for the promotion was well calculated: it wanted to "buy" customers, at about $50 a head (the retail value of the CDs and DVDs). Drew had first considered renting some high-priced AOL or Yahoo! real estate, where banners could be planted to drive traffic to the 800.com site. But he decided it would be cheaper and more effective to eliminate the middleman and give his promotional budget directly to customers, in the form of a quality $50 value perfectly timed for Christmas. He barely advertised, guessing that word of the offer would make its way around the Web quickly. It did. The resulting traffic loads almost melted the site's servers, and indeed, the site was down, off and on, for several days. Still, the company took in four times its projected revenue for the month (because many $1 customers actually bought a lot of normally priced goods). It was a wild bet, but it launched the company and landed Microsoft co-founder Paul Allen as an early investor.

Drew based his calculated bet on numbers that venture capitalists were throwing around as he was going out to raise money. Private e-commerce companies were being valued at $2000 per customer. At that price, he figured, paying $50 for one customer name, even if that customer made only a $1 purchase, would be a real bargain.

Although he was one of the first on the Net to do it, today 800.com's Drew is not alone in making this kind of calculation.

Customer acquisition costs are rising, as is the value of customer relationships. New business models designed to transform the cost of customer acquisition into a direct customer benefit (or seductive promotion) are proliferating. PCs, cell phones, vacation resort stays, and much more are now being given away over the Internet, in hopes of capturing a new permanent customer.

What do these new business models have to do with privacy, trust, and the role of information technology in our lives? Most reasonably knowledgeable adults of course recognize that these giveaways are transparent attempts to capture personal information about, and ongoing relationships with, potential customers. What's less well known is the fact that venture capitalists and stock analysts are using our names as a fundamental unit of value in the marketplace. And pricing this new value unit at around two grand per name.

Think about this for a moment. Your name in an e-commerce company's database—coupled, of course, with other basic identifiers and facts about you and your preferences—is worth $2000 of market value to that company. This means that your name is worth not just $2000, but $2000 *per company*. Imagine all the companies who might be interested in having this kind of value represented on their balance sheets. Sell your name and a deep personal profile about you to just one hundred such companies, and at even half the fair market value, you too can be an Internet millionaire.

And to think that we've all been giving this stuff away, for years.

In reality, there are no Internet millionaires who have struck it rich on the value of their own PII. The value equation between companies and customers with respect to private data exchange is currently out of whack. It's a clear case of marketplace disequilibrium. The value we provide companies when we "register" as customers is huge; the value we get back is marginal, even negative. Given the law of supply and demand, and absent any extraneous factors, this disparity must in time correct itself. Indeed, in the Internet economy, this correction has already begun—the $500 computer that is being offered to customers for signing up for FreePC's program being a prime case in point.

(It should perhaps be noted that in the FreePC deal, the customer is not just providing a name, but also signing up for an ongoing barrage of ads in a special frame on the side of the computer screen. Free PC also provides demographic information to business partners but it keeps this information anonymous to third parties. One tip for would-be FreePC customers: yes, you can use duct tape to cover the ad portion of your screen. But the disclosure of your PII to "business partners" is another matter.)

In the coming years we will no doubt see many more inventive corporate schemes designed to grow "street value" by accumulating more and more new customer profiles. Many of these schemes will pass along a sizeable payoff directly to the consumer, especially when the customer whose profile has been captured actually sticks with an ongoing program, turning a static name into a dynamic connection. To the extent these dollars-for-data deals are honest and transparent, they may even help to build a market for privacy, by driving the prices paid for personal data, and personalized data exchanges, closer to their true market value.

Practically speaking, price inflation in the market for deep, dynamic PII profiles could lead to . . .

- **New personal tools.** Web entrepreneurs would have the incentive to build tools and systems that not only protect your privacy but also enable you to take the initiative and commercially exploit your own PII. You'd be able to sell information about yourself, through infomediaries and other data brokers, for hundreds to perhaps thousands of dollars. Web wallets and passports could enable you to store private personal and financial data in highly secure "envelopes" that interact online with other entities, under certain specific terms and conditions. Thus these tools would not just protect the confidentiality but also the value of private facts about you. If PII becomes more valuable, new electronic "locks and strongboxes" will be built to protect it.

- **New corporate systems.** Valuing a company based on its PII records could become qualitative rather than quantitative. In other words, valuations would not be based on a crude $2000-per-name calculation, but on sophisticated analyses of both the accuracy of the customer data and the depth and degree of loyalty of the customer relationship. The biggest problem with price-per-name valuations in today's relatively low-trust computing environment is that up to 40 percent of all customer registration data is bogus. Imagine investing in a new company with 100,000 customer names, only to discover that 40,000 of those names are not valid. If you valued the company at $2000 per name, justifying a market cap of $200 million and a stock price of, say, $10 per share, you would be paying $4 too much if you bought stock at that price. Though stock values rarely if ever move with this kind of precision, the fact that customer names are now part of the value equation does point up a discontinuity in the equity markets. This imbalance will get corrected eventually, most likely by Big 5 accounting and assurance firms who will audit PII records and data collection practices, just as they audit company financials today. The companies that build trust with customers will receive deeper, more accurate data from these customers—and the value of the resulting high-quality data will start turning up on balance sheets. This in turn could lead to innovations designed to help customers manage their own records inside a company's online environment—much as Federal Express used the Net to allow its customers to manage their own online package tracking. For if you desire really accurate, up-to-the-minute customer data, who better to manage the PII profiles than customers themselves?

- **New datanet rules.** If the world continues to move more and more business information onto the Web; if the role of the database does substantially weaken in favor of a new datanet; if sophisticated third-party analyses of company-to-customer relationships do become a key part of stock valuations; and if new tools that allow consumers to store and manage their own data do proliferate—what comes next? We're way out on a limb here, but it appears to us that static, fossilized customer records might disappear altogether. Instead, millions of dynamic individual profiles would float around the Net like cells in the bloodstream, functioning largely according to rules set up by the individuals themselves. These new datanet rules would specify how PII is to be used, and personal PII cells would monitor and control data transactions accordingly. By combining the intelligence of the datanet with new enhanced security features, and having this new system operate in a marketplace that fairly valued personal data, a new era of trusted data exchange could emerge.

Sound like a pipe dream? Given the strong strategic demand in today's economy for customer information, and the increasing public unease about privacy loss, something's got to give. Perhaps the changes wrought by the growing market for PII over the Internet will be positive. Unfortunately, demand for personal data also creates a brisk market for PII traded among third-party collectors. The same network efficiencies produced elsewhere in the economy can be utilized in this gray market for PII as well. The result could just as easily be a spiral that moves in a negative direction, with more and more personal information becoming openly available at less and less cost.

Today, the electronic market for PII is relatively inefficient— the data is frequently wrong, and tracking changes in individual lives is very difficult. The market is also relatively shallow in terms of the kinds of information it provides, at least when compared with the power of a true datanet. We spoke with the CEO of one company, for example, that maintains a database containing information on over 95 percent of all households in the United States, with the information in the database modeled to predict buying patterns for financial products and services. Because this information is stored in a proprietary database, and sold to financial services companies only, most of us have had little reason to complain (however uncomfortable we might feel about this database's mere existence). Even if it has been used to target us with direct marketing mailers, this company's database has been an annoyance at worst. In fact, we may have even benefited—for one thing, this database has helped financial companies achieve greater marketing efficiency, thereby allowing them to serve us at more competitive prices.

But what if all the financial indicators currently in this database—plus more new ones—showed up on a new open datanet, in a highly accessible format? What if our bank accounts, our investments, and our credit history suddenly were posted online and made available to all comers, to be used for any purpose? Just a few instances of such data dumping, from closed private systems onto a public datanet, would make privacy protection an increasingly futile exercise. With the exception of laws regarding medical and certain children's data, nothing stands in the way of such data dumpings except the economic self-interest of those owning the data.

In the coming datanet era, the economics of data collection could drive a positive cycle in which the increasing value of personal data creates demand for tools that protect and manage it on behalf of its true owners, we ourselves—the "names." Or, it might push us along a slippery slope where private information becomes an ever cheaper commodity, thereby reducing incentives for technology providers to build privacy protection into information environments. And increasing the likelihood that ever more personal data will come online, accessible via a vast datanet.

One step society can take to tip the scale in support of the former cycle, and away from the latter, is to recognize private information, in some forms, as a kind of personal property. In the database era, intellectual property law in the United States has held that the names in a database are the property of the creator of the database. This may be fine for a database economy, where the value of a database lies in the work necessary to assemble it, but it doesn't work at all in a datanet economy, where information freely floats around the electronic cosmos. For practical marketplace reasons, every bit as much as for the preservation of personal rights and values, it is time to rethink the legal framework surrounding PII collection and use. In order to create the right equilibrium between company and customer, and between a right to privacy and the free flow of information, we should consider deeply personal information to be the property of the individual who is providing it. And then let market forces work their magic. (The theory being that if PII is valuable individual property, strategic demand will be created for tools and systems to protect it.)

In the meantime, it's safe to say that with identifiable customer profiles generating increasing value in both the commercial and equity markets, systems that keep track of these customers behind corporate firewalls will get more and more sophisticated. This will result in many new business models, especially in the e-commerce realm. But, as we move to the coming datanet, another pronounced change will occur, this one involving the "names" themselves, and how they interact with one another.

## *Datanet Rising*

As we mentioned earlier in this chapter, the core technology driving the shift to the datanet is the very important Internet standard known as XML, for EXtensible Markup Language. Like its predecessor, HTML, the Internet protocol format that helped launch the World Wide Web, XML shows signs of completely transforming the

Internet and taking it into a new era. HTML improved visual display and led to banner ads and rich online graphics; XML enhances data exchange and could lead to a quantum leap in the ability of machines to read and compile data, without any direct human intervention.

Passing data through an XML editor creates a series of tags associated with the content inside the data object. An XML-edited Microsoft Word document, for example, would contain certain embedded fields, or "metatags," that could be read by other software applications, thereby greatly assisting an exchange of information between two documents, two applications, or two machines.

If both you and your dentist were running XML-based personal organizers, you could e-mail her your calendar, which would "talk" to her scheduling application and figure out the best time for your next appointment. This would be possible even if you happened to be using different software programs. In fact, you, an assistant at work, the dentist, and her assistant could all view and provide input to the scheduling task—even if you happened to be on the other side of the world, with nothing more than a hand-held appliance. In a fully XML-enabled network, personal information of almost every type and description can be exchanged electronically, with relative ease.

Obviously, having your dentist see your entire datebook might not be a good thing. So, software features that control access to certain types of information are being built into many XML-based products. But given the software industry's record on personal privacy so far, we would be surprised if software development labs were able to plug all the privacy holes that will be created in an XML information environment.

The biggest privacy loss may not come from hundredth window-type system vulnerabilities in XML environments but from the proliferation of seamless data exchange that XML is designed to achieve. Take, for instance, the case of personal electronic address books. Once they can be exchanged easily, and accurately, the sheer number of names in everyone's address book may grow exponentially. And, tied to online identifiers, these addresses may be able to be updated rather effortlessly as well. What will this mean for those with personal histories involving violent criminals, stalkers, ex-mates and ex-lovers, business antagonists, opportunists, and other unwelcome types? At least this: given that the Internet retains information longer than an elephant, it will be harder than ever to shake off unwanted inquiries and to move on after unfortunate personal episodes.

The good news is that XML holds the promise of being a kind of Internet Rosetta Stone, enabling many useful but disparate information sources to finally get in synch. XML gives the myriad proprietary data structures on the Net a common structural architecture, thereby enabling them to speak each other's language. Individual computing systems will be able to retrieve each other's most pertinent data and generally interoperate as never before. The result will be a transformation from World Wide Web to Instant Information Environment. In the latter, highly specific query routines can sift through networked databases, deep website archives, posted Web pages, newsgroups, and even audio and video streams. Such requests will produce remarkable results, with big improvements in search and retrieval capability expected in the 2002–2003 period. As a research and learning environment, the datanet will be unparalleled.

To get a glimpse of the near-term future of the Net, try out the popular NewsTracker feature at Excite.com. With it, you can train your own personalized software agent (or "bot," short for "robot") to search the Internet and retrieve news stories on various topics. NewsTracker scans a body of data—the daily news in important news media—that is a tiny subset of the Internet as a whole, and it no doubt stores considerable information about these news media sites locally in its own core database (rather than hitting all the news sources in real time). But this feature nevertheless does provide an excellent and compelling picture of the near-term future of information retrieval.

## The Near-Term Dilemma

Would a company such as the one mentioned above that houses massive amounts of financially related data ever really consider dumping its data online, so that PII could be searched for on the Net as easily as news? Well, imagine that this data collection company applied the same kind of logic used by our cash-selling Internet e-bank. The business thinking might go like this:

*We have a big, somewhat outdated portion of our database that is not really doing much for us these days. Let's dump all the customer data in that section onto the Web, making it retrievable online by anyone who wants to use it. The promotion will drive traffic to our new Web site, and we'll make our money in banner ads, links, and promotions. More important, we will be transforming ourselves from a back-office list management company to an online e-databank. And our stock price will soar!*

This is but one scenario that could result in new PII being posted directly on the public network, ready to be accessed by the next generation of data snatchers. Actually, the above model is not too far from that of several companies in business on the Web today (*their* identities shall remain anonymous, in hopes that no one ever hears of them and they quickly wither away).

The strategy of re-purposing and capitalizing on historic databases, for some companies, currently offers considerable reward with little or no penalty. It is not illegal to gather information for one purpose and then sell or redistribute the data for another purpose to other companies—unless you promised the customer explicitly that you wouldn't. (Which is one reason why it is important to do business with companies that actually post their data collection and data management policies.)

An online privacy policy is not just a hollow promise — it actually subjects a company to voluntary legal liability, should it promise the customer one thing and do another. And though such policies are a helpful guide when making personal decisions today about data sharing, in the near term more and more personal data will inevitably move from the realm of proprietary control by a single company, out into the public "commons" of the network itself.

Thus, most of us will soon find ourselves in a world where more and more information about us will become available to more and more people, with increasing ease. The net result will be a marked reduction in individual control over private personal information. And unfortunately, because all current information technology systems have a basic privacy flaw in their architecture, this loss of control will also, in the short term, lead to many errors in personal profiles and to much identity confusion.

The flaw is that individual consumers — and citizens, patients, and students — have little or no access to personal data that is being stored about them, and therefore no opportunity to review it and correct mistakes. Screw-ups, lies, and strange anomalies can flow around a network as quickly as a hot joke — except that the kind of mistakes that cause months of delay in a credit application, cancellation of all credit cards, or the denial of a government benefit are not at all funny.

Mistakes create one kind of problem in a highly networked world; certain kinds of facts create others. Medical facts, for instance. When President Clinton signed an executive order concerning the privacy of personal health information in October 1999, it was widely reported in the news media that one in three companies screen employee health records for purposes of hiring and promotion. Obviously, in a datanet environment, the distribution of this kind of information could also proliferate greatly, well beyond the confines of a corporate human resources department, though that seems bad enough.

Today, in most cases, there is not even a uniform way to determine the rules and policies under which medical data, or any other kind of data, has been collected. Trust in such an environment is a purely one-way street leading to the data holder (to the extent that any trust exists in the system at all).

Until true Trust Environments—encrypted data exchange systems, or networks, where access to data is strictly controlled and audited—are constructed, and until more technologies that protect and defend our privacy become available, individual people will find themselves exposed more than ever before. This is true in our current information environment, but the need for individual controls will be even more pronounced in the XML-driven datanet that lurks just around the bend.

The privacy questions raised by the imminent arrival of powerful new networking technologies are not easily resolved. Much personal privacy has already been lost to these technologies, but much, much more is yet to be harvested by them. This is clearly a cause for concern—and yet, the advances these same technologies bring in scientific research, human learning, business productivity, and even national security should not be dismissed lightly. The interplay of personal privacy and modern technology is complex and, at the very least, needs to be guided by some fundamental principles.

If we take the leap from the database to the datanet with the wrong set of rules and norms in place, we will lose a great deal more personal privacy than we have lost to date. We'll also lose what may be a one-time opportunity to bring symmetry and fair value to the company-to-customer data exchange.

In complex systems such as the datanet, enduring rules tend to emerge, rather than be installed from above. While we cannot offer a precise blueprint for bringing the name/value market into equilibrium, or for ushering in an era of greater trust on the Internet, we do have some ideas, and the hope that new privacy-enhancing rules and systems will eventually emerge does not seem entirely misplaced. At the same time, the very real possibility that an XML-enabled datanet, propelled by strong, supportive economic forces, will reduce our already diminished personal privacy to levels barely imaginable a decade ago makes the strongest possible case for continuing to make privacy protection a priority.

For now, the best advice is probably that famously provided by Bette Davis while descending a staircase in the movie *All About Eve*: "Fasten your seat belts. It's going to be a bumpy night."

---

### Tips and Tricks for Chapter 5

**Use financial sites with "time-out" capabilities.** Almost one-third of all stock transactions are handled over the Internet. Because we're likely to be at work during the hours the New York Stock Exchange and NASDAQ are open for business, that means that some of our most sensitive, high-stakes financial data are open to visual snoops or colleagues on our company's local area network. Even if you're trading from home, you may be vulnerable to curious, malevolent eyes.

These highly personal online brokerage—or online banking—sites are usually fairly well protected, but once we open our own account activity screen, it is fully unprotected for the period that we keep it open. It is very important, therefore, that the site have a time-out feature that closes our account after a period of inactivity. Any site built to handle personal accounts that does not have this time-out feature is less than ideal, from a security perspective.

It's also very important as a user of such an online account that you always make certain that you close the account *before* walking away from your computer (especially if accessing your account from a computer that is not your own!).

**Block the ads your children see.** If you wish to block online advertisements on the sites that your children visit, Junkbusters provides a free ad-blocking tool called the Internet Junkbuster Proxy. It can be found at http://internet.junkbusters.com. The Junkbuster site also lists other such software products at http://www.junkbusters.com/ht/en/links.html#filtering. These include Webfilter, Webwiper, and Squid. Cybersitter (http:// www.solidoak.com/cysitter.htm) also provides a filter that blocks ads.

**Enter websites without being followed.** Netscape Navigator and Microsoft Internet Explorer keep a record of every Web address you type into your browser. Here's a way to visit a site undetected: In either browser, press Ctrl-O to bring up a dialog box, then type the URL into it.

**Protect your computer against viruses.** A computer virus is a program that spreads from PC to PC, replicating itself along the way. Here are some useful virus prevention tips:

- *Get some antivirus software, and update it frequently.* For a current list of antivirus programs and links to websites where you can obtain them, type: http://dir.yahoo.com/ Business_and_Economy/Companies/Computers/Software/System_Utilities/Utilities/Virus_Protection/. Many antivirus utilities come with an automatic "clock" that will prompt you to go to their website for an update after a certain length of time.

- Don't insert floppy disks from unknown sources into your disk drive.
- Download files into a special folder on your hard drive. Then, scan those files *before* you open them.
- *Scan e-mail attachments before reading them.* If your e-mail program automatically opens attached files when they're received, disable this function.
- If you're sharing data across a network, save all files in RTF (Rich Text Format).RTF doesn't save macros, so this step will prevent macro viruses (one of the most common types).
- *Back up everything on a separate device.* This way if your system becomes infected, you'll have something to fall back on.

**Make sure your name is suppressed on e-mail lists.** Most e-mail programs allow the sender to hide the e-mail address of all other recipients from the view of each individual recipient. If an e-mailer doesn't do this, they may be revealing e-mail addresses of people who don't want this information known. If you receive e-mail with a long list of "cc's"—especially to different domains—e-mail the sender and ask them to start suppressing other names on the list from appearing to anyone except the specific recipient.

**Encrypt your bookmarks.** Prying eyes in the office or at home can violate your privacy by looking at the names of sites in your browser's Bookmarks or Favorites list. What if you've bookmarked the Web page for a jobs site? Will word get back to the boss that you're looking for other employment? A new product called Webroot's Private Bookmarks can encrypt these lists so they are indecipherable to others (http://www.webroot.com/pb-marks.htm).

# 6
# From E-Commerce to Information Economies

*It is true that the machine has sometimes been used by those who owned it, not to liberate men, but to exploit them. This was never accepted by society as right. . . . The right and serviceable use of the machine always makes unprofitable and at last impossible the abuse of it.*
*—Henry Ford,* The Meaning of Power, *1926*

Consider the strange fate of Nicholas J. "Nick" Nicholas, the former CEO of Time Warner. In one of the most celebrated CEO firings of the 1990s, the visionary architect of the merger of Time-Life publishing with Warner Brothers entertainment ran afoul of internal corporate politics and was unceremoniously shown the door by his board. He left with a hefty severance package, however, and used the money to invest in a variety of Internet start-ups. One of the companies was little more than an idea when an old friend from Time invited Nicholas to lunch. The friend brought his son with him—who in turn brought a friend who had patented an innovative Internet business model. His idea was to turn normal commerce upside down with a new type of e-commerce where the customer, not the company, set the price. In other words, a customer would enter the price he's willing to pay for a product or service, and then participating sellers would be contacted over the Internet to determine whether they could fulfill the customer's offer. Nicholas was intrigued, made an initial investment to help get the company going—and sixteen months later the company, Priceline.com, went public. As a result, Nicholas had his original investment turn into $300 million in market value (subject, of course, to stock market ups and downs). Had he stayed on at Time Warner and turned it into the most efficient corporation on earth, he couldn't have accumulated anywhere near as much personal wealth.

Nicholas's story of good fortune is just one of many in the Internet's great second act, the persistent theme of which, as we have said, has been the rise of e-commerce. But the amazing personal fortunes amassed by some Internet visionaries and risk takers are merely the publicly visible flowering of a new force whose roots go much, much deeper into society.

## The Network Effect

How do we explain streaking NASDAQ comets such as Priceline.com, Amazon.com, Real Networks, E*Trade, and dozens of other Internet high-flyers that have created untold fortunes for their founders and early investors? Is there any remnant of traditional marketplace rationality left in the valuations of these new Internet stocks—or have the financial markets simply fallen victim of late to a kind of millennium fever that leads to "irrational exuberance" about all things Internet?

The Internet start-ups that have been the hallmark of Act II of the Internet clearly are guided by a new set of business principles, internally in how they operate and externally in how they are perceived in the capital markets. The price-per-name value discussed in the previous chapter is one example of a new external yardstick, but there are other factors that are perhaps even more important. Many of these factors are intangible, but they also are playing an increasing role in setting the stock value of Internet companies that have successfully entered the public market.

Those who work with Internet start-ups quickly learn that growth and momentum—much more than profit or size—are what drive employee morale, attract funding, and create value. They learn that early "mindshare" and market positioning in an emerging sector can be decisive and lead to permanent competitive advantage. They learn that fluid connectivity and technical interoperability—the need for the tools, applications, services, people, and companies on the Net to work together seamlessly—is an absolute requirement for success. And they learn that those who most fully leverage what is known as the "network effect"—the awesome growth-propelling power of a network to feed the companies within it—become the most successful of all.

The term "network effect" refers, essentially, to the way massively connected systems tend to create standards that, once entrenched, become very difficult to dislodge. These standards become immensely valuable. On a network, the more people who use a particular product or system, the more valuable it becomes, primarily because of an individual user's enhanced ability to connect and share resources with others using the same system. Microsoft Windows and its interoperable companion, Microsoft Office, are classic examples of marketplace standards that have benefited greatly from the network effect. By far the most valuable thing about both of these products, even to Microsoft's most loyal customers, is simply the huge number of other people who also use them. A Microsoft Word document now can be shared with virtually anyone in the world—and that's a competitive advantage that is awfully hard to overcome, as a long list of Microsoft competitors have discovered.

The growth of the Internet is rapidly accelerating the overall significance of the network effect in the global economy. The more business functions move to an electronic network platform, the more important standards and fundamental interoperability become. In this kind of business environment, the master of the network effect is king.

The rise of fax machines in the 1980s and the free e-mail pioneer Hotmail in the late 1990s provide good examples of how the network effect can be leveraged to expand a market, or grow a company. Fax machines took over two decades to gain a foothold in the marketplace, because fax vendors essentially had to bootstrap the creation of their own network of fax machines linked to the existing telecommunications grid. This "network" of interlinked fax devices at first grew slowly, because there was little reason for a business to install a fax unless its partners and customers had one as well. Eventually, however, a critical mass of users was reached in the mid-1980s, the network effect kicked in, and suddenly every business had to have a fax.

Hotmail's founders, on the other hand, already had a network to leverage: the Internet. Utilizing the Internet's enhanced ability to link people together electronically, company founders Sabeer Bhatia and Jack Smith were able to use the Internet's "viral marketing" properties (essentially, the spreading of a message online, customer to customer, as part of an intentional marketing campaign) to go from zero to 12 million subscribers, and a $400 million acquisition by Microsoft, in eighteen months. Obviously, the viral marketing formula they came up with was quite contagious.

The key to Bhatia and Smith's success story was a promotional message that was automatically inserted at the bottom of every e-mail message flowing through a Hotmail server. The message read,

"Get your free Web-based e-mail at Hotmail," and was hot-linked, meaning that the recipient could click it and go directly to the Hotmail site. Putting an embedded advertising message in private e-mail was definitely a first in Internet circles, where the privacy of e-mail contents had always been considered sacrosanct. But Hotmail users generally understood that the free e-mail ad, and many other advertising intrusions, were the price they were paying for getting e-mail service without paying a fee. So there was no real privacy violation, per se, because the principle of informed consent was adhered to. The link itself worked amazingly well as a promotional device—after all, it often came at the end of an e-mail from a friend or relative, and thus appeared to come with the friend's personal endorsement.

Consequently, Hotmail's e-mail service grew faster than any other subscription-based business, ever, in any market. Today Hotmail has over 50 million users. In August 1999, however, it suffered one of the biggest privacy meltdowns in Internet history, when a major security breach opened not just a "window" in the system but a hole big enough to drive a tank through.

With a simple browser patch that could be downloaded over the Net, virtually anyone could enter the Hotmail domain and gain access to the personal e-mail of anyone using the service. Once unauthorized access to a Hotmail user's personal account had been obtained, not only could a hacker read any Hotmail subscriber's mail, but he could also easily e-mail nasty new notes in the subscriber's name, with his or her actual address, to anyone with an old message in the subscriber's e-mail account. No one knows for sure how many phony messages were actually sent, but the prospect has been unsettling to many Hotmail users (to put it mildly), especially given the relative ease with which anyone on the Net could break into a Hotmail account, once the patch was posted.

The Hotmail saga illustrates several important points about the relationship of privacy issues to businesses operating in a network-effect economy.

First, the success of Hotmail's viral marketing innovation of putting hyperlinked ads in private e-mail messages shows that many people will accept a minor intrusion into their personal affairs if it will save them a few bucks. An ad at the bottom of a private message written to a friend or associate may strike some as a bit tacky, others as significantly intrusive, but millions of subscribers were willing to trade a bit of white space in their e-mail fields for an important free service. In certain circles, notably around college campuses, Hotmail was actually trendy, and the ad link at the bottom became a prestige logo. If you were on the receiving end of an e-mail, clicking on that Hotmail link and registering at the Hotmail site were all it took to get into the club. Thus the Hotmail system literally was spread person to person, like a virus. Hotmail harnessed the network effect—the more people using Hotmail, the more valuable it was to each Hotmail user—to build a system that many people used happily and successfully. That's the positive side of the story.

The problem comes when a system that is a standard, or near-standard, is not working properly. When such a system sneezes, many people catch cold. The security breach that Hotmail experienced didn't just put one person or company at risk, but 50 million users. In an economy that thrives on technical interoperability, seamless integration, and standards building, a single open window can expose a huge slice of the populace.

It is for this reason that the leaders of the Internet economy—those companies that control products and systems that are marketplace standards—have such an important role to play in building and supporting personal privacy standards on the Internet as well. Rigorous, highly transparent (i.e., open, honest, and clear) corporate privacy policies help build an environment that values and demands privacy protection. This in turn can help drive specific industry standards (or benchmarks) regarding data collection, data storage, full disclosure, an individual's access to data about himself or herself, and other elements of customer data collection and use—much in the way that ISO 9000 and other industry-wide process benchmarking systems have helped improve product quality and process efficiency.

## *Privacy Management: A New Core Competency*

The emergence of clear benchmarks and standards in the realm of Internet privacy, backed by industry leaders, will help produce stronger, more secure browsers and operating systems; bring more and better private e-mail systems to market; reduce the number of major privacy-related incidents in the news; and generally help create an online environment that ordinary people come to trust and believe in, more and more. A lack of leadership and commitment on the privacy issue will do the opposite and tend to produce many more Hotmail-type episodes.

The privacy issue is for the Internet industry what safety is for the airline industry—an essential part of the business. The general public probably does not care about online privacy with quite the same passion it has for safe airplanes, but polls clearly show that people using the Internet do care about privacy. And their concern is increasing. Like fleet maintenance and pilot training for the airlines, or airbag design and crash tests for the automobile industry, employee privacy training, privacy and security system testing, and other privacy management programs are becoming mission-critical activities for would-be Internet standard-setters.

Failure to execute well on the privacy issue can lead to public relations damage, customer complaints, legal action, and even consumer boycotts. All of which can translate into a diminishing of the company brand and a loss of trust in it. This quickly creates a significant competitive disadvantage when challenging competitors who have used clear privacy policies, standards, and practices to build their reputation for trust. And such competitive advantages can hit the bottom line quickly in a network economy, because word travels fast, and reputations change all the time. When the network effect starts working against you (as it did, for example, for the short-term Internet wonder Pointcast, which sank quickly after word spread about its failure to work properly on corporate servers), the negative effect it creates for a company can be just as powerful as a Hotmail-type growth spiral—it just takes the company in the opposite direction.

## Beyond E-Commerce

Hotmail and dozens of other Internet marvels have been able to tap into the positive power of the network effect, quickly turning momentum and positioning into substantial financial value. And the key to all this momentum and value creation is the seamless exchange of information.

As the speed and volume of the flow of information through the network increase, so does the ability of new, agile start-ups to grow quickly. New network standards—products or systems that leverage the network effect to become widely adopted—create the highest levels of Internet-wide interoperability, and are the strongest enablers of resource sharing, data transfer, and general communication. Tremendous new investment continually rushes into the market chasing the next new network-effects standard, thus ensuring a continuing growth in information exchange overall.

All of this activity is self-reinforcing. As global business and financial leaders recognize that business activity is becoming increasingly interconnected via a single grid, development of the key tools and systems that make up this grid becomes ever more frenetic. At least until the "pick and shovel" phase of this Internet gold rush ends.

It is axiomatic that when gold is discovered, tool vendors receive the first windfall. Gold is hard to mine, after all, but even unlucky miners need shovels. Eventually, however, the gold is located, and industrial powers with huge resources and know-how move in to exploit the resource.

The rise of e-commerce in the late 1990s was largely an era of the tool vendor and the destination site. The latter term refers to high-flying retail sites operated by Internet start-ups; General Electric CEO Jack Welsh calls them "popcorn stands." His point is that the real marketplace power of the Internet is yet to arrive, and when the GEs of the world begin to fully leverage the Net, look out. But as the big industrial giants like GE begin to move en masse into the Internet gold fields, which will be greater: the way the GEs of the world change the Internet, or the way the Net will change GE?

As with many other Internet riddles, this one will likely be resolved according to how the market develops for the true gold of the Internet economy: *information.*

## From Excellence to Trust

The first things outsiders notice when visiting an Internet start-up is the speed. Plans, business models, competitive landscapes, alliances, travel schedules, prospects, and fortunes change constantly. Just-in-time company presentations are readjusted on the fly, in an airplane or a taxi. Handshakes are often sufficient to get new initiatives going, sometimes even with large companies. Conferences and trade shows spring to life all year long, with deal-making filling the aisles. The demands on workers in this environment are considerable. As Internet executive Pete O'Dell of Supertracks put it, "Our employees are only expected to work half-time—twelve hours a day, seven days a week."

The Hundredth Window

Beneath all this frenzied activity you can also observe something else, if you look closely: the power of coherent, well-organized electronic information. Data, discoveries, and insights collected at one node in a networked corporation are instantaneously shared with many others. New marketing stories travel around the enterprise at the speed of light. Training and education systems leverage online systems to keep organizational learning and developmental growth moving forward at an unprecedented pace.

Networked business systems make it possible to form business units that cut across company boundaries, and time zones, to accomplish a singular task. Outsourcing of software and Web development, data processing, system integration needs, marketing and communications, and many central business functions is now commonplace. All these New Economy hallmarks are enabled by the capacity of all businesses, and the workers within them, to exchange information as never before.

Public networks and related information technologies are vital not just for communication but also for production efficiency. In the Internet industry, no less than in medicine or oil drilling, tight streams of coherent information, properly deployed, can bring new levels of precision to business efforts. Internet news tracking systems scour the Net to deliver up-to-the-minute competitive analysis, which can be used to hone and target marketing messages; news about hot emerging technologies spreads quickly over the network, providing companies with access to faster, better, cheaper ways to solve a problem or improve a system; word of new business models, like those of Priceline or eBay (the first online auction company to become profitable), leaps across the Net like wildfire—a fire fueled by analysts and journalists who are anxious to share the good news (or the threat it may bring to existing businesses). Even very young companies learn how to build internal online strategic research and development sites that can be accessed by all company staff, in real time. Successful Internet start-ups (and this includes Internet groups within large companies) filter, shape, and transmit the resulting huge information flow across their organizations almost hourly, so that it is accessible and useful to everyone in the company.

Once a company puts up a website and begins to offer a unique product or service online, another huge new data stream begins to flow. Suddenly, everyone in the company is reading and using online reports that spell out in great detail how the new product or service is doing: unique visitor counts, stickiness indexes (indications of how long visitors are staying on a particular page), product or content downloads, customer registration numbers, banner ad "click-throughs" (how many customers arrive at a site through banner advertising on some other site), visitor surveys, purchases, etc. Most of this core data is further sliced into time-of-day/day-of-week charts, visitor-by-domain breakdowns, and dozens of other slants on the performance of a company's online products and services.

Never before in the history of commerce have merchants been able to squeeze so much information out of a marketplace. There is so much information flowing through the modern Net-savvy company, in fact, that the sensation is often that of drowning in a sea of opportunity. It isn't getting access to information that's hard, it's making sense of it.

And making good and profitable use of all this data is not easy—especially if the network effect kicks in, and a company's online product or service begins getting some serious play on the Internet. As visitor hits, customer sign-ups, and product downloads start to mount, it's a huge task just to keep the server loads balanced and responsive, the credit card gateways up and running, and the customer support backlog under control. Information management at such times is a low priority—but the job of updating and maintaining the data flow gets done eventually, and as it does, whole new waves of information begin to flow through the organization's internal arteries.

To make this relentless data-flow function effectively, Internet companies hire design engineers, chief information officers, and system administrators to be responsible for the company's information plumbing. As a class, these hard-working information system mechanics are overly maligned and underappreciated; their yeoman's labors, in fact, have provided the underpinnings of all Internet and e-commerce prosperity. But it is also safe to say that this group, as a class, tends to be rather desensitized to issues of information propriety. They tend to be as interested in the nature and content of the data that flow through their pipes as your typical telephone lineman is in the conversations running through phone wires. For the techno-plumbers of the network, it's enough that the pipes stay connected and the system stays "up." The privacy of the PII in their pipes is usually an afterthought, at best. In fact, the norms and even the laws relating to personal privacy may be unknown to them.

What most Internet system architects and administrators don't yet realize is that because of the private nature of some of the data flowing through their internal systems, they are soon going to have to get serious about managing, protecting, and controlling PII, and treating it as a very special kind of data. Before they know it they will be complying with a whole new array of data policies, ranging from the data protection directive of the European Union to the online privacy policies of their own company website (or websites). They will have to learn, in many cases, how to provide customers with secure access to their own individual PII records. They will have to learn to destroy PII routinely, in accordance with certain policy terms and conditions. And they are going to have to maintain much higher standards of data protection with respect to third-party access to this data, whether these third parties are outsource vendors, strategic partners, or internal employees.

Net marketers are also going to have to understand and appreciate the dynamics of privacy protection and data civility much better than they have to date as well. In his groundbreaking book *Permission Marketing*, Seth Godin counsels New Economy marketing types that they'll soon need to learn to ask permission from their marketing targets before bombarding them with messages. Godin, now a vice president of direct marketing at Yahoo!, believes that traditional marketing concepts don't work in a network environment, in part because there is such a glut of information floating around that we have all gotten quite good at ignoring it. His idea is to ask people to volunteer their attention—their willingness to receive ads and e-mail messages—in exchange for tangible benefits. In essence, he is proposing an exchange of information in exchange for value, and always with informed consent. Such permission-based marketing, he contends, leads to strong customer relationships built on the most important word in the New Economy: trust.

Godin has hit the nail squarely on its head—not just in terms of marketing but indeed for all network business activities. In a networked economy, trust not only builds goodwill and brand loyalty, it actually increases efficiency in business overall. Among other things, it opens the portals of communications with customers wider than they would otherwise be; a customer gives more personal information about her wants and needs to a company she trusts than to one she doesn't—to cite just one example of how increased access to information can be profitably exploited in a networked world.

But the same accelerated flow of information through our world that gives rise to a Hotmail or Priceline.com, and which delivers numerous overall economic efficiencies, also raises public concerns and personal anxiety levels. Personal privacy is clearly under siege, on a variety of fronts. This siege is only beginning, as the technologies of information collection, storage, and retrieval become fully networked and interconnected. Privacy gaffes and security meltdowns will likely increase not only in number but in seriousness, as more and more of the overall economy and communications infrastructure moves online.

In such an environment, one thing we can say with relative certainty is that public distrust of Internet sites and services will generally increase as well, at least in the short term. When a service such as Hotmail is hacked in such a way that 50 million users suddenly find their most private and personal e-mail communications exposed to all comers, we are talking about high anxiety indeed. And, as we have argued, the essential vulnerabilities of the network infrastructure mean that such incidents will not only continue but proliferate.

It is in this context that trust—customers' reasonable expectation of "regular, honest, and cooperative behavior" by companies—becomes so important. The last two decades in business have focused on building the global information marketplace and maximizing the efficiencies and procedural advances that could be wrung from rapidly evolving information technology. The catchword of this era was *excellence*: doing things right. Today, the Internet is poised on the threshold of a new era where, with the information circuits in place and working well, the industrial-strength mining of information on the network will now proceed. In this environment, it is a constriction in the data flow—especially in the flow of data from customers who will increasingly expect fairness and honesty in all information transactions—that companies will fear most. The watchword of the next several decades, we therefore predict, will be *trust*: doing the right thing.

## Making a Difference

For information system workers, direct marketers, corporate executives, and just about everyone else in business, complying with the raising of the bar with respect to customer privacy and consumer trust is going to mean a ton of new work. It is going to require nearly as much rethinking as corporate reengineering efforts of the early 1990s, and the same kind of system redesign occasioned by the Y2K bug (if on a somewhat smaller scale). Broadly speaking, though some businesses understand the new business requirements and opportunities occasioned by the new public need for trust, many do not. For the notions of personal data privacy protection, online trust, full disclosure, and fair data exchange have only very recently begun to make their way into the server rooms and boardrooms of the New Economy.

Unfortunately, generic government laws are of little help in moving these kinds of notions forward. Compared to the quick development pace of potentially privacy-violating technologies, the pace at which statutes move from conception to enactment to enforcement remains positively glacial—which is not necessarily a bad thing, given the impact they sometimes have. But the Internet treats most constraints (laws included) as a form of damage anyway, and quickly routes around them. On the Internet, the action takes place at the level of real-time electronic data exchange, which, for the moment, is an arena that is well removed from the centers of political lawmaking.

So, with our governmental leaders on the sidelines, are there new rules that online businesses themselves should adopt as core elements of a personal data exchange? Well, as it happens, there are. They go under the heading of fair information practices, and as general principles of the kind of fair play necessary for the new information marketplace to survive and thrive, they are winning wide acceptance.

The Online Privacy Alliance (OPA) is a leader in this area in the United States. More than eighty companies and trade associations belong to this alliance, including America Online, AT&T, Bank of America, Bell Atlantic, Compaq, Hewlett-Packard, Microsoft, and Time Warner, plus the American Advertising Federation, the Direct Marketing Association, and, for good measure, a few recent Internet start-ups, such as Wine.com.

Working with their membership, the OPA has issued a list of privacy guidelines for business engaged in e-commerce and other forms of Internet activity. The guidelines are based on a set of fair information practices that are being endorsed internationally, most particularly in Europe. The OPA's guidelines fall into several key categories: notice and disclosure, choice/consent, data security, data quality and access, plus refusal to collect information from children under the age of thirteen without parental consent.

The basic principles the OPA endorses are:

- *Notice.* Businesses should inform you that they are collecting data about you.
- *Disclosure.* You should be informed why this data is being collected and how it will be used, and especially whether it will be shared with other parties.
- *Consent.* No data should be collected from you and used without your permission.
- *Security/integrity.* Online companies should take reasonable steps to ensure that the data they are using on your behalf is accurate and is protected from unauthorized access and tampering.
- *Access.* Upon verifiable request, you should be able to access the information a company maintains about you.
- *Oversight and redress.* There should be a way for you to redress and seek remedies if you feel that a company has violated its posted privacy policy.

These OPA principles are a good start—although the commitments and actual practices of many of the businesses in the OPA, not to mention those outside it, fall far short of fully abiding by all of these principles today.

# Tips and Tricks for Chapter 6

**Watch out for Windows 98's Registration Wizard.** In 1999, it was reported that not only is it possible for any website to read information that uniquely identifies you and your PC, but that information can be modified and/or sent to Microsoft without your consent. The culprit was the Registration Wizard, or RegWiz for short. Windows 98 uses RegWiz to process your product registration form and submit it to a Microsoft server over the Internet. Two identification numbers are generated based on your PC configuration and the data you enter during registration. The first number, called the hardware identification number (HWID), can in most cases uniquely identify the computer. A second number, called the Microsoft ID (MSID), uniquely identifies you and is placed in a browser cookie for access to services on Microsoft's website.

Although Microsoft has removed this feature, it may still be present on machines that were sold before the new policy was implemented. It is possible to disable RegWiz and remove the information manually by using the Windows 98 registry editor. To do so, click Start, then Run, and then type in the following command: regsvr32.exe -u c:\windows\system\regwizc.dll.

**Some e-commerce "shopping carts" aren't secure. BugNet can help.** Often, the problem isn't malfeasance but inexperience. Some electronic "storefronts" install shopping carts without the proper safeguards. In one recent month, the software-problem report site BugNet logged more than hundred sites with improperly installed shopping carts that could expose customer information such as names, addresses, and credit card info. To check on whether a site you're thinking of buying products or services from has had such problems recently, visit and do a search on the free BugNet site: http://www.bugnet.com/.

**Delete mail as you read it.** Deleting messages after you've read or sent them at least makes them harder to access. Be sure to check the preferences in your e-mail program and choose any option that allows you to delete mail from a central server. (For example, the Eudora mail program's Special menu allows you to change the settings for checking mail; make sure you select "Delete from server when emptied from Eudora trash.")

**Surf anonymously with anonymizers.** These programs work by acting as an intermediary between you and the sites you visit, hiding your identity from invasive tracking measures. You access their "proxy server" site and then type in a Web page URL for the site you ultimately want to visit. Essentially, you're now coming to your desired site through the anonymizer's gateway. Because you are, your targeted site's servers won't be able to identify who you are. Most anonymizers will let you turn off these safeguards for sites that you trust. There's a list of anonymizer programs at http://www.privacyexchange.org/tsi/anonlog.htm.

**Use anonymous remailers.** Clicking a link embedded in an e-mail message also passes along information about the browser and e-mail program you use, your remote address, and your Internet service provider. Anonymous remailers help you circumvent these digital (and at times, human) prying eyes. These systems either give you an anonymous address, to which other people can send you mail, which is then forwarded to your real address (this is something referred to as a pseudonymous server), or they post or mail your message without any trace of your name or address. There's a good list of anonymous remailers at http://www.stack.nl/~galactus/remailers/index-anon.html.

**Jumble, then encrypt your password.** A seemingly nonsense string of letters and numbers is more effective than familiar terms, such as the first name of your favorite uncle or the birth date of your spouse. For maximum effect, mix and match them as in this example: fgs453kb5. To ensure that you don't forget your passwords, store them in a program such as Password Keeper, Password Safe, or Password Manager or your real-world wallet (avoid desk drawers—the first place a snoop would look). The password storage programs take your passwords, encode them with the near-unbreakable Data Encryption Standard (DES) cyphers, and then prompt you with hints so that you can remember your password.

**Does your state have a "no-call" law? Use it!** Several states, including Florida, Georgia, and Oregon, have laws requiring telemarketers to be fined if they call people who have requested that a "no-call" asterisk or other designation be placed next to their names in the phone book. Your phone company will charge you a $5–$10 fee for this listing—but $10 can be a worthwhile trade-off for a year's freedom from phone solicitors. You can bet that telemarketers hate this law, but most will comply rather than pay hundreds or even thousands of dollars in fines.

Call your local phone company's customer service line and ask if there's such a statute in your state. If there is, sign up for no-call status and count the days until the next directory comes out with a big, scary, privacy-enhancing icon next to your name. Note: some of these "do not call" laws make an exception for election-related calls, pitches from bona fide charitable organizations, and legitimate, registered pollsters and market researchers.

**Have a private e-mail address at work.** It's easy for spammers to fill your e-mail up at work. All they need to do is go to your company website, figure out what format your company uses for e-mail addresses (such as John_Doe@anycompany.com) and then send you e-mail you don't want. If you reserve a private e-mail address for your really important electronic correspondence, you'll be able to separate the e-mail you need to read and respond to right away from the junk you can toss.

**Don't fall for "come-on" message subject headers in e-mail.** Time was when spammers only used obvious come-ons such as "make money now" or "free nude pics." Now they've become more sophisticated and write messages with headers that sound like business or personal correspondence. Two examples would be "did we go to college together?" or "please confirm meeting next Thursday." Don't be fooled. These are come-ons, usually for quick schemes or porn sites. If you open these notes or reply to them, spammers will tag you as an easy mark and send even more of this junk to your mailbox. If e-mail headers sound fishy, throw the fish overboard. Delete without opening them.

**Hide your PII and camouflage your cookies.** Lumeria is a new software product that helps you hide individually identifiable data and then allows you to charge companies to see it. This company believes that if information about you is valuable to a business, then businesses should pay for it. Lumeria (http://www.lumeria.com) also allows you to obfuscate your Web surfing tracks by providing inaccurate "cookie" information to websites.

# 7
# Who Can You Trust?

*Why do people always expect authors to answer questions?*
*I am an author because I want to ask questions. If I had an-*
*swers, I'd be a politician.*

*—Eugene Ionesco*

The question we, as authors of this book, are most commonly asked
is: How can I know who to trust on the Net? This question usually
breaks down into three related questions:

- Who can be trusted to protect personal privacy?
- Who can be trusted to respect children's special needs online?
- Who can be trusted to deliver goods and services over the Internet responsibly?

These are not academic questions but practical, everyday
dilemmas faced by millions of people. Take the group of parents

who filled a high school gymnasium to hear one of us lead a discussion about the Internet. Yes, some were interested in the next new thing in network technology. Even more were interested in Internet business models—and hot stock tips. But the group's strongest interest by far was in the social issues raised by the Internet: getting answers about trust, privacy, security, and public safety.

It was easy to appreciate the parents' dilemma. They grew up in an era when "wired" certainly did not mean Internet access. In their youth and adolescence, they never faced issues related to on-line flirting, porn sites accessible from inside the home, or the ready availability of bomb-making recipes. For that matter, they never even faced the more mundane question of just how much information on the Net can be downloaded and used in school assignments before it becomes cheating.

Today's adolescents, on the other hand, take to the Net like birds to the air. Their mothers and fathers stand on the opposite side of a great cultural and ethical abyss. For teens, the Net is cool, important and exciting; for many parents, the Internet is something alien, scary, unsettling. They don't know who to trust, how to trust, or how to teach their children to use the Net prudently.

As authors addressing tough questions about the trustworthiness of websites on the Net, we certainly can empathize with the frustration that Ionesco felt when having to come up with answers. Data collection activities of Internet companies often take place furtively, and PII trading generally occurs behind locked doors, out of the public view. Site security, certainly a key factor in trustworthiness, is almost impossible to ascertain from the outside (short of a hack attack). A company's general reputation and the relative quality and reliability of its online product and service offerings can clearly increase or decrease public trust in that company's website, but in addition to being largely outside the scope of this book, judgments about a company's products, brand, and general image do not necessarily correlate with its actual trustworthiness online.

Trust, in the Internet sense, requires a whole new perspective and a new set of tools and measurements. For public networks to grow and thrive without invading our privacy, it's essential that new methodologies for answering the "who can I trust?" question become part of the Net's infrastructure. We need a framework not just for protecting privacy but for generally measuring trust—tools and subsystems within the Net that can help individual users make practical decisions about the trustworthiness of specific websites.

For better or worse, trust-related decisions are a part of nearly every Internet session—but a network-effect-like standard for making trust-based decisions on the Net has yet to emerge. Admittedly, building such a system—whose purpose would be to help users make real-time decisions about the data collection practices and general trustworthiness of individual websites—would be no trivial task. Copious amounts of data about website operations, policies, and practices would have to be collected, organized, and analyzed; overall company policies and practices would have to be monitored, even those behind its security firewall; and a very sophisticated back-end operational infrastructure would be required to serve up pertinent information upon demand. Such a "trust solution," to use the industry jargon, would also have to support a simple, user-friendly desktop interface (a software application or browser plug-in), so that ordinary users could easily and simply take advantage of it.

All in all, a big order—but the good news is that most of the technology needed to construct such a system already exists. Consider the big personal credit rating companies, such as Experian and Equifax. They maintain huge databases with information about the trustworthiness of millions of individual people, at least insofar as their reliability in paying their bills is concerned. Many of the people whose daily bill-paying activities are tracked in these huge data banks frequently move, change jobs, get married, and otherwise become moving targets. A good number have the same names, and others change their names for various reasons. Maintaining records of the trustworthiness of the most important fifty thousand websites would seem easy by comparison.

Consequently, we would like to submit a modest proposal: the very tools of information collection and data management that have put us all in the digital crosshairs of the data snatchers should now be redeployed to put the collectors of information in our crosshairs as well. We who are being tracked must fight fire with fire, and start using the Net to learn as much about the data snatchers as they know about us.

## Re-aiming the Data Telescope

The first step in tracking the trackers is to look for their traps. In the case of surreptitious data snatchers, we'd want to look for technologies and websites that capture information about us without our knowing it. Unfortunately, unless you are a technologist, monitoring a Web session or some other digital information exchange can be difficult, if not impossible. Everyone, however, can read a privacy policy—and searching for such policies may be a better way to track the trackers than you might think.

Covert data-gatherers dislike the trend of posting privacy notices on websites because posting such policies actually increases legal liability. A company that secretly gathers personal data in Web sessions or sells personal data without disclosing this practice is much less at risk, legally speaking, than those who post policies but don't follow them. The absence of a privacy policy thus says a great deal about a company's practices, and in our experience, sites operating with responsible, full-disclosure privacy statements and opt-in data policies tend to be more trustworthy overall. Privacy policies are currently the best available litmus test of a website's overall ethics. If a company secretly tracks your Web journeys, secretly sucks up data from your browser or hard drive, buys and sells information about you without your knowledge or consent, refuses to tell you what data it has collected about you—can this company be open and honest in other matters? We think not.

On the other hand, a company that is willing to keep all of its data collection and PII usage open and aboveboard is more likely to deal honestly and openly in other areas as well. Privacy policies, in fact, are just a first milestone on the road to full operational transparency and rules of "full and open disclosure" in company-to-customer relations. Soon we can expect to see posted on websites holistic codes of conduct that address not just privacy issues, but honest advertising, fair dealing, product reliability, customer service and support, warranties, dispute resolution, criminal-activity prohibitions, and other key benchmarks of trust in a company's relationship with its customers. These policies are already popping up in the domains of Internet site aggregators such as Onsite, Microsoft BusinessLink, GeoCities, and eBay. We can expect similar "full disclosure" of internal ethical standards by individual companies soon as well—not necessarily because of an abundance of goodwill on the part of Web operators, but because of the increasing transparency of every activity that takes place on the network.

The Internet inexorably drives companies toward greater transparency for the same fundamental reason that it tends to abrade personal privacy: it greatly facilitates the free flow of information. In the new Internet economy, companies that try to play cards close to the vest, and especially those who engage in less-than-trustworthy activities while doing so, will find they are trying to sail against the tide. Better, more responsible organizations will use the Net to raise the shades on their windows, allowing customers to see more and more of internal operations, for they realize that trying to hide questionable business practices in a highly networked, hundredth-window environment is a dubious plan at best. Increasingly, they will learn to capture customers' loyalty by installing solid, honest internal practices and then bringing them to light. Companies that fail to do so will suffer by comparison.

Regardless of individual company intentions, as the data-scopes aimed at individuals begin to turn and focus on business practices, internal operations will be exposed as never before, like it or not. As a result, companies of all kinds will have even more incentive to engage in activities that promote customer trust and eschew those that do not. Word about a particular company's covert practices or cynical policies will increasingly find its way onto the Net, and traditional advertising and brand development strategies will be hard pressed to overcome the resulting negative fallout.

One way such word might circulate is through an online service that would tag individual companies on the Net with a unique "trust rating"—a ranking of how the company's overall trust policies and practices stack up against a set of industry "best practices." Though this kind of qualitative ranking system today is still in the design stage, a number of new Internet start-ups are making it their business to help consumers and other users of the Internet learn as much about individual company trustworthiness as possible. Companies with a low trust rating will find themselves with a major new incentive to shape up when such programs come online and begin to reverse the normal data flow.

On the Internet, demand for information creates supply. The more we demand information about business (and government) policies and practices, the more such information we'll get. Supporting companies with strong, clear privacy policies not only helps protect your privacy but also encourages the general trend toward full disclosure of all practices that have a bearing on a company's trustworthiness.

Yet even companies with the best intentions often make mistakes. And privacy standards can be among the first to break down when business pressures go up. There are several key reasons why even responsible companies have lapses in privacy protection— none of them, unfortunately, mutually exclusive:

- *It's not yet part of the corporate culture.* Some companies are so new, or are growing so fast, that they haven't yet had enough time to implement a privacy policy, let alone build systems that protect and fence in PII.
- *The company may be overly decentralized.* This often happens when acquisitions suddenly become subsidiaries of existing companies, or when constant reorganization results in isolation of individual product and service teams. In such cultures, managing even conventional policies, from accounting systems to vacation guidelines, is difficult enough. New policies, such as those relating to online PII management, take even longer to be implemented.
- *Marketing aggressiveness goes overboard.* Every successful company prides itself on aggressive marketing, in some form. Yet in the face of such imperatives as performance benchmarks, "must-meet" sales quotas, and other yardsticks, a company can become too aggressive and decide to use the data it has about you to sell you services you don't want, acquire PII without your consent, or even sell it to third parties.
- *There's a lack of drill-down.* We've seen many cases where a company chairman or CEO delivers a keynote speech heavy on privacy imperatives. In some companies, unfortunately, that keynote never gets transformed into privacy directives that move down the chain of command to that harried telemarketer or customer service rep working a weekend shift in a phone room 1,200 miles away from the

home office. Out of sight, out of mind. Senior managers must do a better job at driving down privacy compliance through the organization. The real key is company-wide training about privacy, at a level of seriousness now given to such issues as anti-trust training and compliance with sexual harassment statutes.

- *Too much outsourcing, not enough oversight.* For perfectly justifiable reasons, a company may retain a third-party service to handle customer acquisition (i.e., telemarketing), data processing, or even customer complaints. In many cases, this is done without forethought to the privacy implications inherent when data is shared with other organizations. Too often, there's a lack of consideration of privacy issues during the planning stage and a lack of oversight once the outsourcing contract is granted.

- *Privacy bug prevention hasn't been built in.* Privacy protection should be a feature that is built into products and systems, not just something fixed with a software patch after a *New York Times* reporter calls to ask about an incident. Too often, however, privacy safeguards are a low priority for the developer or technical architect who is under severe pressure to produce an easy-to-use alpha version yesterday and get *something* out to market by next month. When product specifications get drafted and delivered to the lab for development, privacy safeguards should be high on the priority list.

Despite the value of posted privacy policies and pronouncements in support of fair information practices, privacy protection is more than just sincere words on a website, in a privacy statement, or in a CEO's keynote at a trade show. It requires an injection of commitment that flows down throughout an entire organization and out to every other business partner or vendor.

## *Privacy Policies, Privacy Assurance*

In a world where the reasons for breakdowns in privacy protection are many, and where internal compliance with even good policies is often weak, how do you make your way around the Internet without having your privacy violated?

To become fully sensitized to the issues surrounding Internet privacy, it is important to understand the context in which many Internet transactions take place—even down to the most innocuous website visit, which is essentially a live data exchange between a foreign web server and your PC. As you point your browser at different sites around the Net, here are a few things to remember.

**You are wanted.** There is a bounty for your personal data profile. Every day, companies pay for information about you so they can market to you more effectively. Companies are valued in part according to whether or not they can count you as their customer and how much information they have collected about you. Governments want to know about you in order to tax you, license you, protect you, and generally enforce their laws and regulations. Potential employers want to know your life history, potential lenders your entire financial background. Competitors may want to know your strategies or your travel records. Con artists and criminals want your information to take advantage of your good name and credit rating and to separate you from your electronically held assets. Your PII is the gold of the information economy, and the forty-niners of data mining are out in force, ready to stake their claims.

**Data collection is occurring everywhere, almost all the time.** The combined efforts and successes of Microsoft, Intel, Oracle, and other high-tech vendors have reduced the cost of compiling data about you to a small fraction of the value that is derived from collecting it. Sensing, recording, and analyzing daily human activity has become so inexpensive, and ubiquitous, that unless you choose to live the life of an unplugged hermit, much of your daily activity is

157

now being recorded in corporate and government databases, whether you know it or not. As we have stressed earlier, however, it is in the profiling of you that most value creation occurs for the data collectors, and the more information there is in your profile, the more valuable it will be. And the more it will be used and circulated. Conversely, the less information in your profile, the less valuable it is, and the less it will be circulated and used. It is never too late, therefore, to start controlling your own PII and damming up at least some of the data flow about you.

**Public safeguards are few.** At this point in Internet development, the speed of technical change has eclipsed the ability of society to evolve social norms. Legal enforcement systems are not yet in place with respect to notice, permission, usage, accountability, and redress in matters of data collection—and, given the distributed, global nature of the Internet, may never be, in some cases. During this early developmental phase of the Internet especially, you must make up your own norms of behavior and your own rules about who you will trust. Over time, companies will develop more sophisticated, more transparent corporate policies, and legislatures and courts will codify at least some social norms into law. Until then, you are left to your own devices to evaluate the situation and protect yourself as best you can.

## Trust: You Know It When You See It

Like critiquing art or music, evaluating a company's privacy practice is not an exact science. It's subject to a considerable amount of personal judgment and is definitely guided by subjective standards and preferences. What strikes some as merely a creative marketing program will be frowned upon by others as a shocking invasion of privacy. Because we all look at the world through the sum of our own experiences and knowledge, we're bound to have differences of opinion on what is acceptable when passing information back and forth online.

Further complicating the issue, we may feel more willing to share information on certain sites than others. Whereas we may feel that it is way too personal for a general website to ask where we like to travel, at a site that helps manage travel we might feel quite comfortable entering the five cities we plan to visit on our next vacation. Yet we might not want that online travel site to sell our name to timeshare companies with business operations in the cities where we like to relax and have fun.

Because of nosey co-workers, we also may be more privacy-sensitive when logging onto a site from work than from home. Some people are fanatical about guarding the details of their personal health history, while not thinking twice about posting their annual income all over the Web. And vice versa. Yet despite all these differences, we can all likely find common ground on one thing: in terms of privacy policy, some sites (to put it mildly) have plenty of room for improvement.

We've compiled a number of examples of these kinds of sites — along with their opposites — and produced our own highly subjective, fully idiosyncratic list of our Ten Best privacy sites, along with a few other sites that are either "recovering" from privacy gaffes, or could use significant improvement.

Privacy is subjective, but how much notice a site provides, and how much control it extends to individual site users, is not. We have tried to use specific metrics of comparison in selecting these sites, but so little verifiable data is publicly available today that we have had to make educated guesses about some things. Here are some of the specific yardsticks we used.

## Clarity

Does the site tell you in clear and unambiguous language what information it is collecting from you and how it will be used? Does the company intend to sell customer or user lists to third parties? Although this kind of clarity is not required by law, most companies feel they owe you this amount of candor. The worst privacy offenders are anything but clear about their privacy practices and usually fail to notify you when they are collecting, using, and reselling data. At the very least, they are being evasive. At their worst, they are literally stealing from you.

## User Control

Does the site allow you to "opt in" for data collection—or does such collection proceed automatically? (Opting-in means that the default process is that no data is collected; actual permission from the "name" is required before any PII is collected and used.) Opt-in systems offer the highest level of privacy protection, because a conscious, informed decision is required by a consumer before data collection begins. Next best is an opt-out feature which clearly and prominently gives a consumer a clear choice of whether or not to have data collected, or perhaps to have it distributed to third parties once collected. The difference between opt-in and opt-out systems is that with the former, the default is always "no data collected;" while in the latter, the default is always "data collected," and action by the consumer is required to see that no data is exchanged.)

The degree of control a site affords you is a key differentiator in building a trusted relationship. Many sites have realized that if they inform you about what data they would like to collect about you and how they would use it, you may be inclined to provide deeper, more meaningful, and more accurate information.

The best sites allow you to build a relationship over time and, in return for knowing about you, build your trust while providing value, personalization, customization, and good service.

## Does the Site Protect Sensitive Information?

To prevent information from being used for detrimental purposes by third parties, sites that collect highly sensitive information—like medical or financial data—and sites that appeal to children have a responsibility to operate with an especially high degree of care and security. If you go to an online bookstore and purchase a volume about new treatments for a chronic disease, that information is private. If you go to an online chat room devoted to a serious health problem, your Internet address should not be "accidentally" posted. If your children visit a site and chat about how cool Pokémon is, they shouldn't be bombarded with related spam a month later.

## Your Responsibility: Be Knowledgeable and Vigilant

Aggressive and innovative companies alike are testing the boundaries of what is acceptable privacy behavior. The best learn from their mistakes, while the transgressors deflect objections with empty rhetoric, become defensively hostile, or turn a deaf ear.

Still there's no need to be overly cynical or to cower in front of your PC, refusing to buy anything or express any of your opinions online. It's your money and your mind, and you have a right to use both. Yet in order to protect your privacy, you must be a vigilant and knowledgeable customer—one with a good static detector that can warn you when an online privacy hazard appears. You also must be vocal when you feel your privacy rights aren't being protected.

• • •

Now that we have clarified the criteria, here is our list of the good guys.

## The Ten Best Privacy Sites

Each of these sites has a clearly stated, easy-to-read privacy policy that is accessible on their home page. Each is signed up with an online privacy assurance organization, such as the Better Business Bureau Online or TRUSTe, that monitors privacy practices to assure users that business practices stay in line with stated privacy policies. All sites, without exception, give the consumer at least the right to opt out of any data collection practices, and many take the time to explain the difference between PII and aggregate information and how these data are being used.

**Excite.** In an effort to provide customizable information that can be of service to its visitors, Excite asks you to provide your name and e-mail or postal address. Yet "the choice of how much of your personally identifiable information that you choose to disclose to Excite is left completely up to you," Excite notes. "The only way we know something about you personally is if you register for a personalized service or enter one of our sweepstakes." (More info: http://www.excite.com/privacy_policy/.) Note: our selection of Excite.com does not extend to Excite@Home, the cable access site for high-speed Internet access.

**IBM.** The company occasionally requests personal information for commercial purposes, such as processing orders for products you may buy online. Its privacy policy states, however, that if you do not wish to provide this data, your wishes will be respected. IBM says it is "also supporting the development of some technologies that will let you manage and control the release of your personal information wherever you go on the Internet." Furthermore, IBM recently announced a policy that it would advertise only on other internet sites with a proper privacy policy. (More info: http://www.ibm.com/privacy/.)

**Lands' End.** In the privacy area of its website, the popular catalog retailer explains why it's necessary for them to track your movement around a site in a given session (in order to efficiently add items to your shopping basket) and the steps it takes to safeguard your identity. "The way Lands' End deals with this is with a state ID," they note. "Your state ID is the long number you can see at the end of all the URLs on the Lands' End website. The state ID contains absolutely no information about you. It is completely unique to each session and changes each time a new session is created. The sole purpose is to enable us to know that the person who added the mesh shirt to their basket is the same person as the one who wants the denim dress." (More info: http://www.landsend.com/.)

**REI (Recreational Equipment Inc.).** The outdoor gear retailer has a "Mailing Options" checklist on its website. This page (http://www.rei.com/YOUR_COOP/MEMBER_HELP/mailops.ht ml) has five boxes where you can specify your preferences. Two of these choices are specifically privacy-related. They are "please do not provide my name to other mail-order services," and "please do not send me any catalogs or mailers, other than my dividend voucher packet" (a yearly rebate package of money or discounts, mailed to members each February). (More info: http://www.rei .com/reihtml/privacy.html.)

**Playboy.com.** While the content on this site is considered tame by some, there are others who object to it or deem the articles and pictures inappropriate for minors. That's a key reason that Playboy.com has taken pains to offer access-blocking capability. Details are on the Block-Out subscription page of its website (http:// www.playboy.com/ blockme/blockmeaddr.html). Playboy.com also offers updates to parents when site redesign has the potential of defeating previously effective parental filtering software. (More info: http://www.playboy .com/copyright.html#privacy.)

**Yahoo!** The ever-expanding suite of services this website offers has the potential for privacy violation. That's why Yahoo! has taken proactive steps to safeguard the security of this data. Yahoo! Online Banking Access, for example, will, the company notes, "work with your financial institution to present your account balances and history to you on your customized Yahoo! pages. In order to present your financial information to you, Yahoo! receives that information from your financial institution in an encrypted format and presents it to you over a secure-server." A series of health-related self-assessment tools Yahoo! also provides requests potentially sensitive personal data, but Yahoo! will password-protect and encrypt this data, storing it separately from your registration information. Yahoo! Health even has its own data privacy and security policy page at http://health.yahoo.com/health/dataprivacy.html. (More info: http//docs.yahoo.com/info/privacy/.)

AltaVista. This search-engine-turned-Web-portal has an aggressive policy toward its business partners who may have violated the online privacy of AltaVista users. AltaVista provides clear direction to users who may sense such a breach of trust: "If you feel that a site using the AltaVista brand and/or logo does not follow an acceptable privacy policy, please send us an e-mail at search-support @altavista.com. We will forward complaints to the appropriate third parties and may, in particular circumstances, decide to advocate on your behalf to attempt to cause the third parties to change their privacy policies." (More info: http://www.altavista.com/av/content/privacy.htm.)

GO Network. Now owned by Disney, the GO Network has ESPN.com as well as the Disney family of websites under its corporate umbrella. Since the corporate parent is an entity that has held a special place in the hearts of children ever since the earliest days of Mickey Mouse, it's not surprising that GO has a particularly emphatic set of guidelines intended to protect the online privacy of kids under thirteen. "Unless otherwise disclosed during collection," GO Network says on its website, it "does not provide any personally identifying information, regardless of its source, to any third party for any purpose whatsoever from our guests under 13 years of age.

All registrants receive an e-mail confirming their Registration. In addition, when a guest under 13 registers, he/she is required to provide the e-mail address of his/her parent or guardian and that parent or guardian receives an e-mail alerting them to that Registration. The parent or guardian must validate the account, as described in the e-mail, in order for the potential member to use most GO Network interactive services. No information collected from guests under 13 years of age is used for any marketing or promotional purposes whatsoever, either inside or outside GO Network except as explicitly stated during registration for contests or promotions (and in that case, the information collected is used only for the specific contest or promotion)."

While the sports news and athletically related e-commerce site ESPN.com—also a part of GO Network—follows all the privacy policies of the other GO sites, it has some extra cautions. ESPN.com has numerous message boards, and the e-mail address of participating fans may be posted. Spirited and sometimes contentious debate among fans of various teams is a frequent characteristic of these areas. Unfortunately, a few fans can become vitriolic. That's why the site cautions you against giving out too much personal information in such posts. (More info on Go Network:http://info.go.com/doc/policy/privacy.html. More info on ESPN .com: http://espn.go.com/sitetools/s/privacy.html.)

**The Motley Fool.** Financial advice sites with lots of forums have some congenital privacy risks, but The Fool is anything but that when it comes to protecting your privacy. It will release "aggregate" user data—such as the number of subscribers in a high-income zip code a potential advertiser would like to reach—but won't reveal info about specific users. Instead, The Motley Fool explains, "it will take the ad and display it to users who've told us they meet those criteria. In this process, the advertiser never has access to individual account information." It also provides a special page where you can sign up to

block unsolicited e-mail (http://www.fool.com/community/never
mail.htm). (More info: http://www.fool.com/community/register/
privacystatement.htm.)

**VeriSign.** The company provides public keys and digital certificates to protect the confidentiality of your online transactions. It
does so by collecting certain customer details in its digital ID as-
signment process, but offers you the option of not including or removing this information. The company's site stipulates that for
certain types of digital ID's, "VeriSign may compare some of the information in the certificate application to information contained
on a third party database. VeriSign does this in order to authenticate
the applicant's identity and other attributes. All such third parties
have executed confidentiality agreements with VeriSign that pro-
hibit the further sharing or use of such information." (More info:
http://www.verisign.com/truste/.) VeriSign also provides a Frequently Asked Questions list where their privacy policy is thoroughly described: http://www.verisign.com/repository/Privacy FAQ/
index.html.

## A Few Sites That Need Improvement

Most of the sites listed below are mainstream companies. Some
have data-gathering practices that may serve to neutralize their
stated privacy policies. Many allow you to "opt-out" of their data-
gathering or data-sharing practices. Others have no privacy policy at
all. Each provides an example of a particular shortcoming with respect to high privacy protection standards. Remember, too, that
these shortcomings exist at the date of this writing, and may be corrected by the time you read this. You should check the site's current
policy (if it has one), and make your own decision.

**Penthouse.** No posted policy. Expresses no interest in the personal privacy of visitors to Penthouse.com.

**Amazon.com.** Under the banner of providing highly customized service, Amazon collects more personal preferences and personal information than nearly any other merchant on the Web. The company has bragged about the extent and value of its customer database of (full PII) on Wall Street, and published lists detailing what books employees at certain companies are reading. Although the information was aggregated, many people have objected to the disclosure of their preferences even in that way. Amazon, the leader in mass market e-commerce, should do better.

**US Bank.** One of the largest banks in the midwestern and western United States, US Bank collects your personal information to make products and services to better serve you. It's privacy policy does not, at this writing, explain to whom this information is shown. This is the same bank that recently paid a $3-million-dollar fine to the government for providing private financial information about its customers to third parties without customer authorization. (This information came from customary banking records, not from information collected over the Internet.)

**Autobytel.** In the spirit of true capitalism, Autobytel states in its policy that its intent is to balance its legitimate business interests in collecting and using personal information with the consumer's expectation of privacy. It will notify you of what is being collected and its intended use after it has been collected. In privacy policy, notification is not enough; user consent is what's required.

**DMVs of most state governments.** Much like US Bank, the Department of Motor Vehicles in numerous states collects personal information to be made available to certain organizations. While these agencies are all certainly reputable, their practice of marketing the names and addresses of huge numbers of private citizens without their permission certainly falls for short of contemporary Internet privacy standards.

**J. Crew.** J. Crew may be known for its comfortable clothing, but it should try a new privacy policy on for size. The privacy policy is buried three clicks away from the home page and openly admits to making its customer lists available for "one time use by carefully screened firms." Privacy policies that are not easily accessible by the consumer are barely better than no privacy policy at all.

## "Recovering" Sites

Many companies that have had privacy-related problems have acknowledged and tried to fix them. Some are farther along than others. Here's a look at some of them:

**eBay** has been the subject of several complaints concerning scam auctions on the website. Items were offered that allegedly didn't exist, or were so outlandish (such as human body parts, available for transplant) that their existence was at least questionable. To erase these blemishes from its record, eBay has been working hard with the National Fraud Information Center to resolve what its critics have termed "auction-related deceptions."

The bigger problem from a privacy perspective is that eBay's entire information system security has also been suspect—owing to the fact that its website has experienced a number of public failures.

In October 1999 eBay released a new privacy policy on its website. The revised policy addressed important issues such as the way eBay shares information with business sponsors, service providers, subsidiaries, and joint venture partners. It also clarified some privacy policy clauses which it admitted were "hard to understand." The new policy was a marked improvement.

The Federal Trade Commission charged the 2-million-member online community **GeoCities** with gathering personal information that could be used by third-party marketers to target children. The government agency said that GeoCities' all-ages registration-process request for e-mail and postal addresses, member interest areas, income, education, gender, marital status, and occupation was made available to third parties. The complaint also charged that GeoCities specifically gathered information from children during sign-up procedures for various contests, as well as its Official Geo-Cities GeoKidz Clubs.

GeoCities' settlement with the FTC involved the posting of a privacy notice describing the nature of the information it collects, the identities of those to whom GeoCities sends the information, and a promise to get parental approval before collecting PII from children twelve and under.

GeoCities now has a privacy policy posted on its website, but privacy advocates claim its first attempts at compliance with the FTC were ambiguous. In particular, the statement that "optional registration information won't be shared" has been deemed ambiguous by some.

Ever since its acquisition by Yahoo! in early 1999, however, GeoCities seems to have reformed. Its website now bears the privacy statement of its corporate parent, which says in part: "Yahoo! does not share personal information about users under the age of 13 with third parties and we do not sell or rent personal information about any of our users, regardless of age. In addition, Yahoo! will not send any direct email offers to users who indicate they are under the age of 13."

**Microsoft**'s technology has been subject to several noteworthy breaches. These have not been sins of policy, but of lack of attention to privacy concerns during product and system design and upgrades. To its credit, the software giant fixed the problems speedily. The question remains: could privacy-centric, preventive vigilance have stopped these problems from ever arising in the first place?

One security hole involved the generation of a hardware identification number (HWID) in Windows 98 registration procedures, and their potential for misuse. The problem started with the registration procedure's option for customers to provide computer system information to Microsoft. This information was intended for use by Microsoft's product support unit in order to assist the customer with support issues. Yet if the computer came equipped with an Ethernet network card, an HWID was spawned.

When the customer clicked on the "register" button, Windows then transferred the contact information and HWID to a secure server at Microsoft. Yet a bug existed that transferred the HWID to Microsoft's server, even if the consumer opted out of such transfer.

An investigation was launched by TRUSTe. "This breach of privacy has since been corrected and did not at any time involve the Microsoft.com Web site. Microsoft has acknowledged this breach publicly," the privacy advocacy organization reported.

Security glitches in Microsoft's free Hotmail service (mentioned earlier) were potentially much more egregious.

The significance of these security holes is that private Hotmail accounts became available to anyone with a Web browser: any Web page that contained a short, simple code—visible on most browsers as a type-in form—was able to connect to a Hotmail server simply by typing in a user name without requiring a password.

To the company's credit, it acted quickly to fix these problems. One hopes that the firmest proactive measures will be taken to prevent such vulnerabilities from happening again.

In May 1999, computer-chip giant **Intel** was discovered to have included an identifying processor serial number in each Pentium III-equipped computer. This was done for the purpose of enhancing e-commerce and to help system administrators track individual computer performance in large networks.

The privacy problem was that the machine's unique serial number could be associated with individual registration information. Although Intel reported that this function could be disabled, a writer for a German computer magazine hacked into the serial number's access controls. Consumer groups initiated a Federal Trade Commission investigation.

To its credit, Intel cooperated fully, even noting that the flaw may also have been present in computers running the previous-generation Pentium II chip. Intel has also updated its online privacy policy, which now provides full notice on how personal information is handled.

**United Airlines'** track record on privacy has occasionally been subject to the "mixed-message" phenomenon. In 1999, some privacy champions said that certain "terms and conditions" terminology on its website at least theoretically could result in highly personal information becoming exposed.

While the website avowed that users' personal info would be protected, a "terms and conditions" statement, required to be clicked before online ticket orders were processed, asked customers to agree that by using the service they gave up any expectation of privacy with regard to their personal data. It further said that by clicking, customers grant "express and unambiguous approval" for the carrier to use this personal information "for purposes of solicitations, promotions, and marketing programs."

Privacy watchdogs called this policy "incredibly confusing." As this book goes to print, United Airlines is saying that it is committed to customer privacy and will review the language in both its privacy and "terms and conditions" declarations.

The world's leading online service, **America Online,** has always been known for its energetically enthusiastic marketing persona. Its meteoric rise has not come without periodic privacy-related growing pains, however. In July 1997, AOL announced it might sell subscriber lists to third-party marketers. A firestorm ensued, and AOL quickly disavowed the proposed initiative.

A far more personal privacy problem was encountered by AOL that year as well. Eighteen-year U.S. Navy veteran Timothy McVeigh (no relation to the man convicted in the bombing of the

Murrah Federal Building in Oklahoma City) used an AOL pseudo-nym and sent an e-mail indicating he was gay. It was subsequently revealed that an AOL customer service employee disclosed McVeigh's identity to Navy officials without due process.

Citing policy, the Navy sought to discharge McVeigh without benefits. He sued AOL for breach of privacy. The service settled for an undisclosed amount (estimated to be $50 million) and gave five thousand of its employees "scenario training" in privacy protection. Its privacy policies were rewritten and strengthened—not only on its subscription-based flagship service but on CompuServe, its AOL.com and CompuServe.com websites, and services such as its event guide Digital City and instant-messaging operation ICQ. The company now also requires its AOL Certified Merchants to post privacy policies that adhere to strict standards.

The software utility company **Symantec** has for a long time collected all sorts of personally identifiable information on customers for such purposes as customer service and beta software and electronic software purchases. Yet until the summer of 1999, when Symantec finally posted a privacy policy, they never told customers what if anything, they did with that information. They may be a little late to the table, but lately the maker of Norton Utilities and many other programs seems to be becoming a bit more forthright regarding customer privacy.

## Kids' Stuff

Up to a certain age, children are trusting beings. The innocence and vulnerability they show in their formative years creates a powerful urge to protect them from many of the woes that infect adult society.

As they get older, their vulnerabilities may change, but each age group has its own susceptibilities. And at every age these days, children are spending more and more time online, where they are especially vulnerable to the deceptions of shady marketers. One website for children developed fun cartoon content that was G-rated and even somewhat educational—but the business model was highly objectionable. In the guise of "getting to know you" friendliness, the site paid its bills by luring children into providing a great deal of information about their parents ("What kind of car does Daddy drive?") and then selling the information. Privacy advocates called them to task on it and threatened legal action. Fortunately, the pressure worked and the site stopped collecting information and changed its business model.

The U.S. Congress recognized these sensibilities when, in 1998, it passed the Children's Online Privacy Protection Act (COPPA—not to be confused with COPA, mentioned in chapter 4). The act's central provision requires websites to obtain parental permission before attempting to collect personally identifiable information from children under thirteen years old. Here's how the act's provisions can safeguard your child online:

- *Sites must provide notice about their data collection policies.* Sites must contain prominent and visible language describing what PII will be collected, how it will be used, and in what form that information will be disclosed to third parties.
- *What cereal does Megan like? Sites must check with you first.* With very few exceptions, sites cannot collect, disclose, or use information obtained from children unless verifiable parental consent has been acquired.
- *Data already given? You can put a stop to it.* You as a parent have every right to tell the site not to release any info about your child that they've already collected and to refrain from doing so in the future.
- *Permission to collect PII is not open-ended.* Some sites collect PII from children in order to enroll them in a game or contest. There's a temptation to abuse the privilege. Kids get ex-

cited by the possibility of winning, and in such a state the cautions you've instilled in them may be dulled. That's why the act says that sites aren't allowed to request additional info that isn't directly relatable to enrolling them in such activities.

- *You have every right to see what they know.* Upon request, sites must grant you access to a description of the specific types of PII they've collected from your child.

## Children's Privacy Online: It Starts at Home

As we've said before in this book, laws can go only so far. The best privacy practices are proactive, at the grassroots level. And you can't get more "grassroots" than the Internet access, monitoring, and compliance policies you implement in your own family.

On its GetNetWise website (http://www.getnetwise.org), the not-for-profit public interest consortium Internet Education Foundation (IEF) has posted some excellent guidelines that families can follow to keep their children safe online.

GetNetWise has broken down tips into six age-range classifications, from toddlers to teenagers. Here are some highlights of IEF's advice, by category:

### Children 2–4

This is the age of "lapware," when children start interacting with the computer in the presence of a parent or sibling. There are numerous activities and sites that are likely to be appropriate for this age group but, in most cases, it makes sense for the parent and child to be exploring together. This is not just a safety issue but also a way to assure that the child has a pleasant experience and to help build bonds between the child and the older person who is surfing the Internet with them.

Starting at about age three, some children can benefit by having a bit more independence so that they can explore, experience discoveries, and make mistakes on their own. That doesn't mean that they should be given free access. It's probably best for parents to choose the websites they visit and not let them leave those sites on their own. You don't necessarily need to stand over them or sit with them the entire time that they're in a known safe site.

## Children 4–7

Children at this age begin to explore on their own, but it's still important for parents to be in very close touch with their children as they explore the Net. When your child is in this age group, you should consider restricting her access only to sites that you have visited and feel are appropriate.

At this age it's important that kids experience positive results from sites that can enhance their discovery. The issue here isn't so much avoiding dangerous sites as making sure they are visiting sites that don't frustrate them or lead them down blind alleys or leave them unsatisfied. The Net is about information, and learning how to access information over the Net is a very important skill.

GetNetWise recommends and links to several Internet directories that list sites appropriate for children in this age range:

- American Library Association 700+ Great Sites for Kids
  http://www.ala.org/parentspage/greatsites/amazing.html
- Children's Partnership Recommended Sites for Kids
  http://www.getnetwise.org/kidsites/cpmore.shtml
- Cyberangels' Cybermoms' List of Approved Sites
  http://www.getnetwise.org/kidsites/cybermomsmore.shtml

- Enough Is Enough
  http://www.getnetwise.org/kidsites/enoughmore.shtml
- Net Mom's 100 Hot Sites
  http://www.getnetwise.org/kidsites/netmom100.shtml

## Children 7–10

During this period, children begin looking outside the family for so-cial validation. Peer pressure begins to become an issue for many kids. It's also a time when kids become more independent and be-gin to take flights out of the parental nest. During these years, chil-dren should be encouraged to surf a bit on their own, but that doesn't mean that the parents ignore their children's Web journeys. For this age group, consider putting the computer in a kitchen area, family room, den, or other areas where the child has access to Mom or Dad while using the computer. That way, they can be "indepen-dent" but not wholly on their own.

GetNetWise also suggests you consider installing time-limiting tools on your computer, so kids don't get obsessive about their on-line activities. These can trigger a log-off of your Internet connec-tion after a specified length of time, say, an hour. I-Gear (http://www.symantec.com/sabu/igear/) is one. It can record the amount of time expended on a specific connection, as well as be set up to al-low your child to access the Internet at specified times only (such as 4 p.m. to 5 p.m., right after school).

## Children 10–12

During this preteen period, many kids want to experience even more independence. If children aren't already doing so, this is a time when they should start using the Internet to help with schoolwork and, perhaps, discover resources for their hobbies, sports activities, and other interests. This is definitely an age when you have to be concerned about what kids see and do on the Internet.

At about age twelve children begin to hone their abstract reasoning skills. With these enhanced skills, they begin to form more of their own values and begin to take on the values of their peers. Before that, they're more likely to reflect the values of their parents. It's important at this age to begin to help children realize that not all the information on the Internet is true.

A good way to illustrate this is for them to do a search for sites on subjects they know a lot about—favorite athletes or musicians, subjects they love in school, etc.—and discover just how much false information they can find. As they explore, take the opportunity to explain the ground rules of privacy, teaching them to be very, very cautious about putting their name, address, or phone number on the Net.

## Children 12–14

This is the time when many kids become very social and when they are most likely to be interested in online chat. Go over the basic privacy rules again with your kids, to be sure they understand never to give out information about themselves or to get together with anyone they meet online without first checking with their parents.

Also, emphasize the importance of never exchanging photographs with people they don't know. At this age they need to understand clearly the fact that people on the Internet may not be who they appear to be.

This is also an age when many children start expressing interest in sex. It is natural for them to be curious about the opposite (or even the same) sex. It's natural for them to want to look at photos and explore sexual subjects, at least to some degree. During this early exploratory period, it is especially important for kids to know that their parents are around and aware of what they are doing. You may not need to be in the same room as your kids the entire time they're on the Net, but they do need to know that you and other family members can walk in and out of the room at any time, and will ask them about what they are doing online.

You can use filtering and monitoring software at this age, but you may start to run into some resistance. What's important is that you are honest with your kids and that they know what you are doing and why you are doing it. If you use filtering software, for example, you need to explain to them that you are doing it to protect them from material that you consider to be harmful. And you need to explain that in advance—so that they don't feel that their privacy is being invaded.

Just as you might not let them go to certain places in your community, you are exercising your parental right to keep them from surfing to certain types of places in cyberspace.

## Teenagers 14–17

Teens are more likely than younger people to engage in risky behavior both online and offline. While the likelihood of a teen being abducted by someone he meets in a chat room is extremely low, there is always the possibility that he will meet someone online who makes him feel good and makes him want to strike up an in-person relationship. It is extremely important that teens understand that people they meet online are not necessarily who they seem to be.

Teens at this age often experiment with aliases and other phony or fanciful identities. This is probably a very useful social skill to acquire these days—and can prepare them for their own adult battles with the data snatchers.

## Tips and Tricks for Chapter 7

**Don't fall for the old "customer support" con.** In this scenario, someone will call claiming to be with your Internet service provider. This individual will report some alleged problem that compels them to confirm your password and/or user name. Do not give this information over the phone or via the Internet to anyone you don't know. Contact your Internet service provider *directly* and find out if the request for information is a legitimate one.

**Question the questioner.** A number of websites innocently ask for personal information so they may serve you better. To determine which type of multimedia content to send you, some sites will ask for your Internet connection speed. That's fine. Others, such as Netscape Netcenter's My Netscape, will ask what city you live in and what your favorite sports teams are because they are trying to personalize the content they send to your desktop. That's fine, too, so long as you trust the site to use their information only for its intended purpose. In such case, read the site's privacy policy carefully to determine what they plan to do with this information.

Providing personal data to help a site give you customized service is one thing. Sending personal information to a site that simply wants the data for commercial goals—either to e-mail their own ads or to sell the information to a third party—is quite another.

**Think your info's being sold? Request a credit report.** Some unscrupulous websites will sell info about you, such as your residential status in a classy neighborhood, to businesses in a position to extend credit to you. It is clearly objectionable and occasionally illegal for such companies to run credit checks on you prior to initial contact with you. If there are too many inquiries, it can affect your credit score and your ability to obtain that mortgage refinance or special platinum credit card you actually need. That's because credit grantors tend to look at lots of "applications" submitted within a year of each other with apprehension. They fear you may wind up taking on more debt than you'll be able to repay.

To catch these sneaky unauthorized credit inquirers at their own game, periodically request a copy of your credit report, which lists companies that have asked for credit information about you. Call Equifax at 1-800-685-1111, Experian (formerly TRW) at 1-888-397-3742, or Trans Union at 1-800-888-4213. These companies also offer subscription plans that deliver your latest credit report to you on a quarterly basis. You may be charged a small fee, but it can be well worth it, especially if you are unaccountably experiencing credit problems. If you see unauthorized inquiries, you have the right to ask the offending parties to get in touch with these credit bureaus and expunge these inquiries from their records. Credit reports from Equifax et al. also provide you with an opportunity to check the accuracy of the information in their profile about you. If it is in error there, the mistake is probably being broadly circulated and can cause serious trouble.

**Ask companies you deal with not to sell your name.** To some marketers the real value of membership programs they enroll you in isn't your goodwill or even your continued business, but the potential income they can earn from selling their membership lists to junk-mailers and spammers. Take an afternoon and call or e-mail the following marketers and ask them to take your name off the lists they sell to outside firms:

- Credit card companies
- Websites you may have purchased merchandise from
- Magazines you subscribe to
- All mail-order companies
- Alumni associations you may belong to
- Airline and hotel frequent flyer membership plans
- Your credit union
- Your mortgage broker
- Buying clubs

It's also a good idea to insist on such provisions when you open a new account with such companies or organizations.

For more tips, get a copy of *Stop Junk Mail Forever.* It's available for $3 from Good Advice Press, Box 78, Elizaville, NY 12523.

**Mind Mergers.** When a company with an airtight privacy policy gets acquired by one with a somewhat looser code of ethics, it might be good news for shareholders, but maybe not for you. Privacy policies are rarely addressed in the feverish acculturation that must take place when one company acquires or merges with another. The acquirer may also feel pressure to get maximum return from their new acquisition—and launch highly aggressive marketing campaigns that have the potential to jeopardize the privacy of customers. You may have been a loyal customer, and the acquired company may have been a trustworthy vendor, but don't automatically assume that the safe harbor will still be in effect. Or, as in the case of the AOL/Time Warner merger, individual profiles about you may be combined in a way you'd find objectionable. Be wary of mergers in privacy matters.

**Not just any blocking software will do.** The Privacy Rights Council (http://www.privacyrights.org) stipulates several minimal capabilities for the tools that block access to certain sites containing adult content, violent subject matter, hateful language, or other potentially objectionable material. Effective blocking software should:

- Block "outgoing" transmission of personal information such as name, address, phone number.
- Limit access by time of day and total amount of connect time.
- Have user-definable options, allowing customization of blocked sites.
- Allow user to turn software on and off with password control.
- Be updated frequently.
- Block image files (JPEG/GIF) and binary downloads, which are likely to contain photos and graphic images.
- Block transfer of compressed files likely to contain adult content. These files may have the extension "ZIP" or "SIT."
- Filter offensive language.
- Block gopher and FTP (File Transfer Protocol) downloads.
- Block Internet Relay Chats (IRCs) and Usenet Newsgroups
- Work with online service providers like America Online that state their criteria for blocking sites, and allow parents to read a list of blocked sites.

**Be careful of "Alt" newsgroups.** Be especially wary of any newsgroup that starts with "Alt." "Alt" stands for "Alternative,"

and, while many Alt newsgroups are fine, some contain material that is sexual, violent, hateful, and otherwise inappropriate. Some software tools do exist that can prevent your children from accessing inappropriate newsgroups. To see a complete list of these Alt newsgroups in order to determine which you may wish to block access to, type: http://www.w3.org/History/ 19921103/
hypertext/hypertext/DataSources/News/Groups/alt.html.

# 8
# The Privacy Game

Let us review for a moment the chief conclusions we have drawn from our examination of information technology and modern global networks, and the effect they have on personal privacy and security:

- The Internet has rapidly evolved from an electronic arena of free expression and noncommercial interaction (Act I) to a sophisticated marketing and entertainment platform that is largely driven by e-commerce (Act II).
- The increasing commercial importance of networked information systems has led to innovations and advances in the collection, storage, and distribution of personally identifiable information, or PII; a diverse array of data collectors now use these technical advances to capture copious information about individual people and their tastes, values, and behavior.
- The growing sophistication of PII collection and distribution

is especially troubling because of the essential vulnerabilities of modern computing systems (the hundredth-window problem); consequently, it is much easier to collect and distribute PII than it is to secure its confidentiality.

- Privacy, a revered value in American culture and a central requirement of a free society, is under attack; networked technologies are enabling a whole host of new threats to our personal privacy, security, and peace of mind; and not only are governments ill prepared to thwart these Internet-age abrasions of privacy, but frequently they themselves are major offenders.

- Yet the collection and use of PII by others is not all bad; in fact, in the decades ahead, you will be required to provide deep, specific information profiles about yourself in order to take advantage of some of the most powerful and beneficial new products and services (e.g., highly personalized medical treatment and drug prescriptions, customized financial services, and intelligent job search systems).

- The increasing value of deep PII profiles, to those who collect them and to those who provide them, will lead to the emergence of an open, publicly accessible datanet that will make the exchange of such profiles relatively seamless, quite inexpensive, and, ultimately, a routine part of everyday life; as a result, much of what hitherto has been private will fall into the public realm, but enough core privacy will remain (through individual resistance and technical countermeasures) that most people will be wary of any transactions — commercial or otherwise — that result in further personal exposure on the network.

- The dynamic e-commerce market sector will stabilize and mature, and market leaders will increasingly emphasize customer retention efforts over high-priced customer acquisition programs; in this new business environment, careful, trusted use of personal information will become essential for winning and retaining customer loyalty, thereby making trust an important competitive advantage; and trusted third-party auditors, rating services, rights clearinghouses, fraud control providers, and other online intermediaries will fill important new roles by providing assurance that both companies and customers are acting responsibly.

- But in the short term, determining the relative trustworthiness of organizations that collect and use PII will not be easy, and slowing the proliferation and depth of online PII profiles about you will be harder still; new security holes, new privacy melt-downs, new schemes that covertly manage personal identity behind the electronic curtain will continue to proliferate; and people who care about retaining some modicum of personal obscurity will understand that, for all practical purposes, privacy has become less a right than a skill.

With these points in mind, we now move to a final hypothesis: namely, that the Internet is once again undergoing a major transition—a transition driven by a new imperative to balance the public with the private, and human values with technical efficiency. It is, further, a transition that will result, ultimately, in the emergence of a new network architecture based on two central values: transparency and trust.

## Act III: Toward a Dynamic Equilibrium

If Act I gave us Net culture, and Act II gave us Net commerce, what does Act III of the Internet portend? Before addressing this question, we should caution that if the rise of the Internet has taught us anything, it is the foolishness of trying to predict how information technology will evolve.

As recently as 1994, Vice President Al Gore led a star-studded cast of modern leaders in a day of technology crystal-ball gazing that was, in retrospect, amazingly off base. The event was billed, rather breathlessly, as the Information Superhighway Summit. In a buzzing UCLA lecture hall, assorted Hollywood studio chiefs, actors, producers, and agents—plus a few high-tech wizards and a smattering of politicians—offered their views on the future of entertainment and technology to an audience of several thousand.

Gore, the first speaker of the day, promptly cleared the air about the origin of the term "information superhighway": he had coined it. The vice president then went on to envision and champion an enlightened new world of interconnected information networks that would completely transform (drum roll, please) schools and libraries.

Following Gore, a series of entertainment industry heavyweights (TCI's John Malone, Fox's Rupert Murdoch, Time Warner's Gerald Levin, Disney's Michael Eisner, and Turner Broadcasting's Ted Turner—just to name a few) went on stage, four at a time, to pontificate about the value of content and the power of "convergence" and "synergy"—without painting much of a picture about how all these new buzz words would actually change things. One thing they did know was that technology would always be subservient to star power. And nearly all of them scoffed at the notion that the computer would ever play a significant role in the mainstream entertainment marketplace.

The lone representative of the software industry on stage that day was Alan Kay, an Apple Fellow and one of the fathers of the desktop metaphor for PC operating systems. Kay played the contrarian. He saw the future in terms of something called the Internet. He described the Net—its history, its technology, its culture. Along the way he cited an amazing statistic, a tiny fact quite at odds with that day's conventional wisdom.

Kay reported that the number of people using the Internet—a

number, incidentally, that included very few in attendance at the summit—had recently been doubling every one hundred days. He compared this rate of adoption with that of other mass-market communications media, such as the telephone, television, and radio. His conclusion: the Internet was growing much faster than any previous communications technology, and the Net, not Malone's cable systems running an interactive version of Levin's HBO, would be the true information superhighway. Hollywood's most common response on later panels: the Internet was at best a hot fad, ultimately no more important than the CB radio craze of the 1970s.

Five years later, Kay has been proven right about the Internet, Hollywood dead wrong. Interactive video-on-demand (a favorite of those on the dais that day) is still a mogul's fantasy, while Internet news is among the hottest topics each day in the most important entertainment industry trade papers (*Variety, The Hollywood Reporter,* and *Billboard*). At present, the number of people on America Online alone surpasses the numbers of people watching NBC, ABC, CBS, and Fox TV, respectively; and with AOL's acquisition of Time Warner, an Internet company has now swallowed the largest entertainment company on earth, and Internet start-ups that did not exist at the time of the Information Superhighway Summit are now worth more than any movie studio or television network. Almost all the "experts" failed to foresee this emergence of the Internet as a mainstream medium.

The entertainment leaders shouldn't feel too bad, however. Even the prescient Alan Kay failed to predict the Internet's second act: the relentless rise of e-commerce.

Steeped as he was in the early-adopter world of Internet culture, Kay foresaw the continued rise of the Internet but failed to see that the Net itself would change radically as it grew. Little did he know, then, that the action on the Internet would move from e-mail communication and the free exchange of ideas within newsgroups to the selling of products and services on the World Wide Web—and that the era of the early-adopter Netizen (a favorite *Wired* magazine term, standing for Net citizen) would give way to the era of the Internet multimillionaire.

Of all its unique characteristics, this tendency of the great public network to confound expectations and evolve in unexpected ways ought to be its most predictable trait. It is a system, after all, that grew out of a Defense Department communications experiment, sprang to life as a communications tool for academics, spawned a unique interactive communications subculture, and then evolved into the most important marketplace on the earth. This most recent twist—the significant role of e-commerce in the global economy—has been called "a totally unexpected development" by no less authority than management guru Peter Drucker. What totally unexpected turn is next?

Addressing this very question, Drucker notes that the emergence of the Internet as a vital distribution channel for goods and services is "profoundly changing economies, markets, and industry structures; products and services and their flow; consumer segmentation, consumer values and consumer behavior; jobs and labor markets." While acknowledging the Net's penchant for surprise, he goes on to predict that despite its pervasive influence on commerce and markets, the Internet's impact "may be even greater on societies and politics and, above all, on the way we see the world and ourselves in it."

All caveats about prophecy aside, we believe that Drucker has it exactly right. The next field to be dramatically reshaped by the Internet—after defense planning, university research, personal communications, global commerce, and mainstream entertainment—will be society at large. Including each of us in society, as individuals.

It is in this context that the true nature of Internet privacy comes into focus. The growing debate isn't just about annoying marketing interruptions, or even about proliferating online profiles of us. What's really at issue is our core identity, and perhaps our humanity.

Privacy is not solitude. It is something more fundamental. It's the elbow room we need to grow. The freedom we require to make mistakes, to be peculiar, to create and invent. The curtain we close to become intimate with others. The space where we explore the esoteric, and perhaps discover our true selves. A shield that protects the sword of liberty (our inalienable right to be a singular, individualistic, special human being).

It is this fragile, highly personal realm of identity and individuality that is being squeezed by the new information technologies and the people who wield them. If you, too, cringe when you receive an unsolicited e-mail message from a porn site; when you see yourself caught unawares on a surveillance camera; when you learn that someone has been listening to your phone calls; when your unlisted phone number turns up online—your discomfort may be due to the fact that you realize, consciously or subconsciously, that an essential part of your humanity has been assaulted.

Our belief is that the great majority of people react instinctively, and negatively, when they feel that their "realm of the personal" is being compromised. Further, as the mainstream of humanity steadily comes online in the decade ahead, fewer and fewer people will be so dazzled by the technology of interconnectivity that they ignore these basic instincts. As the power and reach of information technology grows, so too will the desire to protect personal privacy. Sooner or later, those who ignore mankind's instinctual needs for privacy—be they technologists, business leaders, investors, educators, health care professionals, politicians, or government bureaucrats—will pay a hefty price.

Why? Because, as Peter Drucker maintains, it is not an Internet Revolution that we are living through but an Information Revolution. The real driver of revolutionary change is not the infrastructure of the Internet, per se, but the rapidly rising tide of information that is flooding our world. And this tide cannot always flow merely in one direction. What comes in must go out, and the very tools and systems used today by unseen others to compile detailed information about us will inevitably be redirected to tell us all about them. Soon, the same information circuits that already are spreading information about apparel-industry sweatshops and the side effects of medications will soon be deployed to bring new transparency to the internal practices of companies that are collecting and using our personal data.

In Chapter 7, we offered our "modest proposal" to build a more trustworthy Internet. The idea, you'll recall, was (a) to reverse the data flow by pinning online surveillance bull's-eyes on companies as well as customers; and (b) to leverage the full power of the datanet to circulate this coming information in ways that would be extremely helpful to individual people making trust-based decisions. Admittedly, though, we were rather sketchy on the details.

We now want to take this idea a bit further. Ten years further, to be exact.

What can we predict about the Internet and its related technologies ten years hence? Or, more to the point, what possibilities exist today that, if properly actualized, could make our society, and our personal lives, safer, happier, and more satisfying? To take up the challenge of answering these questions, we first must closely observe the Internet as it is today and take into account the winding path it took to get here. And in so doing, we must look beneath surface events to see if we can discern any underlying principles that are driving it.

Our dilemma in undertaking this task is not unlike that of a visitor from another planet observing a chess match. He (or she, or it) could watch all the early moves—a knight jump here, a pawn capture there, a castle move between king and rook—and conclude that the game had no rhyme or reason to it at all. But if he could patiently watch long enough, he would perhaps begin to see patterns emerge—moves that were repeated, strengths and weaknesses that remained consistent. Despite the fact that the game board would be changing constantly, he would come to understand that the game was not driven by random chaos but by a fixed set of rules.

Today, we are like that alien observer, perhaps halfway through the match. We have seen the Internet jump and move. We have seen it show its strengths and weaknesses. We can even see patterns emerging. But what are its inner rules? What hidden forces propel it forward?

Attempting to answer these questions is perhaps foolhardy, but it's hard not to be curious. What is driving this powerful digital metabolism in our midst? And where is it taking us?

We believe the key to predicting the future course of the Internet lies in three simple words: *follow the data.*

In the early days of the Net, data flowed between academics and scientists, primarily from university to university. The goal was to share research and serious ideas. But inevitably, the data flow quickly extended into the realm of the personal, and the pioneers of the Net began using the medium to circulate (along with their doctoral dissertations) political opinions, movie reviews, jokes, and thousands of other idiosyncratic bits of information. The network application of person-to-person e-mail expanded the personal data flow even further, and among these early users, the Internet began to emerge as a medium for managing many of the details of everyday life.

With personal data now freely flowing through the still-small network, the network began to grow. Early adopters far from university centers began to come online and began using the network to create a new, free-wheeling online culture. Newsgroups formed to distribute free software, to fantasize about killing Barney (the purple dinosaur of PBS), and to share bizarre sexual experiences. The data flow expanded to include much fringe culture, black humor, and libertarian politics, with the result that the reach of the data extended ever further, to a whole new generation of users.

As the number of nontechnical people using the network grew, so too did the realization that the data flow could extend beyond interactive personal communication to the kinds of communication that support commerce. Groups ranging from porn site operators to youthful and intense e-commerce entrepreneurs to established marketing/sales departments of some major corporations—all aided considerably by the arrival of the point-and-click architecture of the World Wide Web—began to plug commerce servers into the network in great numbers. Sales orders, credit card numbers, and ship-to addresses were now added to the data stream.

With the advent of serious online commerce, of course, came new resources. Companies such as Microsoft, Oracle, IBM, and AT&T—Internet latecomers all—suddenly applied their technology muscle to the task of further extending the reach of the Net and further accelerating the rate of its data flow. As they and others joined the game, the processing power and number of nodes in the network took another giant leap forward. Today, Internet growth continues unabated, and the data tide is poised and ready to roll into the new territory of mainstream culture, including, especially, prime-time entertainment.

As aliens observing this phenomenon, what conclusion could we draw at this point in the game? Is there a consistent pattern, a central raison d'être, that we can distinguish in all the Net's twists and turns? There are several possibilities, but let's try this one.

The Internet, essentially, is not about browsers, routers, servers, and backbones. It's not about auctions, banner ads, day trading, or fast shopping. It's not about MP3 players, multiplayer games, or networked video cams—though all these are important outward manifestations of its inner driving force. The Internet, quite simply, is about the exchange of data.

Throughout this book, we have frequently used the term "data flow." And while the concept of data flowing through a network is an essential one in building an understanding of Internet-based systems, it is also less than fully accurate. The Internet is not a highway, and it is not a pipe. Data does not flow through it like water running downhill, through a rigid conduit. If anything, the Internet is more like a massive colony of hyperactive ants who are all somehow able to freely exchange information, ant to ant, one exchange at a time. These exchanges follow certain common routines, but the general condition of this ant colony is decentralized chaos. Every ant is connected, but each to each, rather than one to many. There is no queen in charge.

And these new electronic ants feed on data. In fact, they'll eat just about any form of it in their path.

The electronic ants of the Internet world are, in a sense, human. Actually, "they" are us. Not us in our bodily form, but us in the form of new electronic identities—personal reflections of us that dwell in the mirror world of cyberspace. It is through these identities, and as these identities, that we participate in this great network feeding frenzy, swapping information back and forth in ever increasing amounts.

Whatever the shortcomings of the Internet ant metaphor, and there are some, we can feel confident in asserting that the rapid exchange of data will remain the Internet's most basic function. The data in the network will change, the reach of the network will continue to grow, many new applications for the network will be found, but at its heart, the Internet will remain a huge field of continuous, point-to-point information exchange.

We can also safely predict that the volume of information passing through this electronic grid will grow to enormous proportions. The number of ants in the colony is growing, as is the information processing power of each individual ant. And not only will this colony stay hungry, ever searching for new fields of fresh data, but it will become increasingly adept at swapping the data it collects, from each to each.

It's not hard to see where these Internet ants are headed. They are marching from the fringes of society to its core. Ten years from now, the Internet surely will have arrived at the center of the circle of civilization itself.

The Internet at that point will not just be changing markets and changing institutions. It will be changing people. Changing even our deepest notions of who we are.

## The Digital Handshake

Of all the changes the Internet will bring, we seem least prepared for radical new levels of personal exposure that could be ushered into our world by an Internet a thousand times more powerful, and ten times larger in numbers of users, than the one that is already raising privacy concerns today. Even today, the Internet can seem out of control with respect to the collection of personal data. And yet there is nothing inherent in the technical architecture of the Internet that would prevent privacy protection from becoming a part of its infrastructure. The basic functional building block of electronic networks is the data exchange, and on the Internet—just as in every other major arena of exchange on earth, from a stock exchange to a flea market—we humans have always found ways to develop rules and norms making fair exchange possible.

In many ways, the rules of fair exchange are as old as the public marketplace. The eighteenth-century economist Adam Smith lived two hundred years before the advent of encryption, Oracle databases, and snazzy, Java-enabled electronic commerce websites. Yet Smith defined transactions in a way that is still relevant today, and appropriate to our search for a general framework for trusted data exchange on the Net.

Smith maintained that all honest and fair transactions contribute to the common good. He believed that if Mr. Jones has plenty of bread but no shoes, and Mr. Johnson has lots of shoes but no bread, and they meet in the town square to trade a shoe for a loaf, then both men are better off than before, and the world is a better place for it.

In the age of the Internet, the town square is now global. In most cases, what is bartered in an online transaction is not bread for shoes, but private information about you (a name, an address, a credit card number), and your money, in exchange for a product or service a vendor can provide. As much as if you were trading shoes for bread, you have every right to expect, even demand, fair play. The personally identifiable information you provide to complete the transaction is valuable; you should receive value in return. A privacy policy posted on a website is essentially a contract governing this transaction. If it is taken seriously by the consumer and scrupulously observed by the merchant, a fair exchange is possible.

But fair, value-for-value data exchanges do not yet occur automatically on the Net. If you care about protecting your personal privacy, you must take the initiative, learn what the specific rules of the fair exchange really are, and apply them regularly in your Web journeys. Painful as it may be, do you actually read privacy policies? When entering personal data as part of registration or membership programs, or when purchasing a good or service, do you check to see whether the PII you are providing will be used for certain clearly defined purposes and otherwise kept confidential, or be circulated, forever, to the ends of the earth? These small personal acts not only help protect your privacy, they help build an Internet marketplace governed by the rules of fair exchange, because if repeated often enough by Net users, they will influence the policies and practices of the companies on the other end of the data transaction. An army of citizen consumers determined to protect their privacy on the Net would quickly see their needs and concerns addressed. More privacy policies would be posted, the policies themselves would become fairer and more transparent, and internal company compliance with these policies would improve as well. Learning to use privacy policies as part of your individual data exchange routine can help move the Internet from the era of covert data collection to a time when the terms and conditions of most data exchanges are clear, open, mutually agreeable, and dutifully enforced. At that point, the collection of PII on the Internet will indeed meet Adam Smith's criteria for a fair transaction and thus become an activity that almost always contributes to the common good.

Ah, but the devil is in the details, especially in a system like the Internet, where covert and even coercive surveillance and data collection have become a part of normal operations. Making the Internet an environment that supports the fair exchange of data will take more than good intentions on the part of some merchants and swelling public opinion in favor of privacy protection. It will require a fundamental change in the technology that is the foundation of the Internet: the data exchange itself.

In a very real sense, an Internet data exchange is simply a kind of transaction. And Internet transactions already mirror the exchanges of everyday life more than one might think. Designers of the modem and router protocols that provided the early technical foundation of Internet communications, for example, appropriated the term "handshake" to describe the process used to open a point-to-point connection on an electronic network. A digital handshake involves an introduction and verification sequence not unlike one found when two traders meet, say, on the floor of a crowded commodities market. Such handshakes are, furthermore, an essential part of Internet communications protocol; before a data exchange can take place, a handshake is required. The protocols governing the Internet handshake to date have been purely technical in nature, and do nothing to support or enforce the normal rules of privacy or propriety that guide society at large. Yet for personal privacy protection to become an essential part of the Internet infrastructure, privacy rules must become part of the basic communications protocols that govern data exchange.

The technical architects and netizens in the World Wide Web Consortium agree. For several years, the technical standards–setting body for the Web (based in Cambridge, Massachusetts) has been working on a proposed Platform for Privacy Preferences Project, known most commonly by its nickname, P3P. The Consortium says that P3P will "provide a framework for informed online interactions." P3P standards will, in essence, put your own personal privacy protocols into force when you exchange information with a website.

P3P's goal is to enable you to be informed—online, in real time—of a site's privacy practices, and notified if a site's privacy policies do not match your personal preferences. Based on how your personal rules of exchange mesh with a site's privacy policy, you'll be able to manage the flow of data (including your remote and ISP address, your name, e-mail address, cookies, and click trails) by configuring privacy-related settings in your computer to different levels of protection. With P3P technology and a few other common safeguards, if you want to surf the Net anonymously except when visiting sites with high standards for trust and security, you'll be able to do so.

P3P may sound technical, but using it won't be. It is designed to integrate almost seamlessly into common computing platforms. P3P will also be a major time-saver. That's because at sites that meet the privacy and security criteria you've established in your settings, and which are P3P compliant, common PII can be passed automatically and securely from your P3P-compliant digital wallet directly to the site. Thus you will no longer have to reenter your personal information each time you register with a new site or place a new order. If the site does not meet your criteria, you'll be notified of the site's practices and then have an opportunity to agree to these terms or not. If you desire, you can continue browsing or enter data despite the apparent mismatch of your preferences with their policies.

P3P essentially enables a "digital handshake" agreement between the software in your PC and software at the sites you visit. With this handshake, privacy rules of your own setting become a basic part of your own Internet protocol. With P3P-enabled software, there can be no exchange of data between you and a site until such a handshake has occurred.

P3P, though it has experienced many of the problems that plague and slow large consensus-driven standards initiatives, will likely become part of the Internet infrastructure in the very near future. At this writing, the standard is already at the beta, or "last call," stage, and applications designed to implement P3P are already available on the market (although their value is minimal today, because P3P requires cooperation of merchants to become efficient and practical). But if properly implemented and widely adopted, P3P could be a major step toward making the network a more trusted environment.

P3P is based upon the recognition that different people have widely differing thresholds of comfort when it comes to privacy issues. Rather than enforcing wholesale proscriptions the way both laws and site-blocking software do, it offers flexibility within a context of trust and full disclosure. Still, because it is driving the Internet toward greater standardization in the architecture of PII (solving such practical interoperability problems as whether in a customer registration form, the first name comes first or last), it may well also hasten the day of seamless data exchange. Indeed, some critics maintain that that is P3P's main purpose.

In our view, P3P is an extremely important initiative. It is also a sign that Internet leaders understand that the Net needs an overall privacy upgrade. It is only in its beginning stages, and a great deal of work—and cooperation—will be needed to bring the full promise of P3P to successful implementation. But it is a great first step toward building a trusted, privacy-friendly infrastructure.

P3P is an early step toward what World Wide Web inventor Tim Berners-Lee calls the "Semantic Web." The Web today does a good job of allowing people to interact in a location-independent, seamless way. In the coming era of the Semantic Web, machines (or more correctly, software "agents" inside them) will be able to interact in a location-independent, seamless manner. Trust and privacy must be built into the Internet infrastructure before the Semantic Web can come into existence, for how can we allow "agents" to work on our behalf unless we can trust that there are built-in unbreakable protocols for safe agreements? P3P is both an early example of what will be possible for agents in a semantic web and also a fundamental building block for more advanced and wider reaching agent technology that will be a hallmark of electronic networks in the future.

Here is how it will work:

- When you go to a website, the site will send your computer a privacy "proposal" in which it declares its identity and discloses its privacy practices. This proposal will be in XML format, making it possible to "tag" and categorize various elements of a site's privacy policy. Thus your PC will be able to "read" privacy policies for you and determine whether or not the privacy practices of the site meet your standards.
- The site's "proposal" will be required to define what information it intends to collect, how each piece of collected data about you will be used, who it may be shared with, and whether data will be used in a manner that may identify you as a specific person (rather than as, say, a high-income unmarried resident of zip code 90210).
- Web browsers will have plug-ins that automatically evaluate each proposal to see if it matches the security preferences you have previously indicated. If there's no problem, your plug-in should accept it automatically, and your Web session will proceed normally.
- Should there appear to be a mismatch, you may see a rejection screen or be prompted for a decision as to whether or not you wish to ignore the problem and access the site anyway.

Additionally, some sites may wish to send you an alternate proposal, such as transfer to a more secure portion of their online environment, with a higher privacy standard, should your preferences and their initial proposal not match. For example, a movie listings site might offer to dish up a "movies playing this weekend" page for you, providing local movie times based on the neighborhood zip code it asks you to enter. Yet if you don't want to enter your exact zip code (90210), the site may offer to send you to a clickable list of states, cities, and then theaters within your particular city, with screening times. With a bit more work, you can still find out what's playing in Beverly Hills, but you won't have to disclose your location.

Despite its formidable capabilities, P3P has doubters who are concerned that it only ensures compatibility between a site's stated privacy policies and your privacy preferences. It does not provide a technical mechanism for making sure the site is actually in compliance with its own policies. However, industry self-regulatory programs and new private assurance companies (functioning like accounting firms that audit and certify corporate compliance with financial rules) will undoubtedly fill this void if demand for such verification increases among users. And, ultimately, statutory relief can also play a role. P3P enables what amounts to an agreement between the collector and the provider of personal data, and however fleeting the handshake that accompanies this agreement, it should be upheld with the full force of existing contract law. A deal, after all, is a deal—even if it is consummated by a handshake between pieces of software.

More information about P3P and the current status of P3P initiatives and technology is available on the Platform for Privacy Preferences section of the World Wide Web Consortium's website: http://www.w3.org/P3P/.

# The Privacy Game

So, this brings us to the jumbled state of the Internet privacy game board as we find it today: public concern about privacy is rising; privacy advocates are working hard to build flexible new privacy protection schemes into the grid; some merchants are posting and adhering to clearer, stronger privacy polices and moving toward higher standards of privacy protection in their internal systems; other merchants are going for all the PII they can get, inside the law; and true bad actors are secretly stealing data and lying (if they say anything at all) about their PII collection and distribution practices. The technology itself is full of holes, and no system is fully secure. Government agencies are nervous. Politicians are wagging fingers and writing laws. Big business is beginning to support privacy initiatives, but internal compliance with their own company policies on privacy is spotty at best. Small businesses are all over the map, some acting responsibly, some collecting data like bandits, most confused about the issue to the extent they think about it at all.

Beneath all this *Sturm und Drang* lies the very question considered by Adam Smith two centuries ago: the rules of exchange. No matter how scrambled the privacy game board appears at the moment, the Net is somehow driving to a resolution of how this issue will play out in the electronic networks of modern life—one way or the other. And the decisions all of us make when on the Net will play a large role in the outcome.

One of the founding fathers of modern computing, John von Neumann, also wrestled with the issue of exchange. In the introduction to his book *The Theory of Games and Economic Behavior*, written with Oskar Morgenstern, von Neumann offered a unique approach: "We hope . . . to obtain a real understanding of the problem of exchange by studying it from an altogether different angle: this is, from the perspective of a 'game of strategy.'"

What von Neumann was proposing, essentially, was that transactions could best be appreciated by looking at them as moves in a game—a game where each player follows his or her self-interest in a desire to win. Or at least to produce an optimal result, from the unique perspective of each individual player.

Von Neumann's ideas on this subject led to the development of a new field of mathematics known as game theory. As von Neumann recognized, games have always been simulations of real life, in some sense. Chess, for example, was originally a kind of simulation of feudal wars, a subject of great importance in the medieval kingdoms where chess was born. Similarly, the roots of bridge can be traced to public fascination with a new business tool, the contract. These games and countless others have not only provided amusement and challenge, they have also helped develop skills of strategy and critical thinking that can be applied in the real world.

Modern game theory takes this indirect link with the real world a step further, reapplying the structures of game play and imposing them on real-world problems in ways that have little or nothing to do with parlor games of skill or chance. Students of game theory today do not study the betting in poker so much as the bets businesses might make in a particular competitive market, or those generals might make in a war.

Game theory rests on the premise that transactions—social, political, and commercial—are driven largely by individual self-interest and highly personal preferences. However, it also holds that as we learn to play out strategies in pursuit of these highly personal objectives, we often find that cooperative behavior with other players produces the best results.

Strategic play in mathematical game theory differs greatly from a round of contract bridge; no "game" that has seen Nobel prizes awarded to two of its players is pursued merely for amusement. Today, a half-century after von Neumann's initial insight, the key to game theory is iteration: the repetition of a series of moves, or choices, within a common framework. The basic idea (oversimplified considerably) is that each time a game—or a social or business problem—is played out, players learn more about the consequences of their choices and discover mutual advantages in cooperation.

A classic example of how we humans can move from selfish pursuits to the kind of enlightened self-interest that recognizes the value of cooperation is found in the Law of the Commons that in the seventeenth and eighteenth centuries governed the public squares in small towns in England. In those days, each village of any size had an open, grassy square at the center of town. Farmers would come to town for supplies, news, and cheer, and bring their sheep with them. Before going about their business in town, they would park their sheep on the "commons," where the sheep would happily graze on the grass. However, if one farmer brought too many sheep, or allowed his sheep to remain on the commons too long, the grass would be eaten down to the roots and die. Thus, an informal Law of the Commons evolved which dictated that each farmer moderate his selfish interest of fattening his sheep on the public grass in order to maintain the benefit of having a convenient grazing ground that made trips to town for all farmers more pleasant and productive.

Game theorists often point to the Law of the Commons as illustrative of the core principle of human cooperation in economic systems, a principle now referred to in economics circles as "reciprocal altruism." Briefly, the notion is that people will put cooperation above selfish interests if, and only if, they know that their altruistic behavior will be reciprocated. Reciprocal altruism is greatly accelerated in environments where everyone knows what everyone else is doing and where people are interacting with each other, iteratively, over extended periods of time. If you know that people will know and remember when you have cheated or slighted them, in other words, then it will be in your own self-interest not to do these things.

No environment in human history, of course, compares to the

Internet when it comes to spreading information on what everyone else is doing. That's the double-edged sword of the Internet: it captures and exposes information about us, and it informs us about others who are out to do us ill—thereby helping to prevent such actions. This includes even the antisocial actions of covert data snatchers who are working hardest and most selfishly to capture and sell our private data.

We can safely conclude these two things about the online world in the near-term future: the amount of data about us that is captured and used will grow exponentially (the bad news); and the fundamental data exchanges that fuel this growth will become increasingly transparent to all (the good news). The question is whether these two seemingly opposing trends can be brought into balance in an Internet privacy equivalent of the Law of the Commons.

Personal data about us does indeed have one thing in common with the tall, green grass in an English village square: it is valuable, and tempting. If too much of it is consumed, its value will diminish greatly.

Unless PII collection and use become both measured and monitored, our great new electronic commons of the Internet may itself be put at risk, as people recoil in disgust or fear when learning how vulnerable they are to online surveillance, behavioral profiling, and other data-consuming activities. Data quality will also go down, as individual Internet users become more deceptive (entering only false information, for example) and more anonymous (by employing new privacy-enhancing technologies). A self-reinforcing vicious spiral could take hold, with the Internet becoming less and less valuable to both individuals and companies as a result.

On the other hand, if PII collection does become more fully cooperative, if it is governed, if you will, by a new Internet-Age Law of the Commons, it is easy to see how this vicious cycle could reverse course and become a virtuous cycle. As individual data exchanges became more secure, and more closely governed by individual privacy preferences, people would feel more trusting of their transaction partners and would provide deeper, more meaningful information to them. Vendors could build better products and services, merchants could market them with more precision. More information than ever could flow through the Net, but its impact on our private lives would be greatly moderated.

Sitting in an easy chair, reading this book—or sitting at a computer, writing it—the right conclusions can all seem so obvious. Internet privacy appears to be a straightforward, the-lady-or-the-tiger situation. Go through the right gate, and everyone wins. Go through the wrong one, and look out. Why can't we just pass a law to make sure that we all go through the right gate? Why don't the big businesses with a major commercial stake in the Internet just impose their collective will to do the same?

In practice, at the level of the data exchange, in the realm of millions of ant-like encounters, hour by hour, things are not so simple. The Internet is still at heart a chaotic system. In its short history, this has been part of its value and its charm. It is global in reach, and seems to stretch beyond the jurisdiction of any single government entity. And though the Microsofts, Intels, AOLs, and IBMs of this world do hold great sway, the course of the Net is too spontaneous and chaotic to be directed even by them.

Yet just as game theory teaches us that selfish interests can be transformed over time into cooperative strategies, so too the science of chaos theory teaches us that occasionally a new, more highly ordered system will emerge out of a chaotic one and take on a life of its own. Such an "emergent system," to use the technical term, is guided by a core set of underlying rules that propel the development of the system, much as the rules of chess guide the development of a match. The external picture changes constantly, but the core rules endure.

Emergent systems are never born whole and fully formed. They start small and grow, learning through iteration and driving ahead toward some level of optimization. An emergent system actually has a target vision, or purpose, that seems to guide its way.

In his seminal work *Emergence: From Chaos to Order*, John Holland (another founding father of modern computing) explores how the "laws of emergence" work in real-world systems. Typically in emergent systems, he writes, "we find that (a) the component mechanisms [within an emergent system] interact without central control, and (b) the possibilities for emergence increase rapidly as flexibility of the interactions increase."

Order cannot be imposed on emergent systems from above; rather, it must emerge from within. In terms of the emergence of a new trust and privacy framework on the Net, this means starting at the level of the Net's fundamental building block, the data exchange. From this perspective, it would seem that the P3P initiative does indeed have emergent properties: it is being rolled out as a technical enabler of many types of flexible interactions, rather than being a rigid code of conduct that is produced and controlled centrally.

P3P is still a very small initiative when compared with the huge existing system called the Internet, but Holland also tells us that emergent systems usually begin as a series of "sub-assemblies," which come to fit together over time. The sub-assemblies of an emergent system have different roles and purposes, but they follow a similar organizing principle. Holland uses the example of a Swiss watch, which consists of many moving subsystems which are linked by the common principle of ordered time.

Perhaps in P3P we are seeing the appearance of the first subassembly of a new emergent system—a new and more ordered system that is rising out of the currently chaotic Internet. We have referred to this system previously, in hopeful terms, as a new framework for trust and privacy. Holland might simply call it a new game.

Games are classic emergent systems. The state of the game board changes constantly but is always driven by an internal order, or set of rules, that is governing the changing state of the game.

Chess, for example, has less than two dozen rules but an almost inexhaustible number of board configurations, and even more strategies related to them.

As we complete our survey of the contemporary privacy and security landscape, and the vulnerabilities and opportunities we all face as citizens of the Age of the Internet—the final chapter of this book being a speculation about privacy in the far, far future—we would like to offer a few guiding rules of our own. These are rules that we would not necessarily recommend codifying into law, or even hard-wiring into the Internet infrastructure. They are instead, like the rules of chess, simply a set of guidelines for optimizing the experience of playing the game. And for keeping the grass green in the electronic commons of our global village.

## Rules of the Game

The object of the Privacy Game is to be able to freely exchange personal data for value in the form of money, goods, services, customer care, and anything else the provider of the data feels is worthwhile, without compromising the personal privacy preferences of the player who is making the data-for-value trade. The game is typically played in a "field" consisting of interconnected microprocessors, but can be played virtually anywhere in modern life.

### Guidelines for Individual Players

**Control your data.** The greater your personal mastery of your own PII data flow, the more valuable that data will be to you. The converse is true as well.

**Never exchange data without getting something of value in return.** The value returned can be personal (as in the case of a free subscription) or social (as is the case when you agree to participate in a medical research project).

**Insist on fair use.** Just like businesses that license their products for use only in certain approved situations, you should make sure that your partner in a data exchange fully reveals how your data will be used.

**Check credentials.** The same data exchange that would be a positive trade with one trading partner might be a negative one with another, less trustworthy one.

**Never respond to a cyberspace pitch immediately.** Marketers get paid lots of money to build urgency into the message. Give yourself a four-hour rule: before you respond to any offers, take a deep breath and go on to something else for a while. You'll be amazed how the voice of conscience can enter your mind when you are away from your computer screen and let the nonstimulated parts of your brain process the offer. Sometimes a quiet voice will tell you the offer is too good to be true. And it probably is.

## Guidelines for Company Players

**Control the customer data that you collect.** Playing the Privacy Game without the ability to track and protect your customers' personal information makes you vulnerable to attack.

**Build a privacy-sensitive, privacy-smart culture.** Train your employees to respect private data as if it were as valuable as cash, because it is.

**In privacy matters, one size does not fit all.** Stay flexible, and provide policies that respond to public attitudes about privacy, which vary greatly according to the person and the context in which private information is collected. (Profiling a person's health record is more sensitive than collecting information about the purchase of software, for example.)

**Appoint a privacy ombudsman who will act as the central point of contact.** Have him or her vet offers that seek information from your customers and site visitors before you send them out. Vest him or her with the authority to do something about privacy-related complaints that you receive.

**Watch your outsourcer like a hawk.** If you've hired an outsourcer to handle your e-mail or telephone marketing, bathe them in your corporate ethic that customers' privacy must be respected. Keep them up to date on policy changes and initiatives you make in this area. Have all your outsourcer's employees read your site's privacy policy. Don't simply wash your hands of the problem, using the excuse that your outsourcer has experience in your industry and you trust them. The privacy chain is only as strong as its weakest link. That could mean that new hire on the third shift at your outsourcer's call center in San Antonio.

This is only a very rudimentary list of rules of the emergent Internet Privacy Game. To learn more about this game, and submit new rules or comment on existing ones, visit hundredthwindow.net and help us evolve a brand new framework for building trust and confidence in our Internet commons.

# 9
# Private Lives, Public Networks: The Next 500 Years

*Trust no future, howe'er pleasant!*
*—Henry Wadsworth Longfellow*

At a major computer industry trade show just before the turn of the millennium, several companies debuted strange new mobile computing devices that, unlike current four-pound laptops and the even lighter hand-held digital organizers, are not designed to be carried around. They are, instead, worn like clothing. The producers of these new devices call them "wearable computers."

The first word out of the mouths of many at the trade show when coming upon these new devices was "cool." And yes, there is a certain "coolness" to them. They are still a bit clunky—most resemble either a photojournalist's vest or a huge money belt—but they soon may be just the thing for young, upwardly mobile digerati. A decade or so from now, one can picture a fashion show streaming over MTV.com in which, to the backbeat of thumping techno music, a procession of tall, sleek models prance around a

Paris runway wearing bright, colorful "smart" clothing that actually collects, stores, and transmits data.

The allure of wearable computers is not their ability to solve complex math problems. Designed as wireless transmitting devices as well as computers, they offer the ultimate in full-time, hands-free digital connectivity, and a way to stay jacked into the Internet grid without ever using a plug. (One early product, in an attempt to capture the right superhero spin, is called NetmaN.) You can check e-mail, or even voice mail, while literally on the run. But these are rather mundane uses compared to the wearable PC application that caused the biggest buzz at the trade show: the life-cam.

The wearable PC not only transmits data, it collects it. It collects it the old-fashioned way—with cameras and microphones. Only now with a wearable PC, you can record virtually your entire life, as these miniature digital devices capture and record the world as it passes by, sending it all to the wearable PC for temporary storage, before finally archiving it in some permanent storage media.

Simon & Garfunkel may have prophesied such wearable digital devices in their song *America*, when a couple taking a long bus trip together considers a sinister-looking fellow passenger. "She said the man in the gabardine suit was a spy / I said, Be careful, his bow-tie is really a camera." The thought of a bow-tie camera was a ridiculous notion just three decades ago. Soon they'll be in Wal-Mart. Come to think of it, maybe that gabardine suit was also a computer, programmed to make a complete record of the images and sounds of someone else's life.

The point here is that as wearable computers—and dozens of other sophisticated, lightweight, wireless digital devices—become commonplace, they will have the ability to create a data trail of our lives and experiences that goes well beyond anything we could have imagined even ten years ago. A trail that can, very easily, end up on a public network—the Internet, or some new system to come.

In a way, people in the not too distant future will have the very real option of turning their entire lives into a movie. Which is fine, if that's what they want to do. But what happens when Rebecca enters Jared's movie by virtue of simply having coffee in the same café? What if Tom's baseball-cap PC with the cool fish-eye cam built into the cap logo captures all the conversation at a private business meeting—and Tom later uses it to embarrass the other party after they have a falling-out? What if satellite cams from space can be accessed over the Net to follow a single car around town, or monitor a backyard swimming pool?

Today, as we noted in Chapter 2, there is considerable public debate about the fact that thousands of webcams routinely capture and send out over the Web images of unsuspecting people. Even with a modest level of Internet connectivity, images from these webcams are refreshed every thirty seconds or so. On a high-bandwidth connection, and using the latest video streaming, even today these webcams can provide a picture every bit as fluid and continuous as what we see on TV, only smaller—but that will change as well.

Wearable computers, tiny spy cams, and sky cams multiply this privacy issue a thousand times. If the wearable PC takes off, we won't have to be near a webcam, or drive past one, to become part of someone's movie. Everyone will become a walking webcam, and records of you and your life will be everywhere. Sky cams pose a similar problem.

At the time of this book's writing, there are many research projects under way to develop powerful facial-recognition software that will, much like the document-finding functions on word processing programs today, be able to find images in a file that "map" to the exact digital parameters of the images you load into a search field. A private investigator with an innocent-looking wearable computer could station herself in and around a singles bar and record an evening of banter. Then she'd be able to download the file of the night's snooping, post the file on the Net, and allow visitors to her website to supply photos of mates and search for images of an unfaithful partner.

Such records, as we know, will have to be stored somewhere. And where there is storage designed for electronic access, some bits almost always end up somewhere they shouldn't. When we are talking about storing the data of everyday life in audio-visual form, and when data is available over networks and interpretable through neural nets that simulate all the deductive power of the human brain and much more, the digital defenses will have to be raised much higher if privacy protection is to have any meaning.

However invasive a world with millions of people walking around wearing clothes that suck up the data around them may be, even these only capture images of us that are external. Networked information technology, at least, cannot get inside us.

Or can it?

By the end of 2001, the Human Genome Project will have concluded its primary task of mapping the location, characteristics, function, and hereditary indicators of the more than 100,000 genes in our bodies. Genome enthusiasts point to a happy time some years after the mapping is complete, when we'll be able to identify, very early in life, our predestined physical and perhaps even psychological fates. Then, they say, we'll be able to seek corrective therapies for everything from multiple sclerosis to chronic depression. It will be a matter of altering the faulty gene so that its message—whether it be predicting death by liver cancer or a life with a toupee—never gets delivered.

It is hard to imagine any information more personal, or more private, than a map that outlines our genetic makeup. For genes are not *about* us. They *are* us. And not just us, but our offspring as well. A single privacy loss involving your genetic information could have consequences for your grandchildren!

The privacy debate over genome research has been raging for well over a decade. Let's drop in on one of many contentious exchanges and explore what it might mean for the future.

In 1996 a brilliant molecular geneticist named Dennis Drayna was on a roll. The National Institutes of Health (NIH) researcher had just discovered the gene that indicates a tendency for its carriers to develop a disease called hemochromatosis. With this malady, the body absorbs too much iron, leading to an imbalance that can eventually damage the vital organs—and increase the risk of liver cancer, diabetes, heart disease, and many other often fatal illnesses. The standard treatment, bloodletting, doesn't sound pretty, and it isn't. But it does greatly reduce the risk of serious disease, of death.

In a debate at the NIH that fall, Drayna—also on the scientific board of Mercator Genetics—argued for widespread genetic testing for hemochromatosis. Some in the audience took note that Mercator had recently filed a patent application for ownership of the hemochromatosis gene—and stood to make millions of dollars should the U.S. government encourage hemochromatosis screening. "I'm going to play the capitalist here and say if there was ever a case for genetic screening, this is it," Drayna said. He recommended that the entire population of the United States be tested, and whenever the faulty gene was found, those at risk could be bled twice a week to start, then twice a year as a follow-up.

In the magazine *Lingua Franca*, Arthur Allen described the audience's reaction to Drayna's suggestion: "Immediately, his presumptions are questioned: What about the loss of health insurance if you test positive for hemochromatosis? Will HMOs pay to draw blood from a healthy person?" One senior scientist on the genome project implied that Drayna and his colleagues had gotten carried away "with the elegance of their science and the desire to recoup their research costs." To this Drayna repeated the potentially dire consequences that lie ahead for people who carry the hemochromatosis gene.

Drayna was talking only about genetic screening for a disease, not how the hemochromatosis gene might somehow be repaired or even removed. Yet even this small first step raised the hackles of many in the audience that day—and not just because of Drayna's potential conflict of interest. Calls for mass genetic screenings of major segments of the population raise the specter of genetic engineering—an invasion of privacy that strikes most of us right to the core.

Someday in the distant future, well after the genome project is complete and all of its secondary implementation issues are resolved, it is very likely that detailed genetic information about virtually every human on earth will exist in digital form. Unfettered, it will reside in digital networks, all connected to each other via some vast new public grid. Biometric entry devices, most likely those requiring a handprint to gain entry, will guard the data portals—but only if we want them to. Many of the same economic trade-offs involving the exchange of data that we find ourselves pondering today will still exist in the future—as will, we certainly hope, individual preferences. Perhaps huge bounties will be offered for providing your genetic map—and why not? It would have to be much more valuable than any digital profile that can be created today. Maybe the less fortunate in society will offer up their genetic data for money, in much the same way some homeless donate blood today.

Even within the next decade, e-commerce websites will pop up offering a most personal service: working with commercial, genome-mapping labs to build your unique genetic map, and then delivering it to you via the Internet. Along, perhaps, with considerable information about what these genetic tea leaves have to say about your future well-being.

This is no science fiction scenario. The entire human genetic map can be stored in about one gigabyte of hard drive space. Even now, that's only a fraction of the room available on most PC hard drives, and soon network transmission rates will be fast enough and compression algorithms strong enough so that personal genetic maps could be sent over high-bandwidth networks as easily as we now download software, taking the flow of PII to a whole new threshold.

The mushrooming storage capacity of computing devices and the accelerating rates of data transmission portend a world where most of us walk around with at least some elements of our genome map encoded in smart cards and stored in a file on an all-purpose, hand-held digital device (Palm XXXV, perhaps?). Maybe we won't be carrying our entire genome map around with us anytime soon, but certain small files that indicate a vulnerability to a specific disease would provide valuable information to doctors in an emergency room. Or even to the pharmacist during a routine visit, as prescription drugs become highly tailored, according to one's DNA profile.

What happens to this most personal of information if it is intercepted while being transmitted, or if we misplace our smart cards? Will a cottage industry arise in which hackers and thieves sense potential profit in acquiring such information and then selling it to unwitting insurers or infomediaries? What about the jilted boyfriend who, recalling an earlier conversation with his ex in which she confided a genetic fault, conspires to have that information published on a network?

Will gray or black markets for this kind of information emerge — say, with insurance companies secretly paying large sums to discover just who has which cancer gene? Will employers — mirroring the logic of pre-employment health screenings today — insist on seeing your genome as a precondition of hiring?

Untoward consequences aside, the Human Genome Project raises privacy issues of an entirely new kind, even if we ourselves are the only ones receiving the information. Will it be considered an invasion of privacy in the future if someone tells us things about ourselves, even if we do not want to know?

Clearly, there will be medical benefits in gene testing. At the same time, the health of the body will have to act in concert with the health of the spirit. The balance is in play for us even now, but the stakes will become much higher. What will be the vulnerabilities of knowing what our genes or our fates have in store for us, or for ones we care about? If someone could tell you today that you'd likely develop a fatal condition in such and such a year, would you want to know? Would you want others to know?

Medical ethicist Thomas E. Colonna, Ph.D., has framed the issue succinctly and well: "The right to maintain meaningful control over what information is divulged, to whom and for what purpose is critical to one's self-conception. To be a person means, at a minimum, that one has control over the information that defines him or her. An individual must retain a kind of ownership of such inherently personal information, and thus must maintain a measure of decision-making power over its dissemination, especially when such information could be used to discriminate and to stigmatize."

Today, we are profiled according to our social standing (upper middle class), where we live (upwardly mobile Sunbelt suburb), outward physical characteristics (5'10", 180 pounds), age (46), political affiliation (Independent), and ethnicity (7/8 Caucasian, 1/8 Native American), to name a few of the common categories. In the future, our genome will define us, and perhaps add literally thousands of new characteristics about us that can be captured, managed, and actively used by others.

Wearable computers and genetic records are merely two of many new frontiers where a right balance between privacy concerns and information technology benefits has yet to emerge. One MIT project, for example, is experimenting with nanocomputing in ways that could lead to tiny, bubble-like computers being injected into the human bloodstream in order to enhance nervous system functioning—including, notably, the functioning of the human brain. When the day comes when nanocomputing injections become commonplace, will we want the world to know that our brain is no longer entirely our own?

Most prophecies that extend far into the future amount to little more than wild guesses or leaps of fantasy, but we will hazard one prediction in which we have complete faith: far, far into this new millennium, the debate about information technology and personal privacy will still be raging.

# Appendix A

# Playing It Safe on the Web: Consumer Dos and Don'ts

Good company-to-customer relationships are built on trust. More and more companies are addressing users' concern about privacy by developing clear internal privacy policies and by posting privacy statements about these policies on their websites. The better companies also get your consent before collecting or sharing personal information. In the end, however, you are the single most powerful protector of your privacy online. It's your voice and your choice that will make the difference.

There are plenty of commonsense rules and take-charge tips for safeguarding your privacy online; TRUSTe has compiled some of the most basic ones (grouped by subject) to help you along. These guidelines are presented below, and together constitute a good summary of solid privacy protection practices for the average Internet user.

## *Privacy Statements and Seal Programs*

Read the posted privacy statements of individual websites to find out what personal information they gather, how it is collected, and with whom it will be shared.

Look for third-party seals, such as the TRUSTe trustmarks. These seals indicate that the website has agreed to submit to third-party oversight and compliance review. In other words, an outside agency checks to make sure that the website actually adheres to its privacy statement. These seals usually link to the privacy statement and to the oversight agency's website.

If you can't find a website's privacy policies, contact the site directly and ask for a copy of its privacy collection and dissemination practices.

## *Bulletin Boards/Chat Rooms*

Be aware that when you provide your name and/or messages to others online through a bulletin board or chat group, they'll probably be able to find out how to communicate with you—whether you want them to or not.

Ward off e-mail messages from strangers by not participating in online chats and bulletin boards. Or consider using a screen name that doesn't directly identify you.

## *Children*

Establish a clear set of online rules for your children. You can always modify or add to the rules as you and your children become more comfortable on the Internet.

Teach your children not to give out their names or other personal information online without your permission—just as they should not talk to strangers! Tell your children to get your permission before responding to online surveys or to games, clubs, or prizes that require personal information for eligibility.

As an added measure of protection, look into purchasing parental control software, which can assist you in supervising online activity when you can't be with your children.

There are software tools that block children from transmitting personal information online, give them Internet access to only those sites predetermined by you or only at certain times of the day, and provide you with a report of the places your children visit online.

Parental control software is inexpensive and easy to install on your computer.

Find out whether your Internet service provider has the technology to restrict children's access to specified sites and prevent online data transactions. A number of commercial online providers have this technology, and all you need to do is request that it be activated.

## Cookies

Check to see whether cookie files have been deposited on your computer. If you have a PC, look for a file on your hard drive labeled "cookies.txt" for Netscape browsers and the directory \windows\cookies for IE browsers; look for a file called "magic cookies" if you use a Macintosh. You can remove these files from your hard drive.

If you have a new version of browser software, you may be able to specify that you don't want to receive cookie files or that you wish to be notified when a website is about to deposit a cookie onto your hard drive. Look under the headings Preferences or Options in your software package for such choices, if available.

## Credit Reporting Agencies

Periodically request a copy of your credit report, which lists companies that have asked for credit information about you. Call Equifax at 1-800-

685-1111, Experian (formerly TRW) at 1-888-397-3742, or Trans Union at 1-800-888-4213. You may be charged a small fee.

Remove your name from credit reporting agency mailing lists to stop receiving unsolicited "pre-approved" credit card offers. Under a new law, the three national credit reporting agencies provide a toll-free number for you to call to be removed from their mailing lists: For Equifax, 1-888-567-8688; Experian, 1-800-353-0809; Trans Union, 1-800-680-7293.

## Credit Cards

Ask your Internet service provider how it protects its database of customer credit card numbers, especially if you have monthly charges billed to your card. Shop around if you don't get a straight or satisfactory answer.

Don't send your credit card number or other sensitive, personal data by e-mail unless you're assured that the data is encrypted with the latest software technology. Encryption technology scrambles the information you send online.

Contact the software company to verify whether or not the website actually uses the encryption technology. If in doubt, request an alternate payment method for your online transaction.

Don't believe websites that tell you that your credit card number, or other personally sensitive data, doesn't have to be encrypted.

## Direct Marketing

Scale back on grocery purchases with a credit card or savings club card. Once scanned, marketers know your buying habits and may target you for solicitations.

Remove your name from national mailing and telemarketing lists with the help of the Direct Marketing Association (www.the-dma.org). The site's consumer section tells you how to delete your name and provides downloadable forms.

## *Identity Theft*

Don't list your full name in the telephone book or get an unlisted number. Avoid putting your address and driver's license number on personal checks, if possible. Keep your mother's maiden name private, as it's often used by companies to verify your identity.

Shred financial, medical, and other personal, important documents before discarding them.

Request security codes (a password or number) for your telephone and bank accounts. A prospective thief would have to repeat the code to gain access.

Be especially cautious about giving out your social security number. Employers, banks, and other businesses that are required to report your income to the IRS have legitimate need for your social security number. Very few other businesses do.

If you suspect that someone is using your identity fraudulently, alert all your creditors, contact the fraud division of the three major credit reporting bureaus (see "Credit Reporting Agencies," above), and report all incidents to your local law enforcement agency. Get a copy of your police report and keep the number of your fraud investigator handy. Credit card companies and banks may require you to verify the crime with a police report.

If you believe that your social security number has been misused, report it to the Social Security Administration (look in the white pages of your telephone directory for an area listing) as well as your local law enforcement agency.

## *Junk E-Mail (Spam)*

Help stave off potential spammers by using an online identity that is different from your e-mail address, when possible.

No matter how tempting, don't reply directly to spammers, even to their invitations that you be removed from their e-mail lists. Your reply will, unfortunately, just serve to inform them that they've "got a live one."

Look into technological tools that help you weed out junk e-mail. Most e-mail packages and online services offer filtering programs that scan through your e-mail to receive messages only from users you've specified, or to weed out specific people or services that you've identified as offenders.

Speak up! Most large Internet service providers have set up internal mechanisms to prevent people from spamming from their domains. Therefore, it's likely that if you recognize the domain, the spammer is using a forged header. Report the spammer to that Internet service provider by forwarding spam to customer support so they can investigate.

## *Opt-Out*

Find out whether a website that requests information from you has an "opt-out" policy, which will allow you to prevent your personal information from being shared with others or used for promotional purposes.

Look for the site's posted online privacy statement for its procedures on opting-out.

Instruct the three national credit reporting agencies (Equifax, Experian, and Trans Union) to refrain from sharing your personal information with others or using it for promotional purposes. The Federal Trade Commission's website (www.FTC.gov/privacy/protect.htm) has a sample opt-out letter you can use to put your request in writing.

## *Passwords*

Don't create a password that's similar to your real name, commonly used nickname, or online screen name.

Guard your online password vigilantly. Never give it to anyone who asks for it, even to someone who says they're calling on behalf of your Internet service provider. Change your password often by contacting your Internet service provider.

Don't store your password near your computer or in your desk.

# Appendix B

# Online Privacy Incidents

GeoTrust, an Internet trust and authentication service provider, has been tracking online privacy issues and incidents since 1998. Below are just a few of the incidents recorded by GeoTrust researchers during a four-month period in 1999. For an update on more recent incidents, go to *www.geotrust.com*

### Is the Internet Driving You Crazy?
7/7/99

You think *you* have privacy concerns. The Net can be scary for anyone who's never used it, but for patients suffering from paranoid delusional psychosis, it can be an extreme torment. The June issue of the *Southern Medical Journal* featured two case studies of patients at the University of South Florida College of Medicine in Tampa who felt so vulnerable to the Internet that it substantially contributed to their paranoid delusions. A forty-year-old man shot himself in the face in a suicide attempt because he thought his friends had placed images on the Internet of him masturbating and having sex with his girlfriend. He was also under the delusion that the CIA could read his mind and control his thoughts because they had placed "Internet bugs" in his ears. With the help of medication, the patient's psychosis is now under control. With ever-increasing media coverage of the Internet and the growth of the medium in more sectors of our lives, researchers believe that more patients who are vulnerable to psychosis will incorporate the Internet into their delusions.

For more information: *http://www.wired.com/news/print_version/ email/ explode-infobeat/technology/story/20591.html?wnpg=all*

### Third Voice Rips Holes in Web
7/9/99

A Web software program known as Third Voice was found in 1999 to have the unintended ability to violate personal privacy of computer users as well as the capability of generate bogus Web pages. This came to light when software programmers in the United States and Europe detected security holes in the program that, when utilized by mischievous parties with the right knowledge, could transform Third Voice into a cracking tool.

Its inventors never intended for that to happen.

On its own merits, used as its authors planned, Third Voice is a plug-in program that works with a Web browser such as Microsoft Internet Explorer or Netscape Navigator. When you're running it, you can make comments on a Web page — similar to the sticky notes you put on your office bulletin board. Other people visiting the site can use their Third Voice software to read what you've written.

Software programmer Jeremy Bowers suspected something was wrong, however. Bowers found out that a vulnerability in Third Voice made it possible for users not only to post their own comments to websites, but to sneak in some potentially privacy-violating programming code. When other Third Voice owners read the site tagged with this code, many real and potential privacy problems were spawned. Bowers said his research showed that bogus versions of a Web page could appear to Third Voice users. Someone running Third Voice and reading and clicking on the commentary on this fake page could transmit his or her ID and passwords unknowingly to a bogus site, though no such incidents have been reported.

Preliminary attempts to fix the problem were found to be lacking by Internet security experts from the Mediterranean island nation of Malta. The group, who go by the name Netfishers, demonstrated that the revised version of Third Voice could be adjusted from benevolent to malevolent by the simple insertion of some JavaScript code. They tested their experiment by placing JavaScripts into selected Third Voice sticky notes. Then, when users entered their site IDs and passwords, the scripts successfully dug out passwords from site submission forms, collected this information, and e-mailed it back to the Netfishers. Acting on the information uncovered by Netfishers, Third Voice instituted new security measures intended to block JavaScript from accessing the system.

"The Web is not exactly foolproof, and people will be tempted to break in. People tend to find ways to break into Third Voice software. We will work to fix them," a company official said.

For more information: *http://www.wired.com/news/print_version/email/ explodeinfobeat/technology/story/20636.html?wnpg=all*

More info: *The Web's New Graffiti?* For more information: *http:// www. wired.com/news/print_ version/technology/story/20101.html?wnpg=all*

### Giving Voice to Net Security
6/29/99

In July 1999, the Home Shopping Network became able to use voice-recognition technology to automatically identify individual customers when they called in. This was possible via "speech-print" service from Nuance Communications.

The capability was integrated into the product order function. The voiceprint system requests a contact phone number from each caller. After you provide this info, you're then transferred to a human order-taker to complete the purchase. This technology is not entirely new. Similar voice-recognition systems are in use in prisons, for security purposes.

The voiceprint technology will allow the company to identify and collect data on individual members in a household, Bill Meisel, editor and publisher of the monthly newsletter *Speech Recognition Update*, told Wired.com. However, for outside parties to penetrate the system and build a record that matches your voice with your phone number, they'd have to crack into it, a feat that would be extremely difficult, Meisel implied.

For more information: *http://www.wired.com/news/print_version/email/ explode-infobeat/technology/story/20460.html?wnpg=all*

### Groups Keep Heat on Doubleclick
6/29/99

A proposed merger of a marketing firm and an advertising firm in 1999 was opposed by a coalition of consumer privacy groups. The union they objected to would have combined marketing company Abacus Direct and Internet advertising firm DoubleClick. The privacy groups urged Abacus Direct shareholders to vote against the merger because the combination of the two companies' databases, if used inappropriately, had privacy-violating potential.

The advocates, who included Junkbusters president Jason Catlett and directors of the Electronic Privacy Information Center and Privacy International, warned that Abacus's profiles, which use PII, would permit Web companies to know exactly who has visited their sites. Catlett and other privacy advocates lobbied the Federal Trade Commission to take a close look at the merger.

For more information: *http://www.wired.com/news/print_version/email/ explodeinfobeat/politics/story/20485.html?wnpg=all*

## *Beyond Concern: Understanding Online Users' Attitudes About Online Privacy*
4/14/99

*FamilyPC* magazine and Digital Research Inc.'s Family Panel surveyed 381 Internet users in 1999 about their privacy concerns. Here are some of the canvass' key findings:

- Internet users are more likely to provide information when they are not identified.
- Some types of data are more sensitive than others.
- Many factors are important in decisions about information disclosure.
- Acceptance of the use of persistent identifiers varies according to their purpose.
- Internet users dislike automatic data transfer.
- Internet users dislike unsolicited communications.
- A joint program of privacy policies and privacy seals seemingly provides a comparable level of user confidence as that provided by privacy laws.

You can read a copy of the full report by going to this Web page: *http://www.research.att.com/library/trs/TRs/99/ 99.4/99.4.3/report.htm.*

## *G-Men Subdue "Privacy Gone Crazy"*
7/2/99

Privacy supporters and law enforcement groups both have sincere and well-intentioned goals, but they often find themselves at odds with each other. This happened in June, 1999 when law enforcement advocates successfully derailed a bank privacy proposal that was up before the U.S. Congress.

The issue was a plan to protect the confidentiality of bank records. Several congresspeople noted the opposition of the FBI, the Treasury Department, and the Justice Department, which had indicated it would hogtie their ability to investigate drug smugglers and organized crime. Employing these arguments, several elected representatives termed the plan "privacy gone crazy." The package that included these privacy guarantees was defeated 299-129 and thus was not included in legislation to modernize the banking system.

For more information: *http://www.wired.com/news/print_version/email/ explodeinfobeat/politics/story/20554.html?wnpg=all*

### Study: Online Anonymity Critical
6/29/99

The American Association for the Advancement of Science (AAAS) believes that if the Internet is to thrive as a commercial and communications environment, the right for Internet users to remain anonymous must be protected and preserved. The body made these points in a paper based on a two-year National Science Foundation–funded study entitled "Anonymous Communication Policies for the Internet."

While admitting that anonymity can give cover to Internet users who commit crimes and take part in other objectionable activities such as online fraud and child porn, the study said the best way to handle these anomalies is for online communities to set their own policies with regard to anonymity, and to keep Internet users informed of the extent to which their identity is disclosed online.

For more information: *http://www.wired.com/news/print_version/email/ explodeinfobeat/politics/story/20480.html?wnpg=all*

Link to AAAS Study: *http://www.aaas.org/spp/anon/*

### Your Private E-Mail on Parade?
6/29/99

A security and privacy bug that dated back to 1998 may have exposed more than 10,000 users of Web-based e-mail services MailStart and Mail-Start Plus to code-crackers more than a year later.

236

The programs let you use a Web browser on almost any machine to go to the MailStart and MailStart Plus websites to read and send personal or business e-mail. Yet until the breach was detected and removed, the site was vulnerable to the "::$DATA" bug. That flaw granted unauthorized, as well as permissible, access to the source code used in Microsoft's Active Server Page (ASP) protocol applications running on Microsoft's Internet information servers. A hacker could use this route to penetrate MailStart's database and read subscriber e-mail.

Fortunately, the problem was detected and fixed in the summer of 1999.

For more information: *http://www.wired.com/news/print_version/email/explodeinfobeat/technology/story/20481.html?wnpg=all*

### US Bancorp Pays $3 Million in Privacy Case Settlement
7/1/99

This story does not deal directly with the Internet but has far-reaching implications.

In the summer of 1999, Minneapolis-based US Bancorp, one of the fifteen largest banks in the United States, agreed to stop selling confidential customer information to telemarketers. The state of Minnesota contended that US Bancorp had been selling depositor names, social security numbers, occupational and marital status info, details about revolving account balances, credit limits, and homeowner info to Member Works Inc. of Stamford, Connecticut. Minnesota said this was a violation of various laws that require banks to publish privacy policies telling consumers how their personal information will be used, if the bank intends to supply this information to outside parties, and who will be given access to it. US Bancorp executives said that although they believed this was an industrywide practice, the complaint filed by the company's home state government would cause it to cease these third-party sales. US Bancorp agreed to pay various states and charities $3 million to settle claims.

For more information: *http://cbs.marketwatch.com/archive/19990701/news/current/consumer.htx?source=blq/yhoo&dist=yhoo*

*Appendix B*

### L0pht Releases AntiSniff
7/23/99

"Sniffers" are software programs often used by hackers to obtain unauthorized data from computer systems. To help neutralize this threat, several Boston-based security experts doing business as L0pht Heavy Industries released a product called AntiSniff, which checks computer networks for sniffer attacks.

AntiSniff guards networks by looking for "packet sniffing patterns" and "trails" a hacker might leave while on his motley rounds. The product is available at http://www.lopht.com/antisniff/.

For more information: *http://www.wired.com/news/print_version/technology/story/20913.html?wnpg=all*

### Reading the Privacy Fine Print
7/27/99

The Center for Democracy and Technology released a report in 1999 saying that fair privacy practices are the exception rather than the rule on e-commerce sites. The study, "Behind the Numbers: Privacy Practices on the Web" (http://www.cdt.org/privacy/990727privacy.pdf), determined that less than 10 percent of sites meet the minimum standards called for by the Federal Trade Commission and privacy-certification seal programs. It noted that since private-sector enforcement programs affect only a small percentage of websites, online privacy concerns remain only partially addressed.

The study's findings were presented before a U.S. Senate subcommittee considering the Online Privacy Protection Act of 1999, which was intended to compel websites to provide ways for consumers to obtain and monitor personal data collected about them, and to guarantee the security of that information.

For more information: *http://www.wired.com/news/news/email/explode infobeat/politics/story/20960.html*

### Report: Half of Net Users Mistrust Sites
8/17/99

If you mistrust online privacy policies on the websites you visit, you aren't alone. In fact, 64 percent of people surveyed in 1999 by New York–based electronic commerce analysis and consulting firm Jupiter Communications agreed with you. The survey was conducted not long after questionable privacy practices came to light on several leading websites.

Jupiter estimated that if not addressed, privacy issues could put a major dent into e-commerce—nearly half the projected $40 billion in e-commerce revenue projected for 2002 could be lost without more airtight privacy practices. The study added that largely because a majority of shopping, travel, and finance sites cited their own privacy policies rather than joining a third-party, privacy seal program, consumer trepidations are proving to be "more complex" and difficult to allay.

For more information: *http://www.news.com/News/Item/0,4,40597,00 .html?st.ne.bp..bphed*

### Who Will Regulate the Net?
8/24/99

Whenever Internet security and privacy advocates get together, the question of whether government oversight or industry self-regulation should be the primary force for electronic commerce safeguards is fiercely debated.

But the concept is wrong, according to a panel at the libertarian-oriented Progress & Freedom Foundation's Cyberspace and the American Dream VII conference, which took place in Aspen, Colorado, during the summer of 1999. Panelists said that regulatory and self-regulation approaches could be reconciled and coexist with some creative approaches and "artistic flair." Participants called on attendees to assess ways and formulate specific proposals to achieve this goal.

For more information: *http://www.wired.com/news/news/email/explode-infobeat/politics/story/21393.html*

### In Russia, Big Brother Isn't Watching, He's Reading—Online
8/29/99

"You've got mail . . . and I'm reading it." Without too much of a stretch, that could be a mantra of the FSB, Russia's security service and the main successor to the once-notorious KGB. A government directive lets the FSB tap into the traffic of most of Russia's Internet service providers to monitor e-mail and Internet usage.

Turned out, however, that not all Russian ISPs were pleased when the policy was implemented in the late 1990s. Bayard-Slavia Communications in the southern Russia city of Volgograd sued to have the privacy invasion blocked. "People should be able to use the Internet without fear that someone is watching them," said Nail Murzakhanov, 33, general director of Bayard-Slavia Communications.

The action, which was unresolved at the time this book was written, was widely seen as the first Internet privacy-rights fight ever in that former Communist nation.

For more information: *http://199.97.97.16/contWriter/cnd7/1999/ 08/ 29/cndin/3630-0395-pat_nytimes.html*

### Broken Windows
8/31/99

An online discussion post by a Microsoft manager in 1999 expressed his reservations that the Windows operating system had security vulnerabilities. Windows Script program manager Peter Torr started out his remarks by defending Microsoft's industrial-strength Windows NT operating system as less prone to break-ins than rival systems such as Linux or Unix. But what about Windows 98 or 95?

"If you're talking about Windows 9x, forget it," wrote Torr, using the "x" as the common shorthand for those two systems. "No one ever (seriously) claimed that it was secure." Not long after Torr's remarks, Microsoft posted a security patch on its website that it said fixed two Windows-related "security vulnerabilities" that could be used to "seize control" of a PC through a website visited by, or an e-mail sent to, an unsuspecting user.

240

For more information: *http://www.wired.com/news/news/email/explode-infobeat/technology/story/21524.html*

### New Web Scam Attacks ISPs
9/3/99

If you were a customer of California-based Internet service provider Value Net in 1999 and received a message signed by "Sheila Baker, Administrative Assistant," you may have been targeted with a type of scam that will only become more common.

The message read: "According to our records, your payment for your Internet access account is late. Perhaps you overlooked it? . . . It is very important that you contact us as soon as possible. To update your account information, please go to http://www.valuehelp.net."

It sounded helpful and well-intended, but Ms. Baker never worked there. Even worse, customers were asked to enter a credit card number to make this payment. This payment info would have gone to a bogus address not connected with Value Net. Value Net president Tom Fawcett told the media at least one of the customers who visited the site entered a credit card number. After Value Net told him something was fishy and asked him to check his records, the customer discovered a substantial unauthorized charge on his account.

The moral of this story: when doing business on the Internet, make sure you make payment only to legitimate companies, or to their authorized agents.

For more information: *http://www.wired.com/news/news/email/explode-infobeat/technology/story/21572.html*

### Seattle Weekly *Writer Turns Tables on Amazon*
9/6/99

As we've already noted, Amazon.com came under fire in 1999 for publishing best-seller lists of CDs and books, broken down by sales patterns at corporations and other institutions. That didn't sound right to *Seattle Weekly* writer Mark D. Fefer, whose publication is based in the online retailer's home city. Driven more, he says, by a sense of "fun" than hard-boiled investigatory zeal, Fefer decided to turn the tables by asking his paper's webmaster to use website "log analysis" tools to find out which pages on the *Seattle Weekly* website were most frequently visited by people accessing it from an Amazon.com e-mail address (i.e., Amazon.com employees logging on from work).

Much to his amusement, Fefer found that high on the hit parade were page requests for an archived *Seattle Weekly* article entitled "How I 'Escaped' from Amazon.cult"—a former employee's critical account of his short and presumably unfulfilling career as a customer service representative. Other popular requests were for the *Seattle Weekly*'s online help-wanted section, as well as horoscopes and restaurant reviews. Fefer was quoted in the *New York Times* as saying that his point "was to have Amazon 'find out a little bit of what it feels like' to face such scrutiny."

For more information: *http://www.nytimes.com/library/tech/99/09/biz tech/articles/06data.html*

### "I Promise to Violate Your Privacy . . ."
9/3/99

A year before the U.S. presidential election is the time when the greatest number of candidates are in the race for their party's nomination. It's late enough for most serious candidates to have announced their intent, but too early for them to assess their chances as slim and to withdraw as a result.

That's why eleven major candidates were still in the field as of late summer 1999. This presidential cycle was one in which the Web was a key campaign tool. Information is gold in politics, which is why many presidential candidate sites have asked for increasingly detailed personally identifiable information from supporters, including e-mail addresses, phone numbers, postal addresses, and credit card numbers.

What's being done with this information? A September 1999 study by the Center for Democracy and Technology (CDT) said that six of the eleven major presidential candidates in the field at the time did not have clearly posted privacy policies on their official campaign website. Part of the CDT's concern is related to a federal law that requires that the name, address, employer, occupation, credit card number, and contribution amount of contributors who donate more than $200, be forwarded to the Federal Election Commission. The FEC is then supposed to make this information publicly available.

Of the eleven candidates, the CDT gave Vice President Al Gore and Arizona Senator John McCain A's for disclosing their privacy policies on their home pages. Only Gore, McCain, Senator Orrin Hatch, Bill Bradley, and Steve Forbes posted their policies at all. Ari Schwartz, a policy analyst for the CDT, said that he hoped candidates would realize that privacy is the "number one concern" of Internet users. He added that office-seekers should "become engaged in the issue" and ensure that their campaigns post privacy practices on their websites and enforce them with teeth.

For more information: *http://www.wired.com/news/news/email/explode-infobeat/politics/story/21574.html*

### *Feds OK Cell Phone Tracking*
9/16/99

Late in 1999, the Federal Communications Commission passed a ruling allowing mobile phone companies to distribute handsets embedded with global positioning satellite (GPS) technology that can pinpoint the exact location from which a phone call is made. FCC representatives said the location-mapping technology will speed help to people who call 911 from their cell phones, since callers may be unaware of their exact location or unable to specify it. Manufacturers also said the technology could help provide directions to lost delivery people and other motorists.

As beneficial as cell phone–based GPS tracking may be, though, privacy advocates say the plusses need to be weighed against the risks of being able to track users without their knowledge or consent.

For more information: *http://www.wired.com/news/news/email/explode-infobeat/business/story/21781.html*

### *Russian Hackers May Have Stolen Pentagon Secrets*
9/14/99

*Newsweek* reported in September 1999 that Russian hackers breached U.S. government computers and may have obtained naval codes and classified data on missile-guided systems. Defense and Energy Department systems were targeted, as were computer networks belonging to military contractor companies and universities with defense-oriented research grants. The problems were so serious that for the first time ever, the Pentagon told all its employees to change their computer passwords. "We're in the middle of a cyber war," U.S. Deputy Defense Secretary John Hamre told *Newsweek*.

For more information: *http://www.straitstimes.asia1.com/cyb/cyb4_0914.html*

### *We Know What You Did Last Fall*
9/21/99

WinWhatWhere is a software utility that can track patterns of Web page usage and related computer activity on individual and networked computers. It does so by recording the time, date, and time spent by each user on each page or computer program. Originally, WinWhatWhere was made to help system administrators find and analyze software and network programs, but company founder and president Richard Eaton said the program was also being used by people who suspect their spouses are fooling around in Internet chat rooms.

Privacy advocates, however, have objected most strenuously to the tool's use by companies to monitor the computing patterns of otherwise trusted employees. Some noted a 1998 American Management Association survey, which found that 63 percent of employers electronically monitor their workers by reading e-mail, browsing computer files, and/or monitoring Internet use. Of those employers, 23 percent didn't notify employees they were being watched.

A 1999 bill passed by the California legislature would have put some curbs on the practice but was vetoed by Governor Gray Davis.

For more information: *http://www.wired.com/news/news/politics/story/21847.html*

### New Web Hazard: Page Jacking
9/22/99

The United States and Australia announced raids and a crackdown on people who routed Web users to porno sites instead of the sites they wanted to visit—and would not let them leave. The Federal Trade Commission in Washington characterized the scheme as the "page-jacking" of as many as 25 million of the roughly 1 billion pages on the World Wide Web. At a news conference, FTC officials said when Web users clicked on sites from search engines, they were switched instead to pornographic sites. Attempts to back up the Web browser or shut it down moved the users—including children on game sites—to yet other pornographic sites. The biggest financial impact was on Web merchants, who saw their livelihoods evaporate when their customers wound up at pornographic sites, the FTC said. The scheme was designed to drive traffic at the prono sites.

For more information: *http://www.wired.com/news/news/email/explode infobeat/business/story/21892.html*

# Notes

## Chapter 1: Invasion of the Data Snatchers

On collaborative filtering technology such as that used by Amazon .com, see the article "Augmenting Information Seeking on the World Wide Web Using Collaborative Filtering Techniques," by Don Turnbull, at http://donturn.fis.utoronto.ca/research/augmentis.html. More information about Caller ID is available on the Minnesota attorney general's site at http://www.ag.state.mn.us/home/consumer/utilities/callerid.html. Current information about privacy laws under consideration by the U.S. Congress can be obtained via a keyword search at http://thomas.loc.gov/ home/c106query.html. "Data Mining: What Is Data Mining" is an excellent article by UCLA faculty member Jason Frand at http://www.anderson.ucla.edu/faculty/jason.frand/teacher/technologies/palace/datamining.htm. More information about the Boston Consulting Group survey cited near the end of this chapter is at http://cis.gsu.edu/~rbaskerv/ cis8680/ Lessons/Privacy/tsld008.htm.

# Notes

## Chapter 2: The Hundredth Window

For a searchable database of U.S. Supreme Court decisions, including those about privacy, check Cornell University's Legal Information Institute Supreme Court database at http://supct.law.cornell.edu/supct/. DSL Reports has a Frequently Asked Questions (FAQ) list about the technology at http://dslreports.com/r3/dsl/faq/all. *Computerworld* magazine published a FAQ about the Melissa virus at http://www.computerworld.com/home/news.nsf/all/9903313melissafaq/. Excerpts from Intel Corp. chairman Andrew Grove's book *Only the Paranoid Survive* are posted on the Intel website at http://www.mmx.com/ intel/paranoid/. More information about and contact information for *Mirror Worlds* author David Gelernter (who is cited in this chapter) is at http://electriciti.com/authors/ gelernterdavid.html. An article about Intel's Processor Serial Number is posted on the Privacy Exchange website at http://www.privacyexchange.org/tsi/psn.html. *Net.Gain*, by John Hagel and Arthur Armstrong, was published by the Harvard Business School Press in 1997 (ISBN 0875847595).

## Chapter 3: Something Digital This Way Comes

A synopsis of George Orwell's *1984*, extensively cited at the beginning of this chapter, is on the K-1 website at http://www.k-1.com/Orwell/1984.htm. A similar treatise on Aldous Huxley's *Brave New World* is on a website named for the author and located at http://www.huxley.net/. The Intel Museum website has a definition of Moore's Law at http://www.intel.com/intel/museum/25anniv/hof/moore.htm. A detailed look at the privacy issues of public-key cryptography was written by University of Miami (Fla.) professor Michael Froomkin and can be found at http://www.law.miami.edu/~froomkin/articles/clipper.htm. The best general primer on cryptography is Bruce Schneier's standard text, *Applied Cryptography* (John Wiley & Sons, 1996). More data about the Santa Fe Institute's privacy-related research is on their website at http://www.santafe.edu/projects/-2adaptive-computation/AC.html.

## Chapter 4: Privacy and Net Culture:
## Sex, Spies, and Video-Scrape

The Voyeur Dorm website, referenced in this chapter, is at http://www.voyeurdorm.com. A collection of links to articles about ECHELON is maintained by Paul Wolf at http://home.icdc.com/~paulwolf/echelon.htm. The European Parliament's Science and Technological Options Assessment group's main Web page is http://www.europarl.eu.int/dg4/stoa/en/default.htm. The National Security Agency home page is http://www.nsa.gov:8080/. *The Transparent Society: Will Technology Force Us to Choose between Privacy and Freedom?* by David Brin (Addison-Wesley, 1998), offers good coverage of networked video surveillance issues, as well as a provocative argument generally in favor of increased transparency over privacy protection. Scholarly arguments in favor of strong privacy protection can be found in *Technology and Privacy: The New Landscape*, edited by Philip E. Agre and Marc Rotenberg, (MIT Press, 1997). Bruce Schneier and David Banisar provide a deep look at technology policy and some of the activities of the NSA and other government agencies in *The Electronic Privacy Papers: Documents on the Battle for Privacy in the Age of Surveillance* (John Wiley & Sons, 1997).

## Chapter 5: The Datanet Rules

The PortNet website has a basic explanation of databases and can be found at http://www.portnet.k12.ny.us/port2000/database.htm. The Graphic Communications Association maintains a collection of resources about XML (extensible markup language) at http://www.gca.org/whats_xml/default.htm. The Direct Marketing Association has instructions on how to be removed from phone and mailing lists; this information is linked from the left frame on the page http://www.the-dma.org/topframe/index5.html. *The Dynamic Society: Exploring the Sources of Global Change*, by Graeme Donald Snooks (Routledge, 1996), makes a broad historical case that technology and economics are the real drivers of social change (more than war, conquest, and politics).

## Chapter 6: From E-Commerce to Information Economies

Michael Dertouzos, director of the MIT Laboratory for Computer Sciences, provides an excellent view into the emerging world of what he calls the global information market in his book *What Will Be: How the New World of Information Will Change Our Lives* (HarperCollins, 1997). "Viral marketing" is discussed in an article by venture capitalists Steve Jurvetson and Tim Draper; it's posted on the Draper Fisher Jurvetson website at http://www.DraperVC.com/viralmarketing.html. *Permission Marketing*, by Seth Godin, was published by Simon & Schuster in 1999. The Online Privacy Alliance website is at http://www.privacyalliance.org/. The best, most detailed explanation of network effects can be found in *Information Rules: A Strategic Guide to the Network Economy* (Harvard Business School Press, 1999).

## Chapter 7: Who Can You Trust?

It's possible that some of the "Need Improvement" sites mentioned in this chapter have indeed improved their policies since this book was researched and written. Here's where you can find the privacy policies on these sites: *Penthouse* had no policy when this book was published; site is at http://www.penthouse.com; Amazon.com: http://www.amazon.com/exec/obidos/subst/misc/policy/privacy.html/; The Knot: http://www.theknot.com/privacy.html; US Bank: http://www.usbank.com/privacy.html; Autobytel: http://www.autobytel.com/contentframe/help/privacy.cfm?; Adobe Systems: http://www.adobe.com/misc/privacy.html; J.Crew: http://www.jcrew.com/1-800-851-3189/privacy.jhtml; VerticalOne: http://www.verticalone.com/ privacy.html. eBay: http://search.zdnet.com/cgi-bin/texis/zdhelp/zdhelp/ single

.html?Ueid=920074; United:http://news.cnet.com/new/0-1007-200-343254
.html?owv; The Center for Media Education has details about the Children's Online Privacy Protection Act at http://getnetwise.org. For enforcement information updates, check the Children's Issues section of the Federal Trade Commission website at http://www.ftc.gov/bcp/menu-children.htm.

## Chapter 8: The Privacy Game

The complete text of *An Inquiry into the Nature and Causes of the Wealth of Nations,* by Adam Smith (cited in this chapter), is posted at http://www.shef.ac.uk/uni/projects/gpp/Tapestry/society/aninqu1.html. Details about P3P (Platform for Privacy Preferences Project) are available at http://www.w3.org/P3P/. Various links to the writings of *The Theory of Games and Economic Behavior* coauthor John von Neumann are on Ralph C. Merkle's nanotechnology website at http://www.ubiq.com/nanotech/von Neumann.html. The Law of the Commons is explained on Babson College's website at http://faculty.babson.edu/hotchkiss/publaw.htm#VIII. Law of the/. Francis Fukuyama's books *Trust: The Social Virtues and the Creation of Prosperity* (Free Press, 1995) and *The Great Disruption: Human Nature and the Reconstitution of Social Order* (Free Press, 1999) provide scholarly insight into trust, community, and the trade-offs necessary to maintain a balance between individual and social values. John H. Holland's *Emergence: From Chaos to Order* (Addison-Wesley, 1998) is a highly engaging, imaginative look at emergent systems and their relation to ordinary games.

## Chapter 9: Private Lives, Public Networks: The Next 500 Years

Yahoo! maintains a collection of links to sites about wearable computers at http://dir.yahoo.com/Computers_and_Internet/Mobile_Computing/

251

*Notes*

Wearable_Computers. A thorough library of resources about the Human Genome Project is available on the Oak Ridge National Laboratory Internet site at http://www.ornl.gov/TechResources/Human_Genome/home.html. Virginia Postrel's *The Future and Its Enemies* (Free Press, 1998) makes a compelling and optimistic argument in support of ongoing, creative technological progress.

# Glossary

*Anonymizer* Service that allows you to send anonymous e-mail or browse the Web anonymously by going through its site.

*Anonymous E-mailer* Service that operates software that receives your incoming messages, replaces the headers that identify you (such as john-doe@hometownisp.com), and then sends the message along to its intended recipient.

*Antivirus Software* Programs that are intended to detect, cleanse, and erase harmful virus files that may have infected your computer.

*Automated Surveillance* With respect to telecommunications, technology that lets computers automatically search through millions of intercepted messages for ones containing preprogrammed keywords. Keywords could include certain politically or socially controversial phrases a government objects to.

*Bot* On the Internet, an automated software program that performs tasks at recognized intervals. In just one example, bots can be programmed to scour one hundred shopping sites every business day to look for bargain merchandise offered for sale on those sites.

*Browser* Software that enables you to view text and pictures in a document on the World Wide Web.

*Browser Cache* A memory file in your Web browser that stores the Internet addresses of sites you've recently visited. This capability enables your browser to "pull up" certain sites quicker.

*Caller ID* Technology that lets other people learn your phone number when you call them, and makes it possible for you to do the same. Opposed by some privacy advocates for lack of protective safeguards.

*Cell Phone Camera* A black-and-white pinhole camera built into a nonfunctioning cell phone.

*Cellular Spying* Spying accomplished with the assistance of cell phone microphones, tiny stealth devices that allow you to record conversations around you.

*Click Trail* A record of all the Web page addresses you have visited ("clicked on") during a specific online session. Click trails tell not just what website you've visited, but which pages inside that site.

*Collaborative Filtering* A means of predicting the interests and needs of a specific customer based on previously collected data from a larger group of customers. For example, if Amazon.com discovers that a significant percentage of people who bought Tom Clancy's latest book also purchased John Grisham's latest novel, they may conclude that you, who are about to buy the latest Clancy volume, might be interested in Grisham's newest work. A collaborative filtering system would then display a message or ad informing you about the new Grisham book.

***Compacks*** Highly personalized services that merchants can provide to you based on detailed information they obtain about you. Compacks (from *complex packages*) put you in an aisle or window seat on a flight you have reserved, send you e-mail bulletins when a company you hold stock in makes a major announcement, and not only provide you with information about your favorite music albums but in some cases even enable you to purchase and download your "favorite" new song that you've not heard yet. Unless the company or one of its vendors has your information stored in a database or network where it can be processed, compacks aren't possible.

***Cookie*** A block of data that a website arranges—with or without your consent—to store on your system. The data stored in a cookie could include your credit card number, your aircraft seating preference, or your password.

***Cryptography*** In Internet systems, the use of mathematic algorithms to "lock" and "unlock" files sent over the network, and to provide a secure basis of authentication and verification of people and data.

***Databank*** As used in privacy circles, a large center in which collections of personal and financial data about thousands or even millions of people are stored. Databanks are often composed of multiple databases.

***Database*** A storehouse of digital records that uses a basic query-and-serve architecture to make stored records easily accessible and highly flexible for cross-referencing, analysis, and automated retrieval.

***Data Mining*** The use of sophisticated relational database technology to deeply probe database records for unique patterns, trends, and behaviors of individual people. When data mining is conducted with PII, very detailed personal profiles can be developed.

**Datanet** The concept that the open, public Internet will begin to support database-style information retrieval, with the consequence that much privately stored information could be openly available on the Internet.

**Data Snatchers** A term (invented for this book) for all people and organizations that proactively make the capture of personally identifiable information a high priority. Typically, data snatchers use the Internet and modern information technologies as their primary data-capturing tools.

**Data-veillance** Technology for the real-time collection and monitoring of digital data about you. This can and will include vision technology; bugging and interception techniques; satellite tracking; through-clothing human scanning; automatic fingerprinting; human recognition systems that can recognize genes, odors, and retina patterns; and biometric systems.

**Digital Clearinghouse** A trusted third party that manages digital rights, digital certificates, credit card processing, and other services that facilitate online transactions. Clearinghouses typically provide nearly all their services on a real-time basis.

**Digital Wallet** Electronic commerce software that holds your payment information in encrypted form. A wallet can contain a digital certificate to identify the user as well as shipping information to speed transactions. Wallets enhance personal privacy to the extent they encrypt and protect PII and financial information on a local computer; they raise questions when such information is also stored centrally by the wallet vendor.

**Direct Marketing Association** Trade group formed to promote the business and public policy interests of mass mailers and companies that provide related services. Now has a Privacy Promise compliance guide for its members. It's posted on the DMA's website at http://www.thedma.org/pan7/pripro22.html.

***Direct Subscriber Line*** Technology that works on an existing phone line to provide a fast connection to the Internet. Because the connection is always active, no dial-up is necessary—eliminating the typical delays due to busy signals or time you expend going through the log-on process.

***Domain*** The unique name that identifies the Internet address of Website. Example: *http://www.simonandschuster.com/.*

***ECHELON*** A system designed by the National Security Agency that can detect, listen to, and transcribe the contents of phone calls or data transmissions deemed harmful to a government.

***Electronic Frontier Foundation*** An international organization dedicated to protecting the privacy and civil liberties of people who use the Internet and other public communications networks.

***Electronic Lifestyle Monitoring*** Practice of associating different data about your purchasing patterns to make assumptions. For example, someone who cashes in a lot of supermarket coupons for cigarettes could find his or her health insurance raised.

***Electronic Software Distribution*** Dissemination of software programs via Internet download rather than through purchase at a software or office-supply retailer.

***Electronic Wallet*** Software that conducts secure electronic transactions between you and a merchant. It does so by transferring encrypted authentication information so that the merchant's credit card processing software recognizes you as a valid user.

***E-Mail Spoofing*** Practice of sending an e-mail that has a forged sender address, to create mischief for a person or business.

**Encryption** The process of encoding transmitted data to deter unauthorized interception. One example would be the encryption of your credit card number as you make a purchase over the Internet.

**E-Revenge** Use of e-mail to spread computer viruses or the Internet to post malicious information to embarrass a company or person.

**E-ZPass** Automatic toll collection system that scans your license plate when you pass through a tollgate, and then debits the credit card you have on file with the highway agency.

**Face-Recognition Software** Programs that can identify a particular face in a large database of faces, or even in a video stream of people in a crowd. Such programs can be used for constructive purposes but also have the potential to invade privacy by allowing companies to pinpoint individuals and literally track their movements in public places.

**Federal Trade Commission** U.S. government agency charged with enforcing consumer protection and anti-trust laws by preventing, eliminating, and punishing businesses that commit acts or follow practices that are unfair or deceptive.

**Fiber-Optic Line** A very fast, high-bandwidth transmission method using laser light beams to carry digital information.

**File-Sharing Settings** Settings that regulate who has access to computer files stored on a database or computer network.

**Filters** In e-mail systems, programs or features of programs that can intercept or block incoming data you don't want to be transmitted or outgoing data you don't want to send.

**Finger** An Internet utility that can determine whether or not certain users are online at a given moment. For the program to work, an Internet service provider has to provide access to it.

**Firewall.** *See* Personal Firewall.

**Flames** Angry, accusatory e-mail, chat room language, or newsgroup postings, often about an individual, group, or company. Examples: "That car dealer is a crook," or "Nancy is a tramp."

**HTML** Hypertext Markup Language, the code used to "mark up" or create, documents on the World Wide Web. HTML is primarily a graphics display language.

**Hundredth Window** In the computer security field, a metaphor for the weakest link in a system. Origin is from a computing fable that points out that if ninety-nine windows are well locked and secure, the castle can still be vulnerable if the hundredth window is left wide open.

**Identity Theft** Con artist's use of purloined personal information to assume your identity, then loot your bank account, make costly purchases with your credit card number, or otherwise use your identity for malicious purposes.

**Infomediaries** Persons or organizations that specialize in personal information management for individual Internet users. The term was first coined in 1997 by *Net.Gain* authors John Hagel and Arthur G. Armstrong, who advocated that new intermediaries were needed on the web to handle PII from individuals in ways that would ensure the security and privacy of their data.

**Information Broker** Company or individual who will collect information about you for a fee, often paid by a business that would like to know a great deal more about you than you would likely want them to. Many will do this legally by searching public documents, but others will go over the line and obtain credit reports, phone bills, travel records, banking and other personal information under false pretenses. Though not a new profession, many information brokers are now moving their operations online, with enormous privacy implication.

**Internet Service Provider** A business that provides business or consumer access to the Internet, usually for a flat monthly fee.

**Interoperability** The ability of computing hardware and software components to work together relatively smoothly and automatically and to share resources with each other. For example, Microsoft Word can read spreadsheets created in Microsoft Excel. Similar examples exist in the office computing world, making information easily exchangeable across software and platforms with different functions.

**Lifestyle Tracking Systems** Software programs that can take personal data about you, such as your shopping habits, and then help build a database about your assumed lifestyle, health risks, etc.

**Linda Tripping** The undisclosed recording and distribution of supposedly private phone conversations. Takes name from government employee who taped personal conversations with presidential paramour Monica Lewinsky.

**Mail Controls** In this context, an America Online feature that, among other capabilities, lets you block e-mail from certain people or cyberspace addresses.

**Mailing List Management Software** Utility that can process, manage, and send e-mail to thousands of people at regular intervals and with one click. Used by legitimate businesses and spammers alike.

**Melissa Virus** A harmful software program that destroyed files in millions of computers in 1999, and is generally considered to be the most destructive computer virus in history.

**Member Profiles** A series of personal information nuggets some subscribers choose to list with America Online or other Internet service providers. For example, Jane Thomassen could list her name and her interest in sewing. Member profiles are often used by direct marketers and others to enhance and target spam campaigns and other online marketing programs.

**Moore's Law** Long-established shibboleth that maintains that computer-chip speed doubles every 18 months. Named after Gordon Moore, the cofounder of Intel Corp, this law is widely held to be one of the prime drivers of the information Age.

**Munge** Internet jargon for imperfectly transforming or inaccurately rewritting information. It traces its lineage to the phrase "Mash Unit! No Good," early computer tech talk in vogue during the 1950's at the Massachusetts Institute of Technology.

**Nanny Cams** Devices that can enable parents at home or at work to watch their children in daycare. This is usually done through a direct Internet connection or over a website.

**Netcams** Similar to nanny cams, with more general usage and wider distribution. An example would be a camera at a major intersection or shopping center entrance, set up to feed images to a local website every thirty seconds or so.

**Netizens** People who actively participate in the Internet as members of a new global community. Netizens are far more active, and more serious about using the Net, than surfers who merely check the baseball scores or the price of their stocks. They will chat, post to newsgroups, buy merchandise, take online polls, and occasionally undertake political action in support of basic rights and freedoms that have been a vital part of the Internet's growth and development.

*Neural Network (Neural Net)* Computer system modeled after the nerve cells in a brain and intended to simulate the way a brain learns, remembers, and thinks. Neural nets are not as efficient as normal digital computing systems, especially in terms of brute force, but they are much better at modeling real-world complexities and improving results through iterative processes.

*"No Call" Laws* Statutes passed in many states that allow consumers to ask their local phone company to enter a symbol next to their name in the phone directory that tells telemarketers not to contact them. Violators are often subject to steep fines.

*Parental Controls* Set of instructions in e-mail software or other programs that allows parents to deny access to websites or to incoming messages that contain certain words or images.

*Personal Firewall* Firewalls are computer security systems with software intended to block access by unauthorized users. Formerly used only in large computing networks, firewalls now come in personal desktop or laptop versions that can thwart attempted access to your computer by hackers and other unwanted intruders.

*PII (Personally Identifiable Information)* Any data in an electronic network that can be tied in some way to a flesh-and-blood human being; to someone with a name, an address, and a life; to you, for example.

*PIN (Personal Identification Number)* Sequence of digits you press, for example, on an automatic teller machine to gain access to your account. Some websites use PINs as well, either as a substitute for, or in tandem with, passwords to control access to information and services.

***Pretext Calls*** Practice used by information brokers and others who wish to obtain private information from banks and other large institutions that house reams of PII. Typically, the info broker calls using either a phony name or a trumped-up excuse for getting access to personal bank records, phone bills, credit information, etc. At this writing, pretext calls are not illegal, although legislation designed to curtail this practice has been proposed.

***Privacy*** The right to be left alone, live a life relatively free of unauthorized intrusion, and keep most personal information secret, unless you specifically approve otherwise.

***Privacy Enhancing Technologies (PETs)*** Software, tools, and related policies that work to safeguard your online privacy and security. An example would be software that encrypts your credit card number or private e-mail so that it won't be intercepted and will be readable only by the person or business you send it to.

***Processor Serial Number*** Technology introduced with the Intel Pentium III microprocessor that allowed third parties to identify an individual user by capturing a unique serial number embedded in his or her computer. Privacy advocates led a short-lived boycott of Intel products based on their concerns that this feature would lead to a universal index of personal identity that was machine readable. Processor Serial Number technology is still in Pentium III chips, but in the default, or normal, configuration, the feature is turned off and inaccessible to outsiders.

***Profiling*** The practice by marketers and other collectors of personal information of building consolidated data summaries of as much information about a particular person as possible. Profiling implies the collection and organization of data from multiple sources.

***Public-Key Cryptography (PKI)*** Dual key system of cryptography that requires both a public key and a private key to decode confidential information. PKI infrastructure systems play a vital role in-building highly-secure trust environments that are essential for the continued growth and development of e-commerce.

**Public Network** Group of communication devices at least in theory accessible to all. The phone system is the best example.

**Retina Scanners** Devices that can vouch for an individual's identity by matching retina scan information with profiles it has stored, including yours.

**Shotgun Microphone** Apparatus that can pick up sounds from a distance of up to fifty yards, sometimes even through walls. Consent to use these tools is seldom obtained. Therefore shotgun microphones are widely considered obtrusive and privacy-violating.

**Slamming** As used in privacy circles, this term refers to the unauthorized switching of your long-distance phone company without your express consent. This is sometimes done by a request from a long-distance provider to your local phone company—which is not supposed to comply without your authorization.

**Smart Card** Card that contains a computer chip—rather than just a magnetic stripe like most credit cards. Smart cards can be used in an almost unlimited variety of applications, such as paying mass transit fares, buying pay-per-view television services, and storing medical information about you that could, in an emergency, enable a hospital to gain access to your medical profile. Because the information smart cards are capable of storing can be very personal, the potential for privacy-violation abuse should the card fall into the wrong hands is very real.

**Sniffers** Tools used by computer experts to extract data from systems they are analyzing. Can be used by hackers to break network security systems. Also called "packet sniffers."

**Spam** Unsolicited e-mail message, usually offering questionable business advice, porn, or schemes. Spam is usually sent out to thousands of unwilling recipients at once. Much spam can be blocked by spam filters.

**Spam Filter** Program that detects and rejects spam by looking for certain keywords, phrases (such as "get rich"), or Internet addresses. These utilities work with various e-mail software applications.

**Spoofing** Faking an electronic mail address or a password on a system-access attempt to make a communication appear to be sent by an authorized user.

**Spy Cams** Cameras that, at regular intervals, feed visual information from a public or private area to a website. Spy cams capture images of people without their knowledge or consent.

**Storage** Device on a computer in which information can be housed. One example would be your PC's hard drive, but increasingly many devices will have their own storage capacity.

**TRUSTe** An independent, not for profit privacy organization whose mission is to build trust and confidence on the Internet. It offers a privacy seal or "trustmark" to websites that adhere to established privacy principles, such as to openly disclose what personally identifiable information about you is being gathered, with whom it will be shared, and whether you, as a user, have the option to control its distribution. Certified companies must agree to comply with TRUSTe's oversight and consumer complaint resolution process. Organizations certified by TRUSTe usually choose to display the trustmark on their websites.

**Trust Environment** Complete online environment of authentication, verification and trust (via public-key infrastructure).

*Universal Identifier* Set of numbers assigned to all or most individuals in a nation or community and then used to identify them in a broad range of settings. In the United States, the social security number most closely fits this definition.

*URL (Uniform Resource Locator)* Address for a website, or Web page on that site.

*User Filter* Most commonly, technology that allows websites to determine the Internet addresses of people that have visited specific pages on the site.

*Vehicle Recognition System* Technology that can identify the license plate on a car, then track the car around a city using a computerized geographic positioning system. Used by intelligence agencies for some time, it is now making its way into the private sector.

*Video-scraping* The process of searching the Internet for certain specific video images. Technology supporting video-scraping is still in its infancy.

*Voice Recognition Software* Programs that can help a computer recognize and execute spoken commands.

*Web Filtering Software* Software that prevents access to specific websites, for example, sites with content deemed unacceptable for children by their parents or the software vendor.

*XML (Extensible Markup Language)* System for defining different types of information—such as text, graphics, and footnotes—on a Web page, and rendering them interoperable among many different applications and devices. Its proponents note that it has wide applicability. A document needs only to be coded once in XML to be able to be read on a computer, shown within a cellular-phone display, translated into voice on a device for the blind, etc.

**ZAG Profile** Presumed information about you that is based on the demographics of your zip code plus your age and gender. This practice unfortunately makes it possible for companies to screen out certain less affluent, "more risky" demographic groups.

# Index

Aladdin Knowledge Systems, 17
Abacus Direct, 234
Access, 144
Accountability, 70
Adobe Systems, 250n
Advertisements, blocking, 126
Aliases, 16. See also Anonymity
Allen, Arthur, 217
Allen, Paul, 113
AltaVista, 41, 110, 164
Alt newsgroups, 182–83
Amazon.com, 5, 60, 109, 130, 250n
   criticism of, 242
   trustworthiness of, 167
*America* (song), 214
American Advertising Federation, 143–44
American Association for the Advance-
   ment of Science (AAAS), 236
American Civil Liberties Union
   (ACLU), 87
American Library Association 700+
   Great Sites for Kids, 175
American Management Association, 244
America Online (AOL), 17, 28–29, 143,
   153, 189

Mail Controls of, 52
Member Profile of, 79–80
trustworthiness of, 171–72
Anonymity, 101–2, 146–47, 236. See
   also Aliases
Anonymizer.com, 51
Anonymizers, 146
AntiSniff, 238
Antivirus software, 126–27
AOL. See America Online
AOL.com, 172
*Applied Cryptography* (Schneier), 248n
Archive of Hacked Web Sites, 78
Armstrong, Arthur, 47
Article Nuke Form, 79
AtGuard 3.1, 17
AT&T, 143, 194
Audit trails, 101
Autobytel, 167, 250n
Automated surveillance, 92
Automated teller machines (ATMs), 34,
   98

Back-up, 127
Banisar, David, 249n

# Index

Banking. See Online banking
Bank of America, 143
Bayard-Slavia Communications, 240
Bell Atlantic, 143
Berners-Lee, Tim, 200
Better Business Bureau Online, 48, 162
Bhatia, Sabeer, 132
*Billboard*, 189
Blocking software, 182. See also Filters
Bookmarks, 127
Boston Consulting Group, 16, 247n
Bowers, Jeremy, 232–33
Bradley, Bill, 243
*Brave New World* (Huxley), 56, 57–58, 248n
Bright Mail, 19
Brin, David, 66, 249n
Browsers. See Web browsers
Brute force attacks, 77
BugNet, 145–46
Bullet cameras, 95
Bulletin boards, 224

Cable modem systems, 28
Caller ID, 8, 247n
Carrey, Jim, 84
Carroll, Lewis, 21
Catlett, Jason, 234
Celebrities, 44–45
Cell phone camera, 95
Cell phone microphones, 96
Cell phones, 3–4, 34, 43, 243–44
Center for Democracy and Technology (CDT), 238, 242–43
Centraal, xx
CGIMail, 101–2
Chaos theory, 207
Chat rooms, 104, 224
Child Online Protection Act (COPA), 86–88, 173
Children
  age-appropriate monitoring for, 174–78
  blocking ads for, 126
  eBay and, 168–69
  e-mail and, 103
  GO Network and, 164–65
  Internet safety rules for, 102
  laws protecting, 86–88, 173–74, 251n
  online behavior contracts for, 100
  Parental Controls and, 52
  parental dos and don'ts, 224–25
  privacy of online journeys, 85
  trust and, 161, 172–78
Children's Online Privacy Protection Act (COPPA), 173–74, 251n
Children's Partnership Recommended Sites for Kids, 175
Clarity, 159–60
Clinton, Bill, 123
Clock radio cameras, 95
CNN.com, 109
Cockroach implants, 96
Collaborative filtering, 5, 247n
Colonna, Thomas E., 220
Compacks, 69
Compaq, 143
CompuServe, 172
Con artists, 157
Conference information, 7
ConSeal Private Desktop, 46
Consent, 144
Constitution, U.S., 22
Cookies, 42, 50, 148, 225
COPA. See Child Online Protection Act
COPPA. See Children's Online Privacy Protection Act
Corporate culture, 155
Corporate systems, 116
Coupling, 110
Credit cards, 2, 4, 9, 40, 47
  porn sites and, 87–88
  protecting, 226
  trust environments and, 74
Credit rating companies, 151–52, 226, 228
Credit reports, 179–80
Crime, 15
Critical Path, xx
Cryptography. See Encryption
Customer support con, 179
Customized health care, 69
Cyberangels' Cybermoms' List of Approved Sites, 175
Cyber-dating, 69–70
Cybersitter, 126

*Darwin among the Machines* (Dyson), 60
Databases, 13, 107–10, 119
DATA bug, 237
Data Encryption Standard (DES), 147
Data-mining, 108
Datanet, 107–27, 249–50n
  defined, 110
  economic trends and, 111–19
  increasing importance of, 119–22
  near-term dilemma and, 122–25
  new rules for, 117
Data-veillance, 91
Data Zone, 2–3
Davis, Gray, 245
Decentralization, 155
Deja.com, 79
Denmark, 45
Department of Motor Vehicles (DMV)
  sites, 167
Dertouzos, Michael, 250n
Digital certificates, 110
Digital City, 172
Digital faceprints. See Facial recognition
  capability
Digital handshake, 198–200
Digital metabolism, 35, 60, 63, 64, 71
Digital Research Inc., 235
Digital signatures, 76, 77
Direct marketing, 22, 48–49, 226–27
Direct Marketing Association, 48–49,
  144, 226, 249–50n
Direct subscriber lists (DSL), 27–28
Disclosure. See Full disclosure
Discount cards, 7–8
Disney, 162, 164, 188
Diva Futura, 86, 89
DoubleClick, 234
Drayna, Dennis, 216–18
Drew, Greg, 113
Drill-down, 155–56
Drivers' licenses, 9, 34, 227
Drucker, Peter, 67, 190, 191
*Dynamic Society, The* (Snooks), 250n
Dyson, Esther, 66
Dyson, George, 60, 61, 66

Eaton, Richard, 244–45
eBay, 60, 138, 168, 250n

ECHELON, 90–93, 249n
e-commerce, 114, 119, 129–37, 186–87,
  250n
  beyond, 136–37
  network effect and, 130–35, 136, 139
  privacy management and, 135–36
  shopping carts in, 145–46
Egghead Software, 62–63
800.com, 112–13
Eisner, Michael, 188
Electronic badges, 4, 7
Electronic Frontier Foundation, xx
Electronic Privacy Information Center,
  234
*Electronic Privacy Papers, The* (Schneier
  and Banisar), 249n
Electronic software distribution (ESD),
  62–63
Ellison, Larry, 93
e-mail, 5. See also Spam
  aliases for, 16
  anonymous address for work, 101–2
  attachments to, 127
  children and, 103
  come-on messages in, 148
  conference information on, 7
  deletion of, 146
  encryption of, 76–77
  filters for, 49
  forwarding of, 104–5
  legal liability and, 13
  monitoring of workplace, 41
  munging, 80
  name suppression on lists, 127
  private address for work, 148
  security bug in, 236–37
  trust environments and, 74
*Emergence: From Chaos to Order* (Holland), 208, 251n
Emergent systems, 207–8, 251n
Encryption, 226, 248n
  of bookmarks, 127
  of e-mail, 76–77
  of passwords, 147
  public-key, 73, 76–77
  subscription-based services for, 51
  technology of, 93–94
  upgrading equipment for, 49

# Index

ENIAC computers, 63
Enough Is Enough, 176
Equifax, 151, 180, 225–26, 228
Erasing entries, 17–18
e-redlining, 41
e-revenge, 43
eSafe Protect Desktop 2.1, 17
ESPN.com, 164, 165
E*Trade, 109, 112, 130
Eudora mail program, 146
European Union, 140
Excite.com, 121, 162
Expedia, 24
Experian, 151, 180, 226, 228
*Exposing the Global Surveillance System* (Hager), 90–91
Extropia, 102
Exxon, 61–62
E-ZPass toll booths, 3, 34

Fabs, 61
FaceIT, 98–99
Facial recognition capability, 35, 97–99
False identities, 68. See also Identity theft
*FamilyPC*, 235
Fan/flame sites, 44–45
Fawcett, Tom, 241
Fax machines, 132
Federal Communications Commission (FCC), 243–44
Federal Express, 116
Federal Trade Commission (FTC), 12, 45, 168–69, 171, 228, 245
Feedback.com, 102
Feedback forms, 101–2
Fefer, Mark D., 241–42
Fields, 107–8
File-sharing settings, 100–101
Filters, 19, 46–47, 49, 163, 178. See also Blocking software
Financial sites, 125–26
Finger, 77
Firewalls, 17, 27–28, 46
Flaming, 79
Florida, 147
Focus on the Family, 103
Forbes, Steve, 243

Ford, Henry, 129
Fox News Channel, 85, 188
France, 90
"Free" goods and services, 70
FreePC, 23–24, 115
Frequent user cards, 34
FTP (File Transfer Protocol), 182
Fukuyama, Francis, 251n
Full disclosure, xix–xxiii, 144, 153, 154
*Future and Its Enemies, The* (Postrel), 252n

Game theory, 203–5, 207
Gates, Bill, 5
Gelernter, David, 37, 248n
General Electric, 137
Genetic research, 216–20
GeoCities, 45, 100, 153, 168–69
Georgia, 147
Georgia Tech University, 38
GeoTrust, xx, 231
Germany, 45
GetNetWise, 174, 175–76
Gilder, George, 67
Global positioning satellite (GPS) technology, 243
Godin, Seth, 141, 250n
GO Network, 164–65
Gopher downloads, 182
Gore, Al, 188–89, 243
Government, 14–15, 24, 93–96
Graphic Communications Association, 249n
Gray Mail, 19
Great Britain. See United Kingdom
*Great Disruption, The* (Fukuyama), 251n
Grove, Andrew, 35, 248n
@Guard, 50

Hacking, 43, 78, 244
Hactivism, 43
Hagel, John, 47
Hager, Nicky, 90–91
Handles, 79
Handset interface, 96
Hardware identification number (HWID), 145, 169–70

Hatch, Orrin, 243
Health information, 8–9, 68
  customized care and, 69
  datanet and, 123–24
  identity reverse-engineering and, 44
  possible abuses of, 72
  technological solutions for dispersal of,
    72–74
Hemochromatosis, 217
Hewlett-Packard, 143
History files, 17–18
HIV-positive citizens, 72
Holland, John H., 208, 251n
*Hollywood Reporter, The*, 189
Home address, 18–19, 47–48
Home Shopping Network, 233–34
Hooks, 9–10
Hotmail, 72, 132–34, 135, 136, 142, 170
HTML, 110, 119
Human Genome Project, 216, 217, 219,
    252n
Hundredth-window problem, 26–30,
    186
Huxley, Aldous, 1, 56, 57–58, 59, 64, 65,
    76, 83, 248n

IBM, 12, 108–9, 162, 194
ICQ, 172
Identification (ID) numbers, 70
Identity reverse-engineering, 44
Identity spoofing, 40–41
Identity theft, 14, 40, 227
Image files, 182
Imagefish.com, 98
Industrial espionage, 42
Infomediaries, 47
Information, 137–44, 250n. See also Per-
    sonally identifiable information
  as power, 61–66
  trust and, 141–43
Information brokering, 2, 14, 22
*Information Rules: A Strategic Guide to
    the Network Economy*, 250n
Information Superhighway Summit,
    188–89
*Inquiry into the Nature and Causes of the
    Wealth of Nations, An* (Smith),
    251n

Insurance companies, 43–44
Integrity, 144
Intel, 30, 35, 45, 62, 70, 157, 170–71,
    248n
Intellectual property law, 119
Interception of communications, 92
Internet. See also Datanet; e-commerce;
    Websites
  consumer dos and don'ts, 223–29
  crime on, 15
  as Data Zone, 2–3
  dynamic equilibrium for, 187–96
  as an electronic bazaar, 24–26
  fair exchange on, 196–202
  power of information on, 61–66
  privacy incidents on, 231–45
  reason for existence of, 58
  safety rules for, 102
  scraping, 99
  sentient, 35–36
  social tumult caused by, 60–61
  sophistication of data collection on,
    32–35
  speed of information dispersal on,
    30–32
  twenty reasons to care about privacy
    on, 39–45
  workplace monitoring of, 5
Internet Education Foundation (IEF),
    100, 174
Internet Explorer (IE), 18, 49, 50, 77,
    78, 126, 225
Internet Junkbuster Proxy, 126
Internet Relay Chats (IRCs), 182
Internet start-ups, 129–31, 137–39, 189
InteRosa, 105
Ionesco, Eugene, 149, 150
ISPs, 103, 241
Israel, 94
iVillage, 97

J. Crew, 167–68, 250n
Japan, 35
Jeopardy fulcrum, xxiii–xxiv
Junkbusters, 126, 234
Jupiter Communications, 239

Kay, Alan, 188–89

KidShield, 103
Kindercam.com, 67–68
Knot, The, 250–51n

Lands' End, 162–63
Laptop cameras, 96
Laptop computers, 43, 92
Law of Increasing Returns, 62
Law of the Commons, 205, 206, 251n
Lawsuits, 13, 237
Legal liability, 13, 152
Levin, Gerald, 188
License plate numbers, 3, 41, 47, 92
Lifestyle monitoring, 43–44, 68
Linda Tripping, 44
*Lingua Franca*, 217
Longfellow, Henry Wadsworth, 213
L0pht Heavy Industries, 238
Lumeria, 47, 148
Lurking, 104
Lying, 16

Macintosh computers, 50, 225
Mail Controls, 52
MailStart, 236–37
MailStart Plus, 236–37
Malone, John, 188
Marketing
  aggressiveness of, 155
  direct, 22, 48–49, 226–27
  tele-, 147
  viral, 132, 134, 250n
Massachusetts Institute of Technology
  (MIT), 220
McCain, John, 243
McGraw-Hill, 12
McNealy, Scott, 39
McVeigh, Timothy, 171–72
Medical information. See Health infor-
  mation
Meisel, Bill, 234
Melissa virus, 28–29, 89, 248n
Member Profile, 79–80
Member Works Inc., 237
Mergers, 181–82
Merkle, Ralph C., 251n
Metatags, 120
Microprocessors, 60, 62

Microsoft, 12, 113, 143, 145, 157, 194
  security problems in, 240–41
  trustworthiness of, 169–70
Microsoft BusinessLink, 153
Microsoft.com, 170
Microsoft ID (MSID), 145
Microsoft Internet Explorer. See Internet
  Explorer
Microsoft Office, 131
Microsoft Windows. See Windows
*Mirror Worlds* (Gelernter), 37, 248n
Mobile computing devices, 81
Moore's Law, 59, 248n
Morgenstern, Oskar, 203
Motley Fool, 165–66
Mouse-prints, 42
Mr. Payroll, 98
Munging, 80
Murdoch, Rupert, 188
Murzakhanov, Nail, 240
MyExcite, 16, 24
My Netscape, 179

Names
  economic value of, 111–19
  removal from lists, 48–49
  requests not to sell, 180–81
  suppression on e-mail lists, 127
  on voice mail, 103–4
Nanny cams, 67–68
Nanocomputing, 220
National Centers for Disease Control,
  45
National Fraud Information Center, 168
National health ID, 45
National Institutes of Health (NIH), 217
National Security Agency (NSA), 90,
  93–94, 249n
Negroponte, Nicholas, 107
Netfishers, 233
*NetGain* (Hagel and Armstrong), 47
NetmaN, 214
Net Mom's 100 Hot Sites, 176
Netscape Communicator, 17–18, 49, 50,
  77–78, 126, 225
Netscape Netcenter, 179
Network effect, 130–35, 136, 139
Network Neighborhood, 28

Network Solutions Internic WhoIs
  Server, 51
New Economy, 138, 141
Newsgroups, 78–79, 182–83
NewsTracker, 121–22
*Newsweek*, 244
New York City, 35
*New York Times*, 96
New Zealand, 90
Nicholas, Nicholas J., 129–30
*1984* (Orwell), 55–58, 248n
Nixon, Richard, 56
No-call laws, 147
Norton Utilities, 172
Notice, 144
Nuance Communications, 233–34

Objects, 110
O'Dell, Pete, 137
Ombudsmen, 211
One-from-many search, 98
onestopinfo.com, 41
One-to-one match, 98
Online banking, 112, 125–26, 163–64,
  235–36
Online Banking Access, 163–64
Online behavior contracts, 100
Online Privacy Alliance (OPA), 143–44,
  250n
Online Privacy Protection Act, 238
Online relationships, 69–70
*Only the Paranoid Survive* (Grove), 35,
  248n
Onsite, 153
Opt-in, 160
Opt-out, 160, 166, 228
Oracle, 93, 108–9, 157, 194
Oregon, 147
Orwell, George, 55–58, 59, 64, 65, 76,
  248n
Outlook Express, 103
Outsourcing, 156, 211
Oversight, 144, 156

Pacific Bell, 27–28
PalmPilots, 81
Parental Controls, 52
Party line-style online snooping, 44

Password Keeper, 147
Password Manager, 147
Passwords, 81, 101, 147, 228–29
Password Safe, 147
Pen camara sets, 95
Pen microphones, 96
Penthouse, 166, 250n
Pentium II, 171
Pentium III, 45, 170–71
Penzias, Arno, 58
PeoplePC, 112
*Permission Marketing* (Godin), 141,
  250n
Personal identification numbers (PINs),
  4
Personally identifiable information (PII).
  See also Names
  accountability and, 70
  debates about ownership of, 84–85
  defined, xvii
  economic value of, 70, 111–19
  hiding, 148
  hooks for, 9–10
  increasing use of, 10–11
  license plates as source of, 3
  near-term dilemma and, 122–25
  ongoing collection of, 157–58
  packaged products for, 41
  from porn sites, 87–88
  sensitive, 161
  significance of, xvii–xix
  sophisticated collection techniques
    for, 32–35
  technological solutions for dispersal of,
    72–74
Personal profiles, 30–32, 85
Personal tools, 115–16
Philpot, John, 66
Phone Manager, 96
Platform for Privacy Preferences Project
  (P3P), 199–202, 208, 251n
Playboy.com, 163
Pointcast, 136
Pornography sites, 5, 83–84, 85–88, 89
  forced entry onto, 245
  revenue from, 86
PortNet, 249n
Posting of information, 109

# Index

Postrel, Virginia, 252n
Presidential candidates, 242–43
Priceline, 130, 138
Privacy
  as a fundamental right, 22
  lack of built-in safeguards, 156
  lack of public safeguards, 158
  online incidents, 231–45
  price of, 23–24
  twenty reasons to care about, 39–45
Privacy game, 203–11, 251n
Privacy International, 234
Privacy laws, 13, 238, 247n
Privacy management, 135–36
Privacy policies, 6, 152–56, 157–58, 162,
    166, 179
  automatic evaluation of, 201
  broken promises and, 45
  checking validity of, 224
  fair exchange and, 197–98
  mergers and, 181–82
  reasons for lapses in, 155–56
Privacy Rights Council, 182
Privacy statements, 224
Privaseek, 47
Private Bookmarks, 127
Problem solving, 66–71
Processor Serial Number (PSN), 45, 70,
    248n
Progress & Freedom Foundation, 239
Proxy sites, 51
P3P. See Platform for Privacy Prefer-
    ences Project
Public-key encryption, 73, 76–77
Public opinion, 12, 24, 37–39, 235

Query routines, 108, 121
QVTech Inc., 105

Racal, 92
Rand Foundation, 43
Real Networks, 130
Real-time monitoring, 84
Reciprocal altruism, 205
Redress, 144
Registration Wizard (RegWiz), 145
REI (Recreational Equipment Inc.), 163
Remailers, 146–47

Ripper, John, 112–13
Rogers, Will, 55
RTF (Rich Text Format), 127
Rumsfeld, Don, 21
Russia, 94, 240, 244

Saffo, Paul, 36
Santa Fe Institute, 75, 248–49n
Scams, 241
Schemas, 108
Schicci, Riccardo, 86
Schneier, Bruce, 248n, 249n
Schwartz, Ari, 243
Science and Technological Options As-
    sessment (STOA), 91–92, 96, 249n
Seal programs, 224
*Seattle Weekly*, 242
Security, 144
Security codes, 227
Security Info, 78
Seeding, 17
Semantic Web, 200–201
Sensitive information, 161
Sentient Internet, 35–36
Shopping carts, 145–46
Shotgun microphones, 96
Simon & Garfunkel, 214
Singapore, 35
Smart cards, 52–53
Smith, Adam, 196, 198, 203, 251n
Smith, David Lee, 28–29, 89
Smith, Jack, 132
Smoke detector video cameras, 95
Snap.com, 97
Sniffers, xvii, 238
Snooks, Graeme Donald, 111, 249–50n
Social security numbers, 1–2, 9, 47, 227
Sony 960 time lapse VCR, 95
*Southern Medical Journal*, 231
Spam, 38, 148
  amount of, 39–40
  AOL Member Profile and, 79–80
  filtering, 19, 46–47
  tips for avoiding, 227–28
Spam Buster, 46
SpamKiller, 46–47
Spy-cams, 36, 42
Spying, 89–97

Squid, 126
*St. Petersburg Times*, 72
Stalking, 22, 41–42
State ID, 163
Sticky-cam, 96
Stock transactions, 125
*Stop Junk Mail Forever*, 181
STRIP (Secure Tool for Recalling Important Passwords), 81
Sun Microsystems, 39
Supertracks, xx, 137
Supreme Court, U.S., 22, 248n
Surveillance
    automated, 92
    telephone, 95–96
    video. See Video surveillance
Symantec, 172
SyShield, 46

Talon system, 92
*Tampa Tribune*, 72
TCI, 188
"Technologies of Political Control" (report), 92
*Technology and Privacy: The New Landscape*, 249n
Technology transfer, 93–96
Teleconferences, 6
Telemarketing, 147
Telephone numbers, 18–19, 47, 227
Telephones
    caller ID and, 8
    cell, 3–4, 34, 43, 243–44
    message services and, 9
    recording and surveillance, 95–96
    teleconferences on, 6
Terrorism, 65–66
*Theory of Games and Economic Behavior, The* (von Neumann and Morgenstern), 203, 251n
Third Voice, 232–33
Time-out capabilities, 125–26
Time Warner, 129, 143, 188
TML.com, 41
Torr, Peter, 240
Transparency, 66, 89, 153
*Transparent Society, The* (Brin), 66, 249n
Trans Union, 180, 226, 228

Travel sites, 6–7
Tripod, 100
Trust, 141–43, 149–83, 250–51n
    children and, 161, 172–78
    clarity and, 159–60
    personal responsibility for, 161
    recovering sites, 168–72
    sensitive information and, 161
    sites needing improvement, 166–68
    ten best sites, 162–66
    user control and, 160
*Trust: The Social Virtues and the Creation of Prosperity* (Fukuyama), 251n
TRUSTe, xix–xxiii, 16, 17, 48, 162, 170, 223, 224
Trust environments, 74–76, 124
Trust ratings, 154
Truth, when to tell, 16
TRW. See Experian
Turner, Ted, 188
Turner Broadcasting, 188
Twelve-hour telephone recording system, 95–96

United Airlines, 171, 251n
United Kingdom, 35, 90
United Parcel Service (UPS), 48
Universal identifiers, 45
Universal Resource Locator (URL), 51, 59, 68
UNIX, 108
US Bancorp, 13, 237
US Bank, 167, 250n
Usenet, 79, 80, 182

Value Net, 241
Vandalism, hacker, 43
*Variety*, 189
Vehicle recognition systems, 92
VeriSign, 77, 166
VerticalOne, 250n
Video surveillance, 4, 7, 35–36
    equipment for, 95
    useful purposes of, 67–68
    at workplace, 41
Virage, 97
Viral marketing, 132, 134, 250n

# Index

Viruses, 126–27
Visionics, 98–99
Voice mail, 103–4
Voiceprints, 234
von Neumann, John, 203–4, 251n
Voyeur Dorm, 84, 85, 89, 249n

*Wall Street Journal*, 61
*Washington Post*, 72
Wearable computers, 84, 213–15, 252n
Web browsers, 49, 126, 201, 225
  deleting cookies with, 50, 225
  erasing entries with, 17–18
  securing websites with, 77–78
  updating, 78
  upgrading encryption strength of, 49
Weberaser, 18
Webfilter, 126
webmd.com, 74
Webroot, 127
Websites
  duplication of, 51
  family, 100
  hacking on, 78
  mistrust of, 239
  needing improvement, 166–68
  prevention of following on, 126
  recovering, 168–72
  securing, 77–78
  ten best, 162–66
Webwiper, 126
Wedding registries, 6

wellmed.com, 74
wellpartners.com, 74
Welsh, Jack, 137
*What Will Be: How the New World of Information Will Change Our Lives* (Dertouzos), 250n
Windows, 46, 131, 169–70
  break-ins on, 240–41
  Registration Wizard, 145
Wine.com, 144
WinWhatWhere, 244–45
*Wired*, 189
Wireless clock video cameras, 95
Witness protection program, 68
Workplace, 14
  anonymous address for, 101–2
  corporate systems for, 116
  electronic monitoring of, 5, 41
  private e-mail address at, 148
World Wide Web, 59, 109, 119, 121
World Wide Web Consortium, 198–99, 202
Wright, Steve, 92
WRQ, 17, 50

XML, 110, 119–21, 124, 125, 201, 249n
X-no-archive option, 79

Yahoo!, 60, 141, 163–64, 169, 251–52n

ZAG profiles, 41
Zetetic Enterprises, 81

9 780743 254984